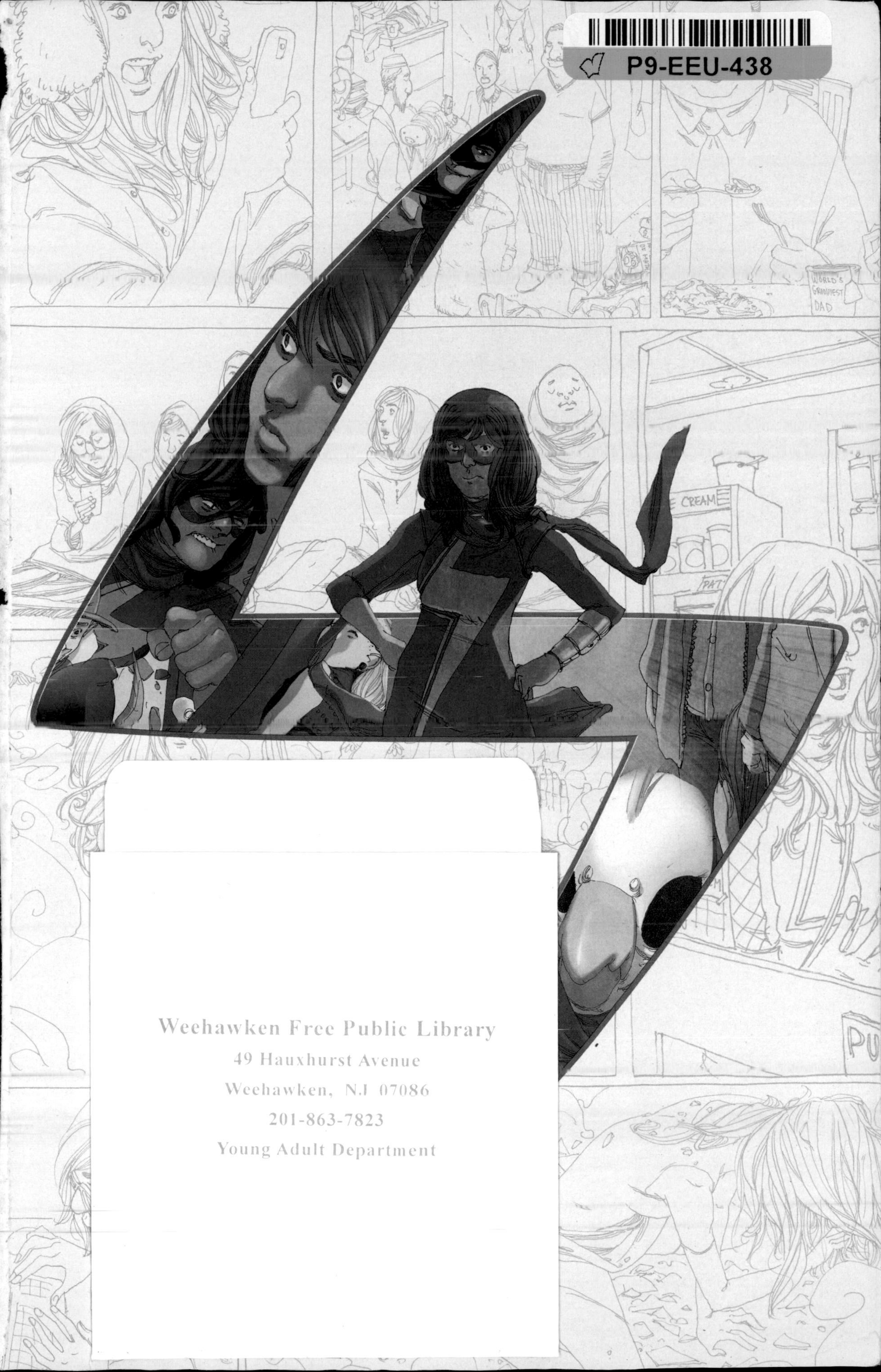
E CREAM

MS. MARVEL VOL. 2: GENERATION WHY. Contains material originally published in magazine form as MS. MARVEL #6-11. First printing 2015. ISBN# 978-0-7851-9022-6. Published by MARVEL WORLDWIDE, INC., a subsidiary of MARVEL ENTERTAINMENT, LLC. OFFICE OF PUBLICATION: 135 West 50th Street, New York, NY 10020. Copyright © 2014 and 2015 Marvel Characters, Inc. All rights reserved. All characters featured in this issue and the distinctive names and likenesses thereof, and all related indicia are trademarks of Marvel Characters, Inc. No similarity between any of the names, characters, persons, and/or institutions in this magazine with those of any living or dead person or institution is intended, and any such similarity which may exist is purely coincidental. **Printed in Canada.** ALAN FINE, EVP - Office of the President, Marvel Worldwide, Inc. and EVP & CMO Marvel Characters B.V.; DAN BUCKLEY, Publisher & President - Print, Animation & Digital Divisions; JOE QUESADA, Chief Creative Officer; TOM BREVOORT, SVP of Publishing; DAVID BOGART, SVP of Operations & Procurement, Publishing; C.B. CEBULSKI, SVP of Creator & Content Development; DAVID GABRIEL, SVP Print, Sales & Marketing; JIM O'KEEFE, VP of Operations & Logistics; DAN CARR, Executive Director of Publishing Technology; SUSAN CRESPI, Editorial Operations Manager; ALEX MORALES, Publishing Operations Manager; STAN LEE, Chairman Emeritus. For information regarding advertising in Marvel Comics or on Marvel.com, please contact Niza Disla, Director of Marvel Partnerships, at ndisla@marvel.com. For Marvel subscription inquiries, please call 800-217-9158. **Manufactured between 1/16/2015 and 2/23/2015 by SOLISCO PRINTERS, SCOTT, QC, CANADA.**

10 9 8 7 6 5 4 3 2 1

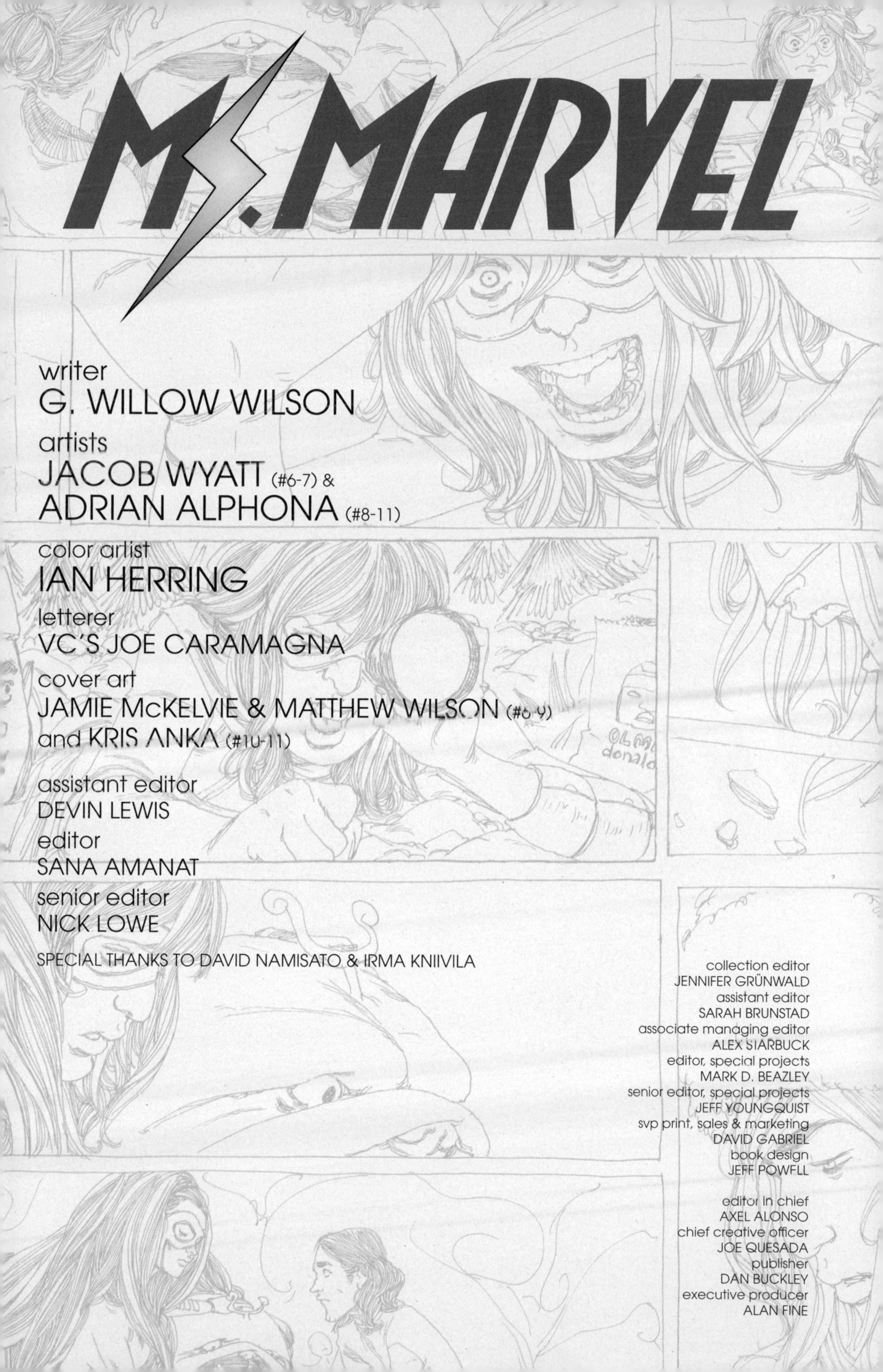

MS. MARVEL

writer
G. WILLOW WILSON

artists
JACOB WYATT (#6-7) &
ADRIAN ALPHONA (#8-11)

color artist
IAN HERRING

letterer
VC'S JOE CARAMAGNA

cover art
JAMIE McKELVIE & MATTHEW WILSON (#6-9)
and KRIS ANKA (#10-11)

assistant editor
DEVIN LEWIS

editor
SANA AMANAT

senior editor
NICK LOWE

SPECIAL THANKS TO DAVID NAMISATO & IRMA KNIIVILA

collection editor
JENNIFER GRÜNWALD
assistant editor
SARAH BRUNSTAD
associate managing editor
ALEX STARBUCK
editor, special projects
MARK D. BEAZLEY
senior editor, special projects
JEFF YOUNGQUIST
svp print, sales & marketing
DAVID GABRIEL
book design
JEFF POWELL

editor in chief
AXEL ALONSO
chief creative officer
JOE QUESADA
publisher
DAN BUCKLEY
executive producer
ALAN FINE

PREVIOUSLY

KAMALA KHAN HAS ALWAYS FELT DIFFERENT. NERDY INTERESTS, STRICT PARENTS AND NOW...STRANGE POLY-MORPHING POWERS.

AFTER RESCUING HER BEST FRIEND BRUNO'S BROTHER FROM A SHADY CREW, SHE DISCOVERS THAT JERSEY CITY HAS A VILLAIN NAMED THE INVENTOR LURKING IN ITS MIDST.

GOOD THING THE CITY HAS A NEW HERO NOW, TOO.

KAMALA KHAN IS THE ALL-NEW...

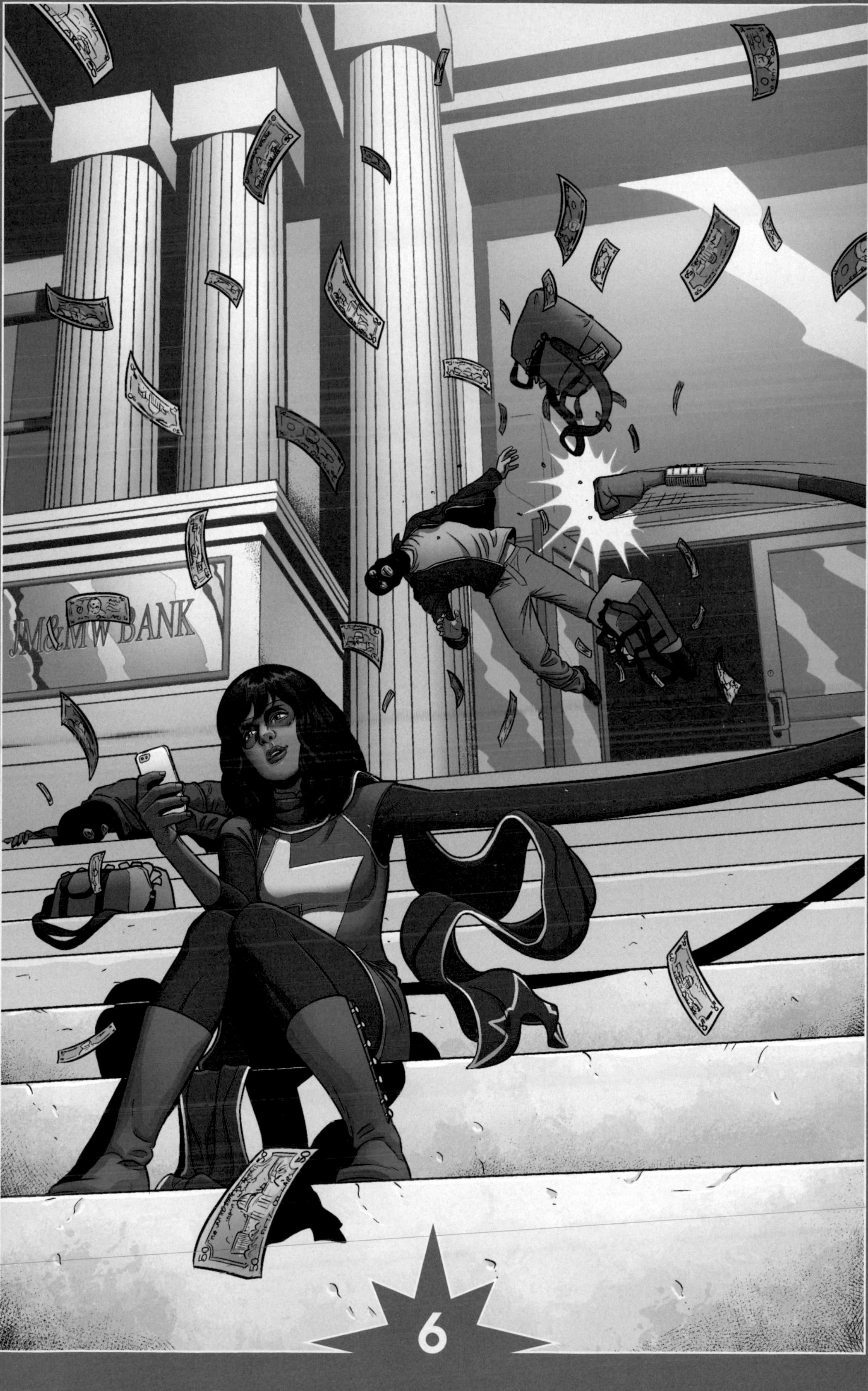
JM&MW BANK
6

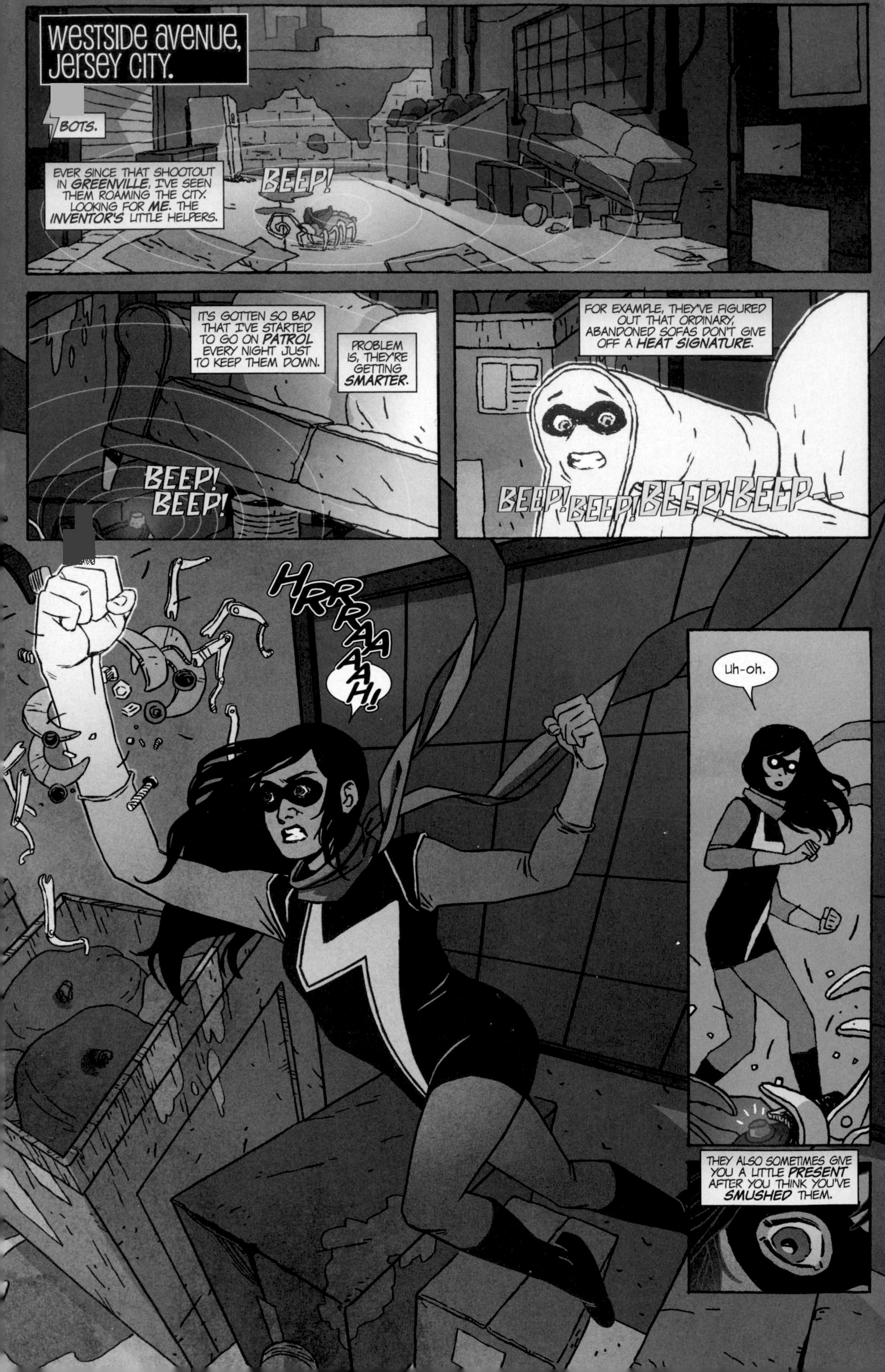

WESTSIDE AVENUE, JERSEY CITY.
BOTS.
EVER SINCE THAT SHOOTOUT IN GREENVILLE, I'VE SEEN THEM ROAMING THE CITY. LOOKING FOR ME. THE INVENTOR'S LITTLE HELPERS.
BEEP!
IT'S GOTTEN SO BAD THAT I'VE STARTED TO GO ON PATROL EVERY NIGHT JUST TO KEEP THEM DOWN.
PROBLEM IS, THEY'RE GETTING SMARTER.
BEEP! BEEP!
FOR EXAMPLE, THEY'VE FIGURED OUT THAT ORDINARY, ABANDONED SOFAS DON'T GIVE OFF A HEAT SIGNATURE.
BEEP! BEEP! BEEP! BEEP--
HRRRAAAAAH!
Uh-oh.
THEY ALSO SOMETIMES GIVE YOU A LITTLE PRESENT AFTER YOU THINK YOU'VE SMUSHED THEM.

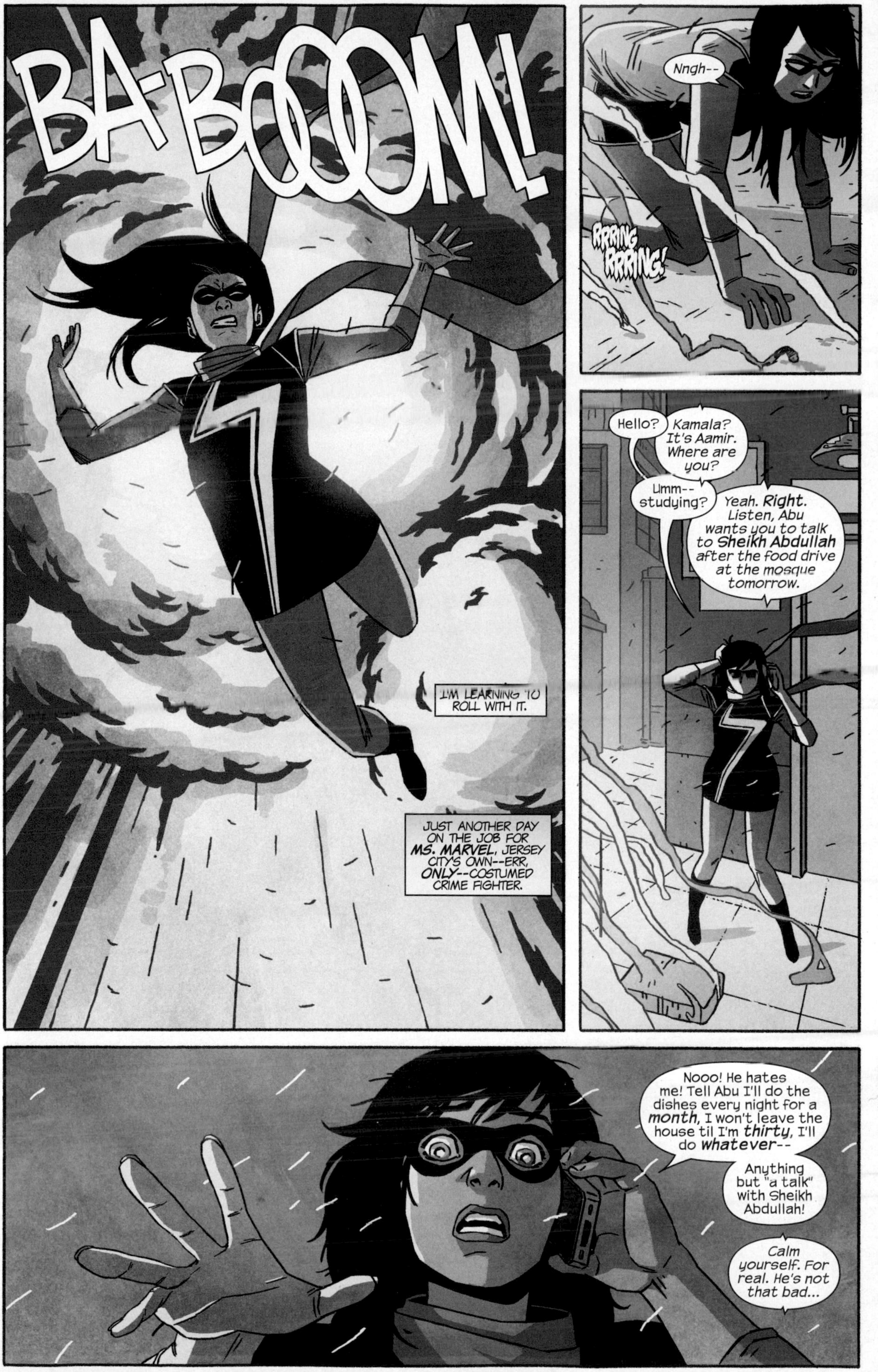
BA-BOOOM!
I'M LEARNING TO ROLL WITH IT.
JUST ANOTHER DAY ON THE JOB FOR MS. MARVEL, JERSEY CITY'S OWN--ERR, ONLY--COSTUMED CRIME FIGHTER.
Nngh--
RRRING RRRING!
Hello?
Kamala? It's Aamir. Where are you?
Umm-- studying?
Yeah. Right. Listen, Abu wants you to talk to Sheikh Abdullah after the food drive at the mosque tomorrow.
Nooo! He hates me! Tell Abu I'll do the dishes every night for a month, I won't leave the house til I'm thirty, I'll do whatever--
Anything but "a talk" with Sheikh Abdullah!
Calm yourself. For real. He's not that bad...

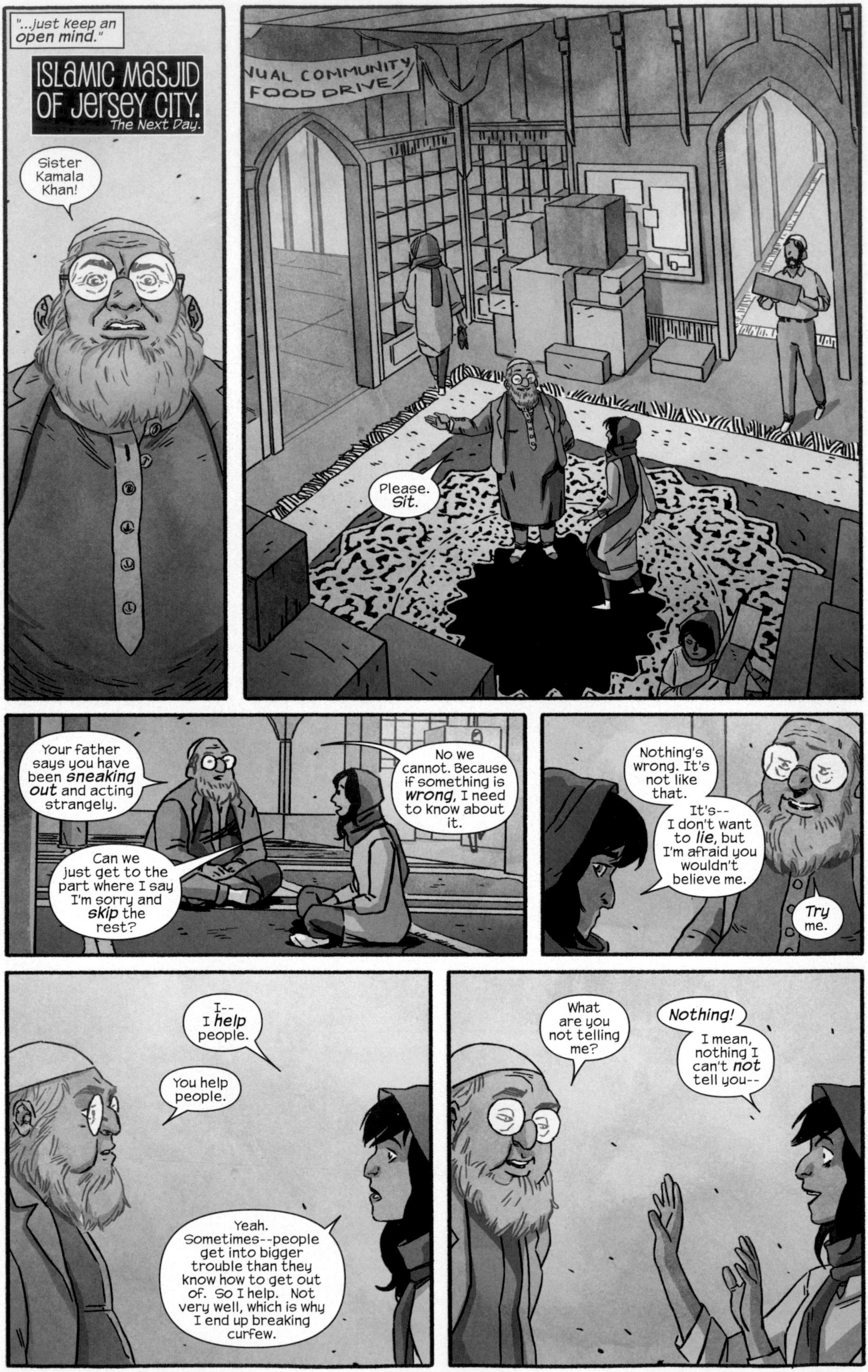
"...just keep an open mind."
ISLAMIC MASJID OF JERSEY CITY.
The Next Day.
Sister Kamala Khan!
ANNUAL COMMUNITY FOOD DRIVE
Please. Sit.
Your father says you have been sneaking out and acting strangely.
Can we just get to the part where I say I'm sorry and skip the rest?
No we cannot. Because if something is wrong, I need to know about it.
Nothing's wrong. It's not like that.
It's-- I don't want to lie, but I'm afraid you wouldn't believe me.
Try me.
I-- I help people.
You help people.
Yeah. Sometimes--people get into bigger trouble than they know how to get out of. So I help. Not very well, which is why I end up breaking curfew.
What are you not telling me?
Nothing!
I mean, nothing I can't not tell you--

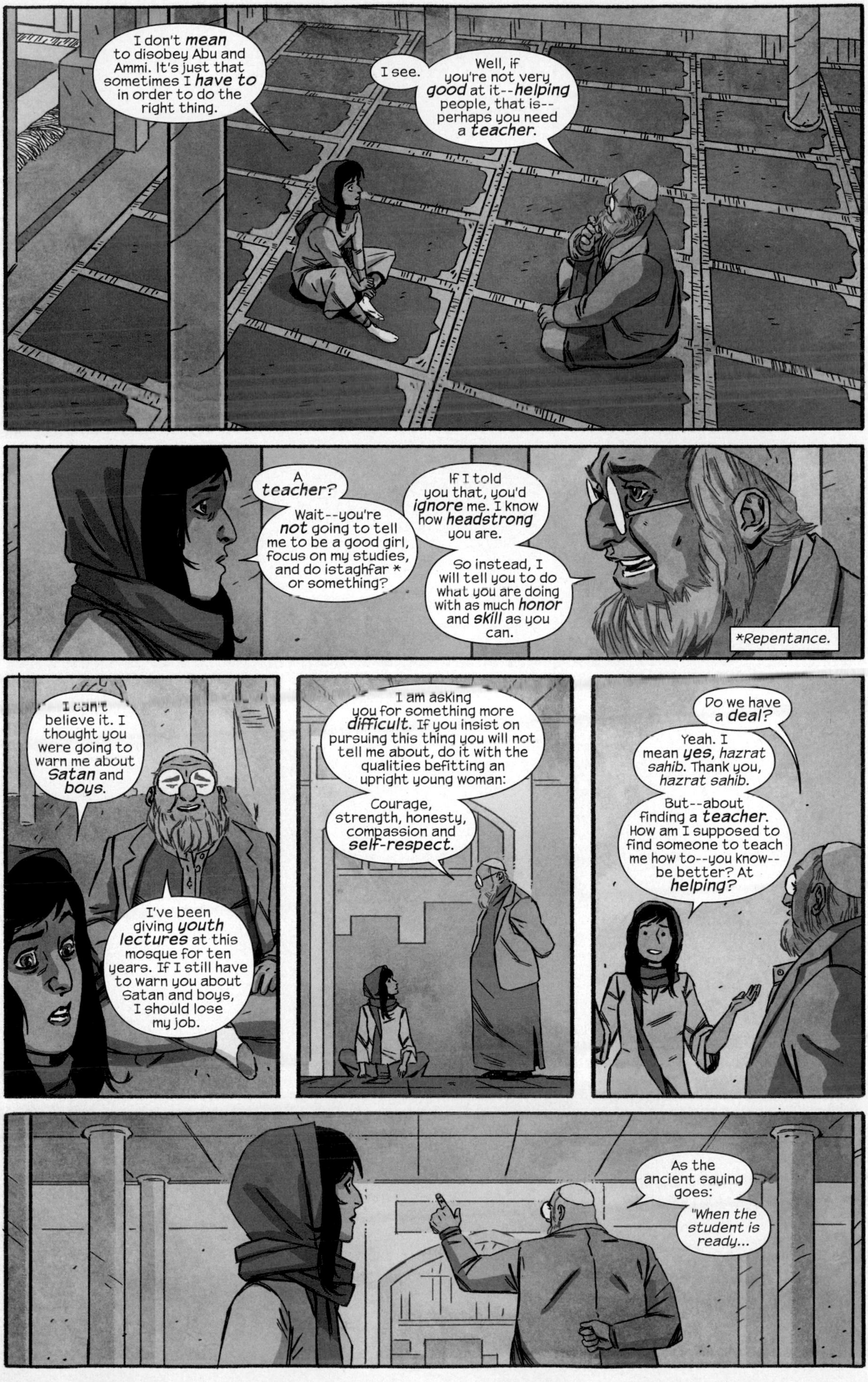

I don't mean to disobey Abu and Ammi. It's just that sometimes I have to in order to do the right thing.
I see.
Well, if you're not very good at it--helping people, that is--perhaps you need a teacher.
A teacher?
Wait--you're not going to tell me to be a good girl, focus on my studies, and do istaghfar * or something?
If I told you that, you'd ignore me. I know how headstrong you are.
So instead, I will tell you to do what you are doing with as much honor and skill as you can.
*Repentance.
I can't believe it. I thought you were going to warn me about Satan and boys.
I've been giving youth lectures at this mosque for ten years. If I still have to warn you about Satan and boys, I should lose my job.
I am asking you for something more difficult. If you insist on pursuing this thing you will not tell me about, do it with the qualities befitting an upright young woman:
Courage, strength, honesty, compassion and self-respect.
Do we have a deal?
Yeah. I mean yes, hazrat sahib. Thank you, hazrat sahib.
But--about finding a teacher. How am I supposed to find someone to teach me how to--you know--be better? At helping?
As the ancient saying goes:
"When the student is ready...

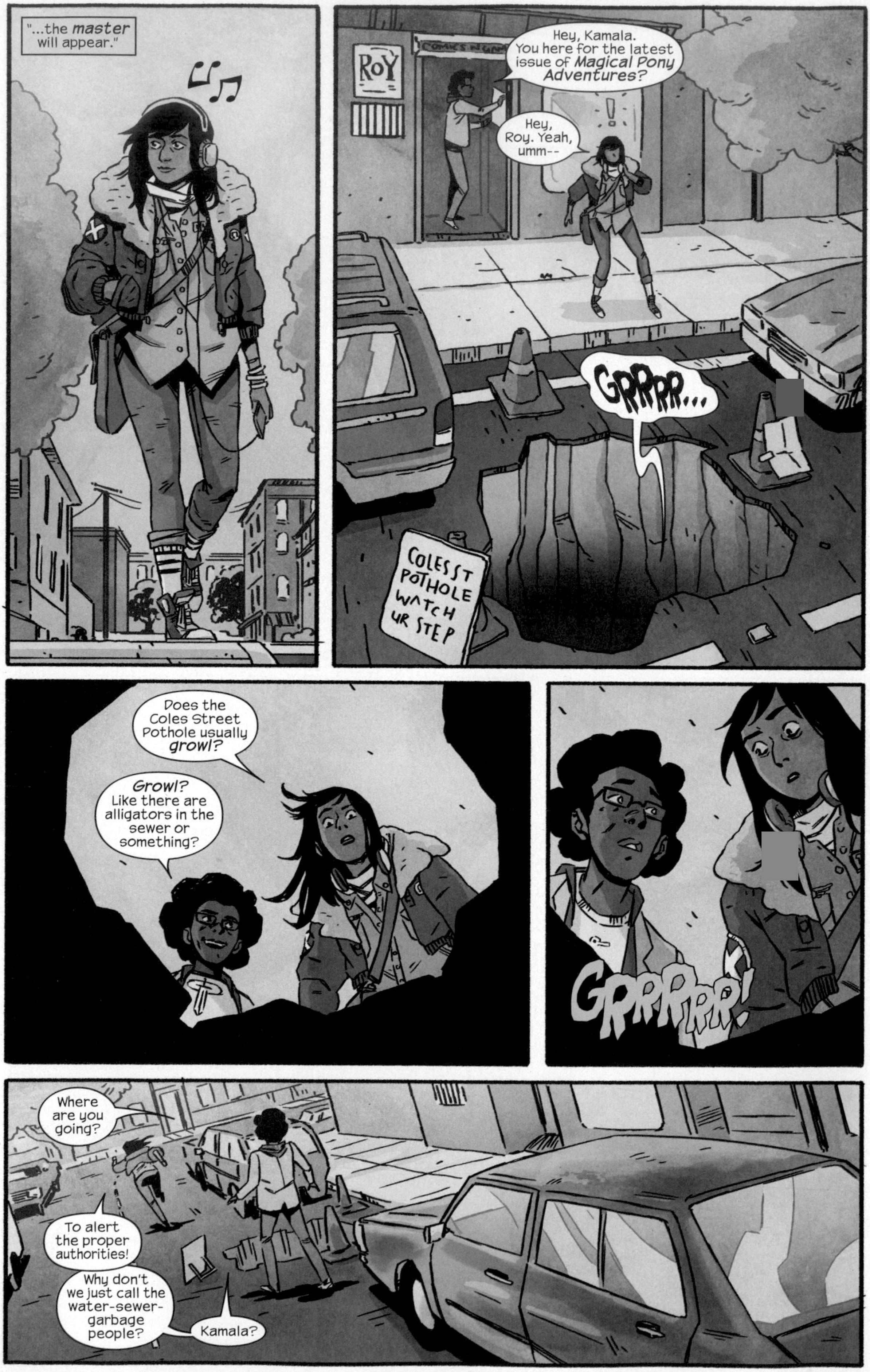
"...the master will appear."
Hey, Kamala. You here for the latest issue of Magical Pony Adventures?
Hey, Roy. Yeah, umm--
ROY
!
GRRRR...
COLES ST POTHOLE WATCH UR STEP
Does the Coles Street Pothole usually growl?
Growl? Like there are alligators in the sewer or something?
GRRRRR!
Where are you going?
To alert the proper authorities!
Why don't we just call the water-sewer-garbage people?
Kamala?

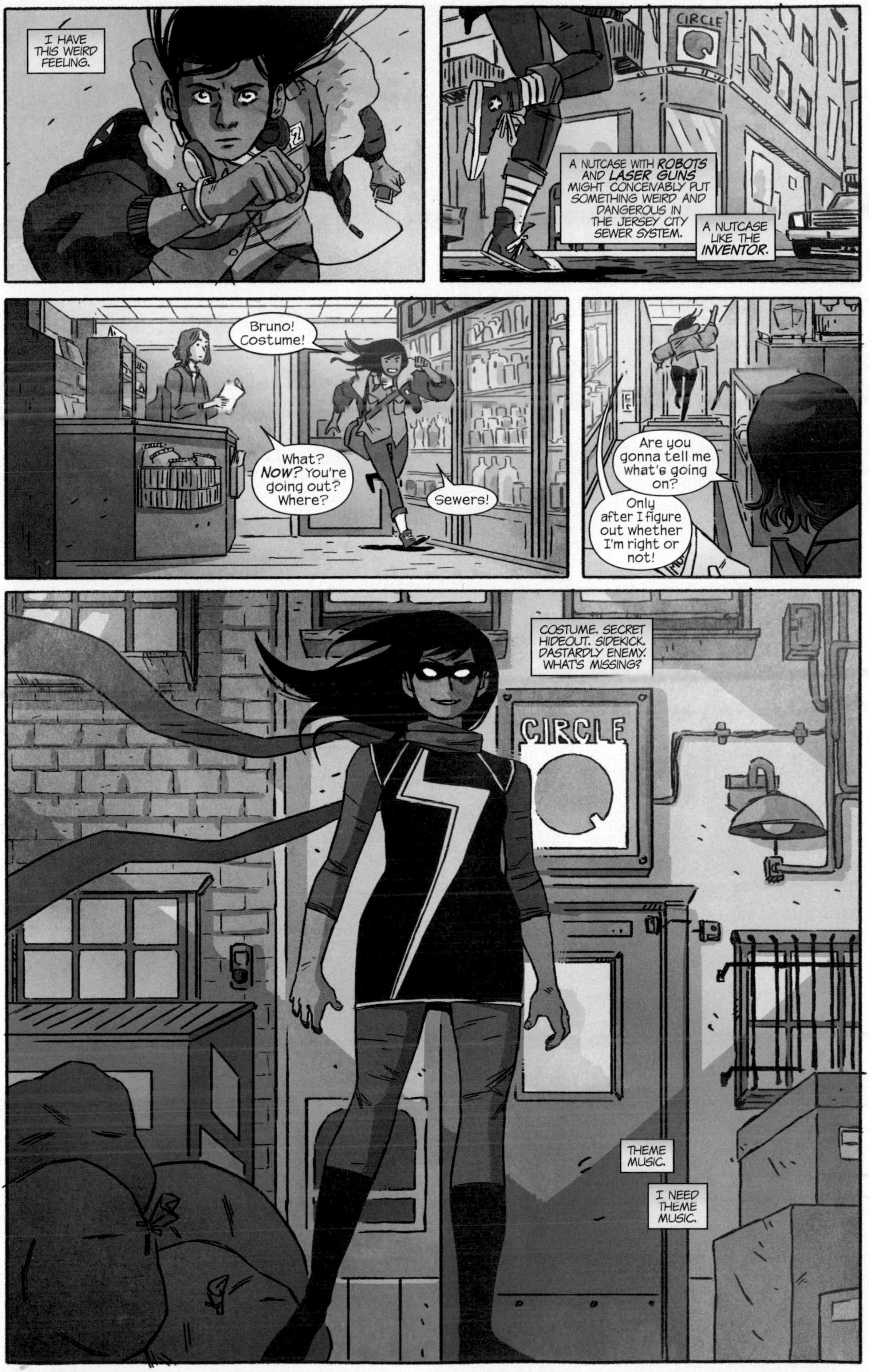

I HAVE THIS WEIRD FEELING.
A NUTCASE WITH ROBOTS AND LASER GUNS MIGHT CONCEIVABLY PUT SOMETHING WEIRD AND DANGEROUS IN THE JERSEY CITY SEWER SYSTEM.
A NUTCASE LIKE THE INVENTOR.
CIRCLE
Bruno! Costume!
What? NOW? You're going out? Where?
Sewers!
Are you gonna tell me what's going on?
Only after I figure out whether I'm right or not!
COSTUME. SECRET HIDEOUT. SIDEKICK. DASTARDLY ENEMY. WHAT'S MISSING?
CIRCLE
THEME MUSIC.
I NEED THEME MUSIC.

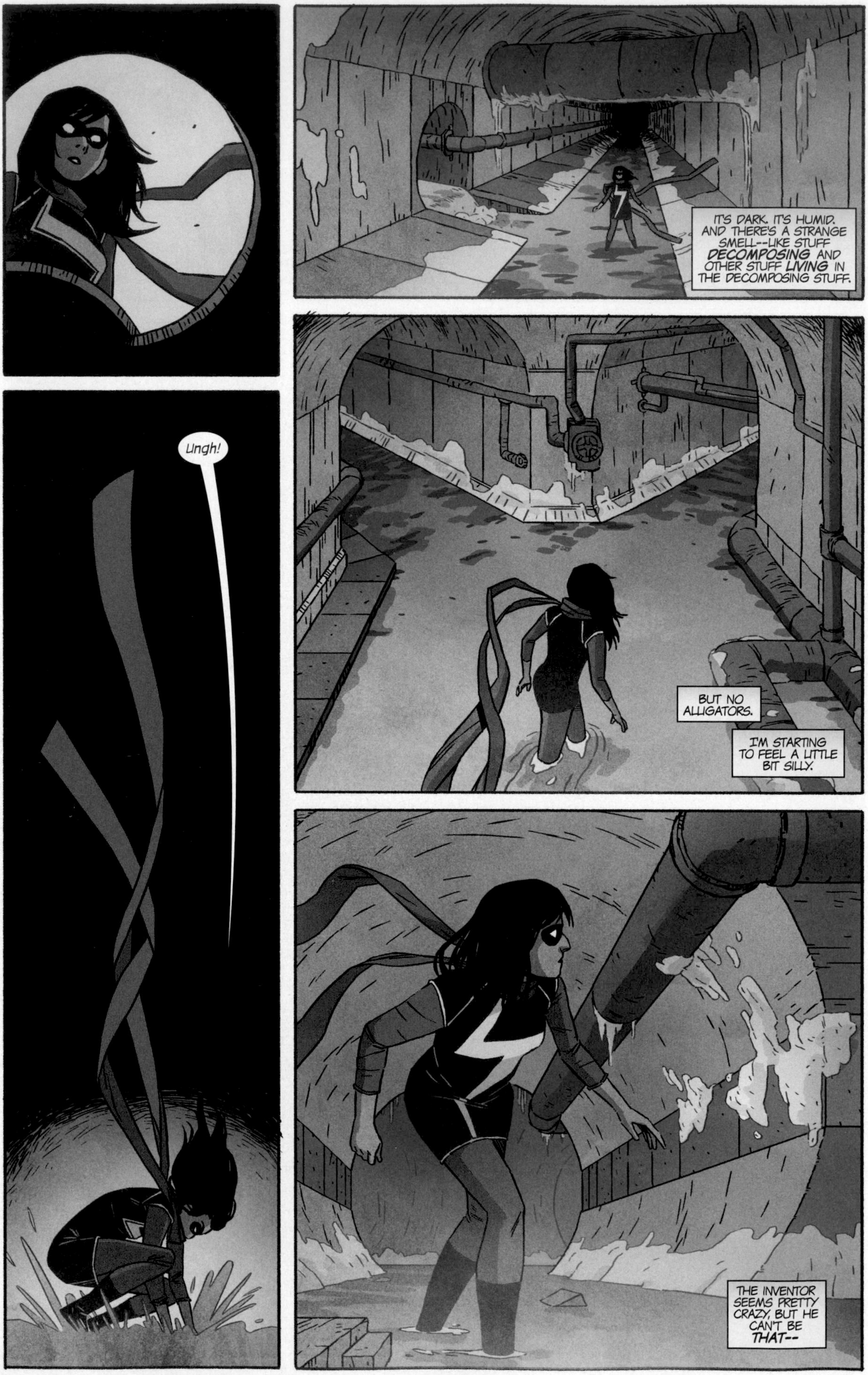
IT'S DARK. IT'S HUMID. AND THERE'S A STRANGE SMELL--LIKE STUFF DECOMPOSING AND OTHER STUFF LIVING IN THE DECOMPOSING STUFF.
Ungh!
BUT NO ALLIGATORS.
I'M STARTING TO FEEL A LITTLE BIT SILLY.
THE INVENTOR SEEMS PRETTY CRAZY, BUT HE CAN'T BE THAT--

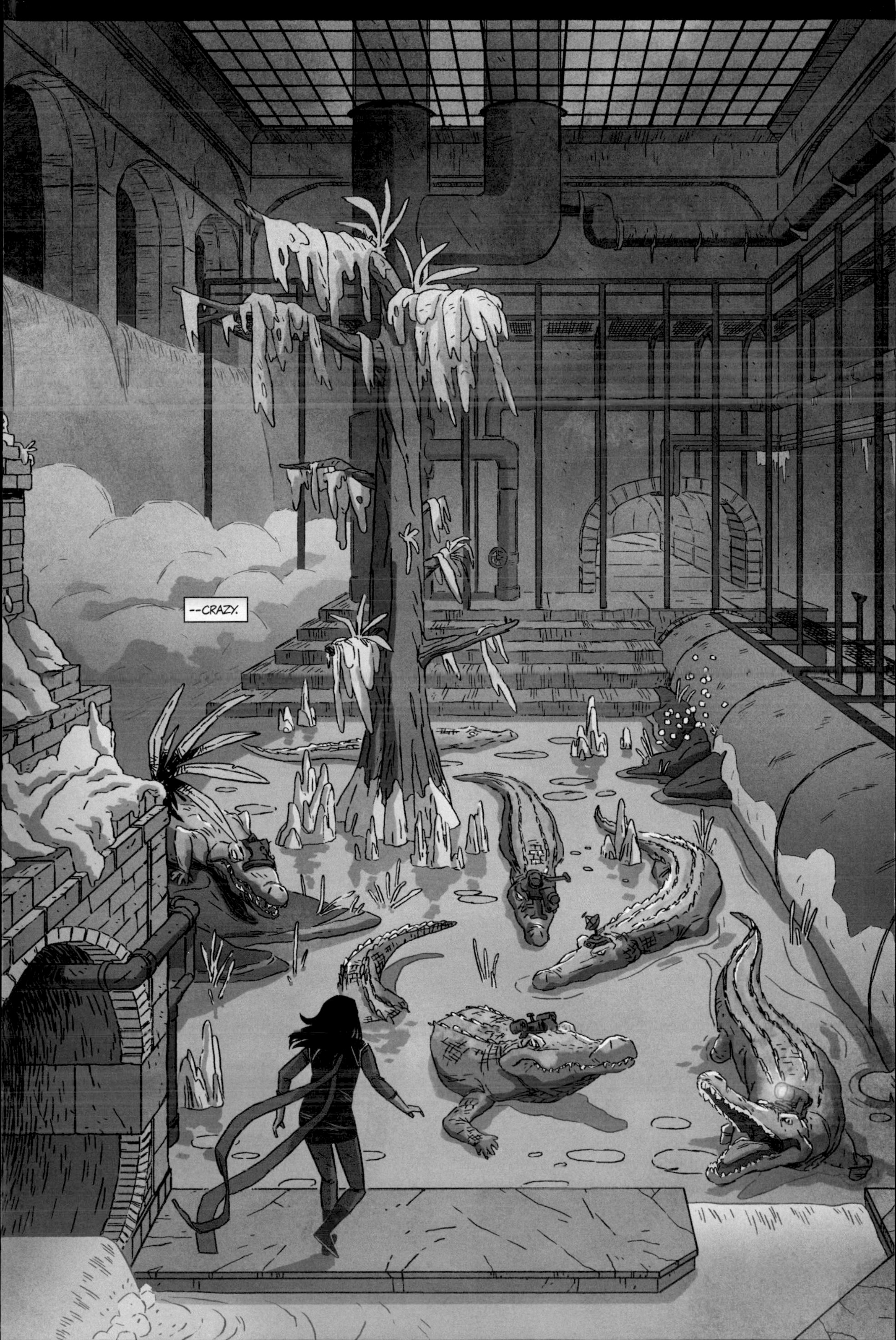
--CRAZY.

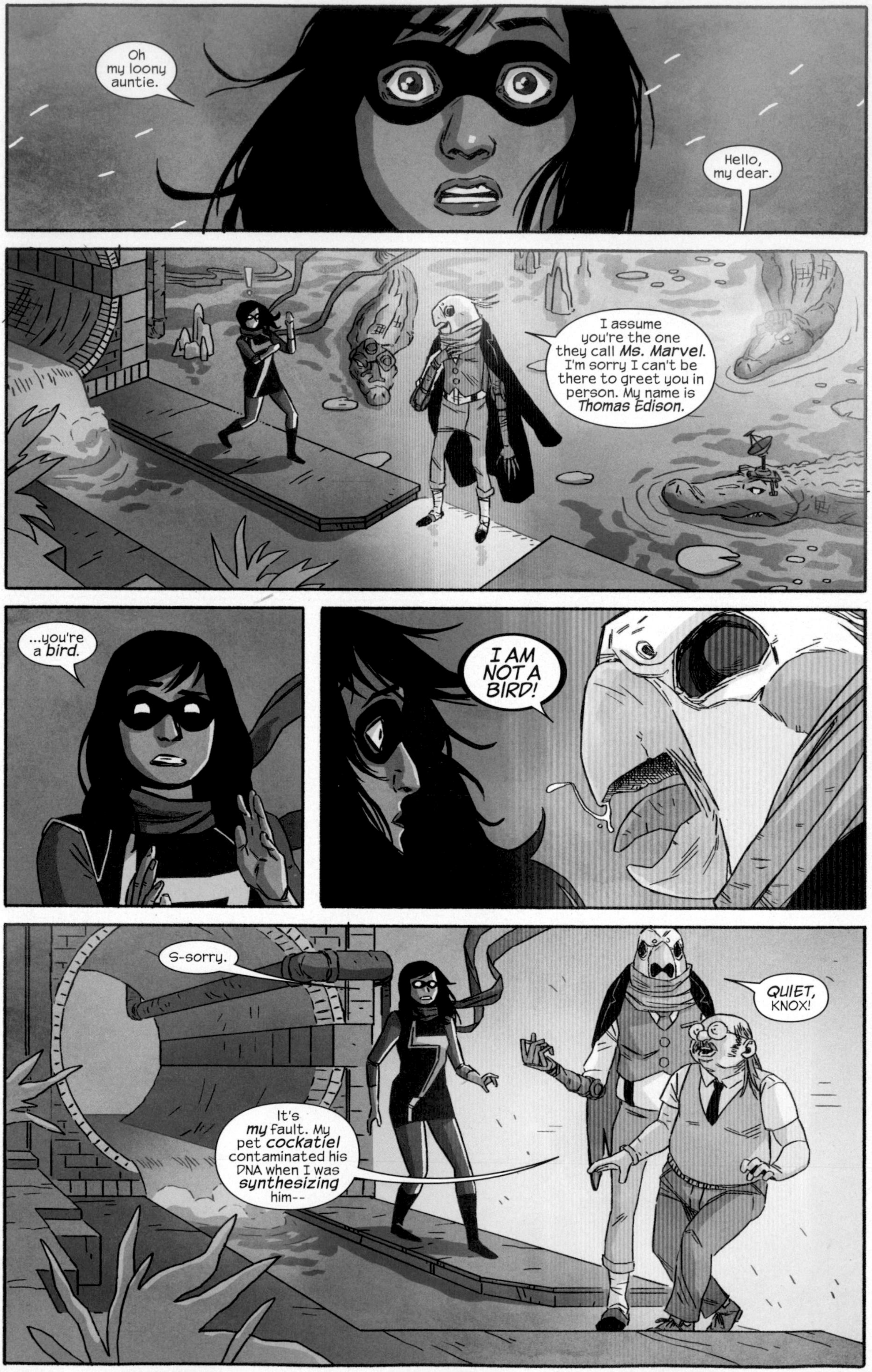
Oh my loony auntie.
Hello, my dear.
I assume you're the one they call *Ms. Marvel.* I'm sorry I can't be there to greet you in person. My name is *Thomas Edison.*
...you're a *bird.*
I AM NOT A BIRD!
S-sorry.
QUIET, KNOX!
It's *my* fault. My pet *cockatiel* contaminated his DNA when I was *synthesizing* him--

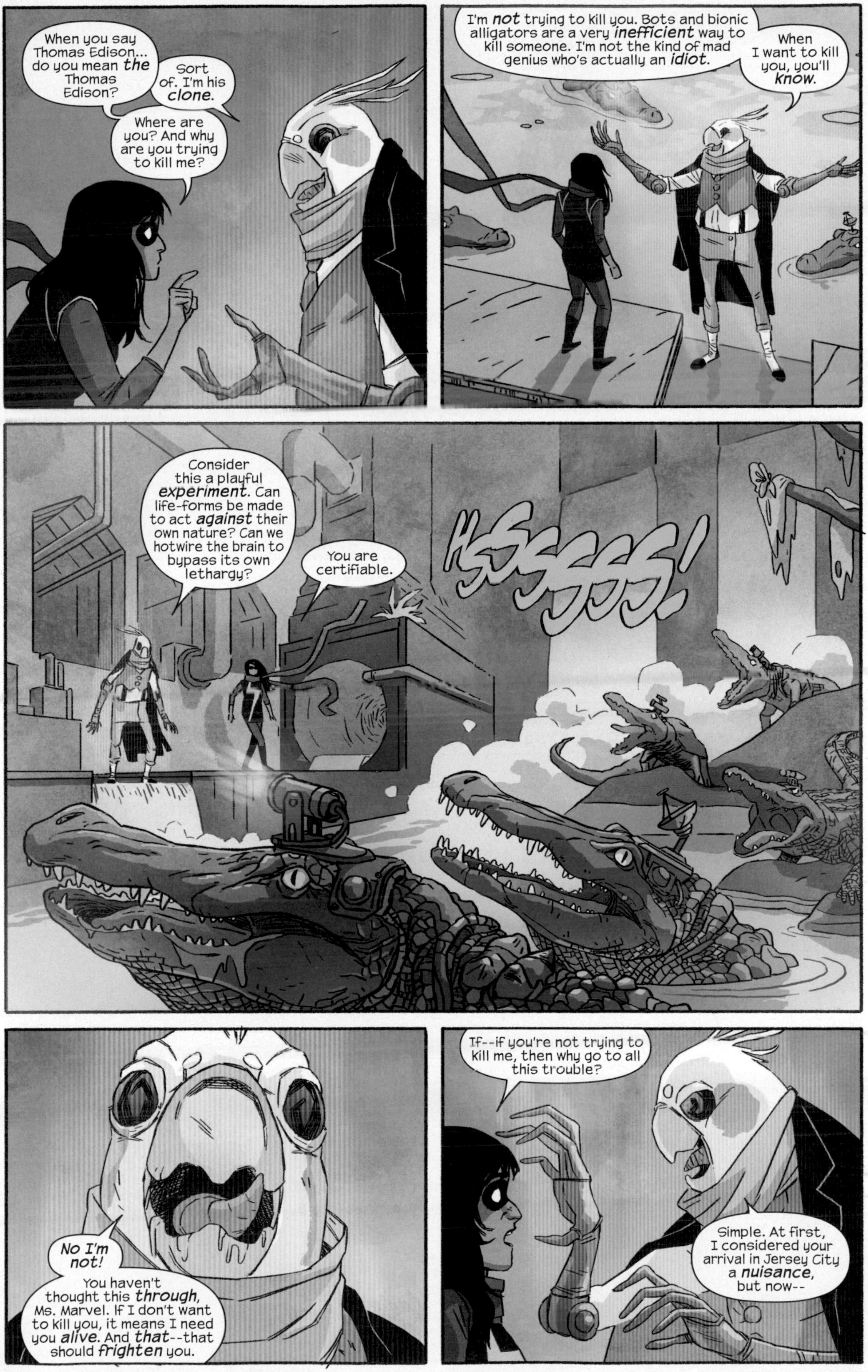
When you say Thomas Edison... do you mean *the* Thomas Edison?
Sort of. I'm his *clone*.
Where are you? And why are you trying to kill me?
I'm *not* trying to kill you. Bots and bionic alligators are a very *inefficient* way to kill someone. I'm not the kind of mad genius who's actually an *idiot*.
When I want to kill you, you'll *know*.
Consider this a playful *experiment*. Can life-forms be made to act *against* their own nature? Can we hotwire the brain to bypass its own lethargy?
You are certifiable.
HSSSSSS!
No I'm not!
You haven't thought this *through*, Ms. Marvel. If I don't want to kill you, it means I need you *alive*. And *that*--that should *frighten* you.
If--if you're not trying to kill me, then why go to all this trouble?
Simple. At first, I considered your arrival in Jersey City a *nuisance*, but now--

Now I see that you are deeply relevant to my *work*.

Fight, little girl. I want to watch you fight for your *life*.

Sir! Infrared has detected someone else approaching the holding tank!

Someone? What do you mean, *"someone?"* This place was supposed to be locked down!

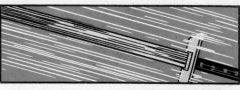

GREAT. MORE BAD GUYS? WITH *SWORDS*?

HOW MUCH WORSE CAN THIS DAY POSSIBLY GET?

GET READY TO *LOSE*, WEIRD SHORT DUDE. I'VE GOT +10 HEALS.

POWER ATTACK!

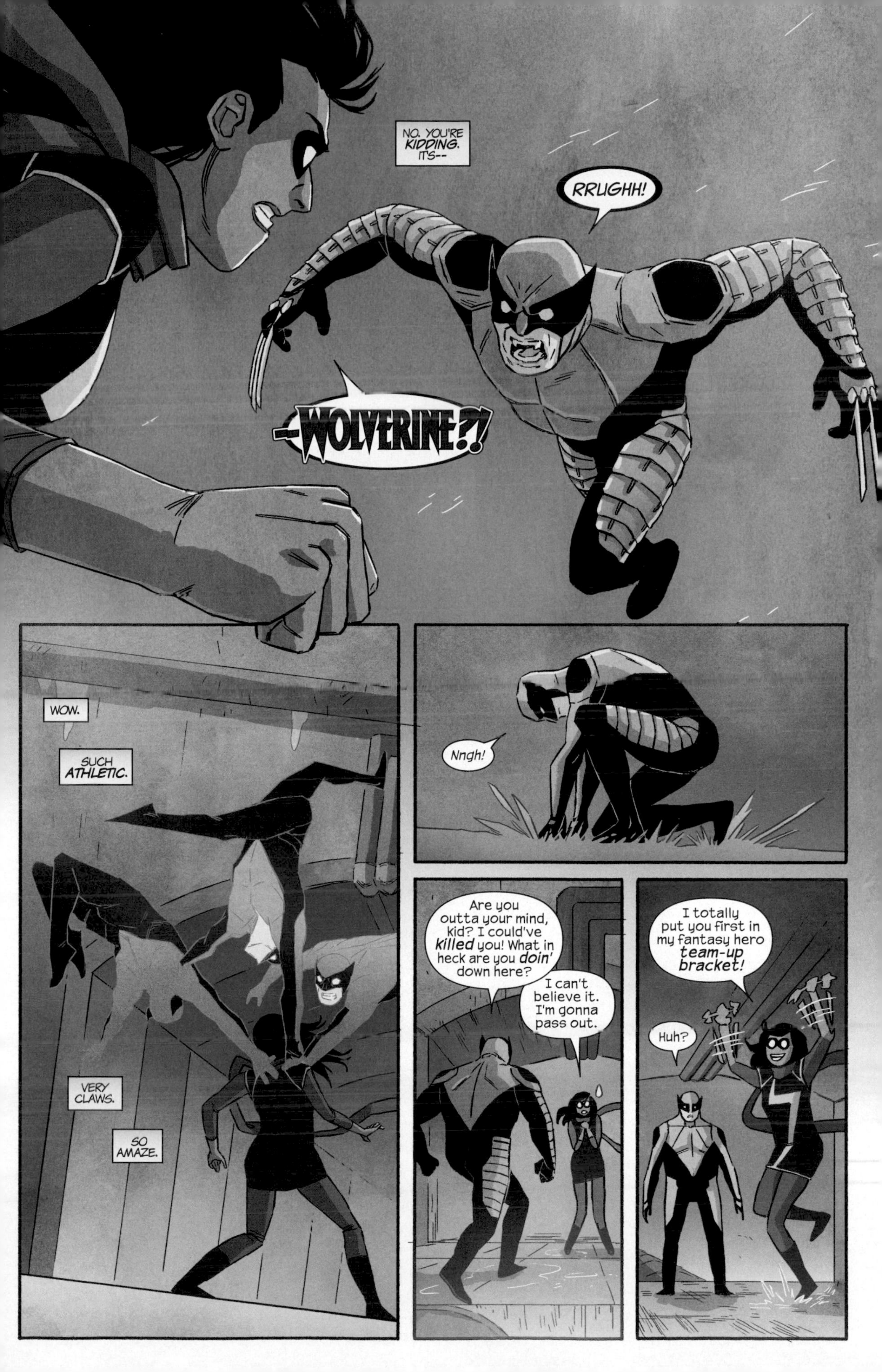

NO. YOU'RE KIDDING. IT'S--
RRUGHH!
--WOLVERINE?!
WOW.
SUCH ATHLETIC.
VERY CLAWS.
SO AMAZE.
Nngh!
Are you outta your mind, kid? I could've killed you! What in heck are you doin' down here?
I can't believe it. I'm gonna pass out.
I totally put you first in my fantasy hero team-up bracket!
Huh?

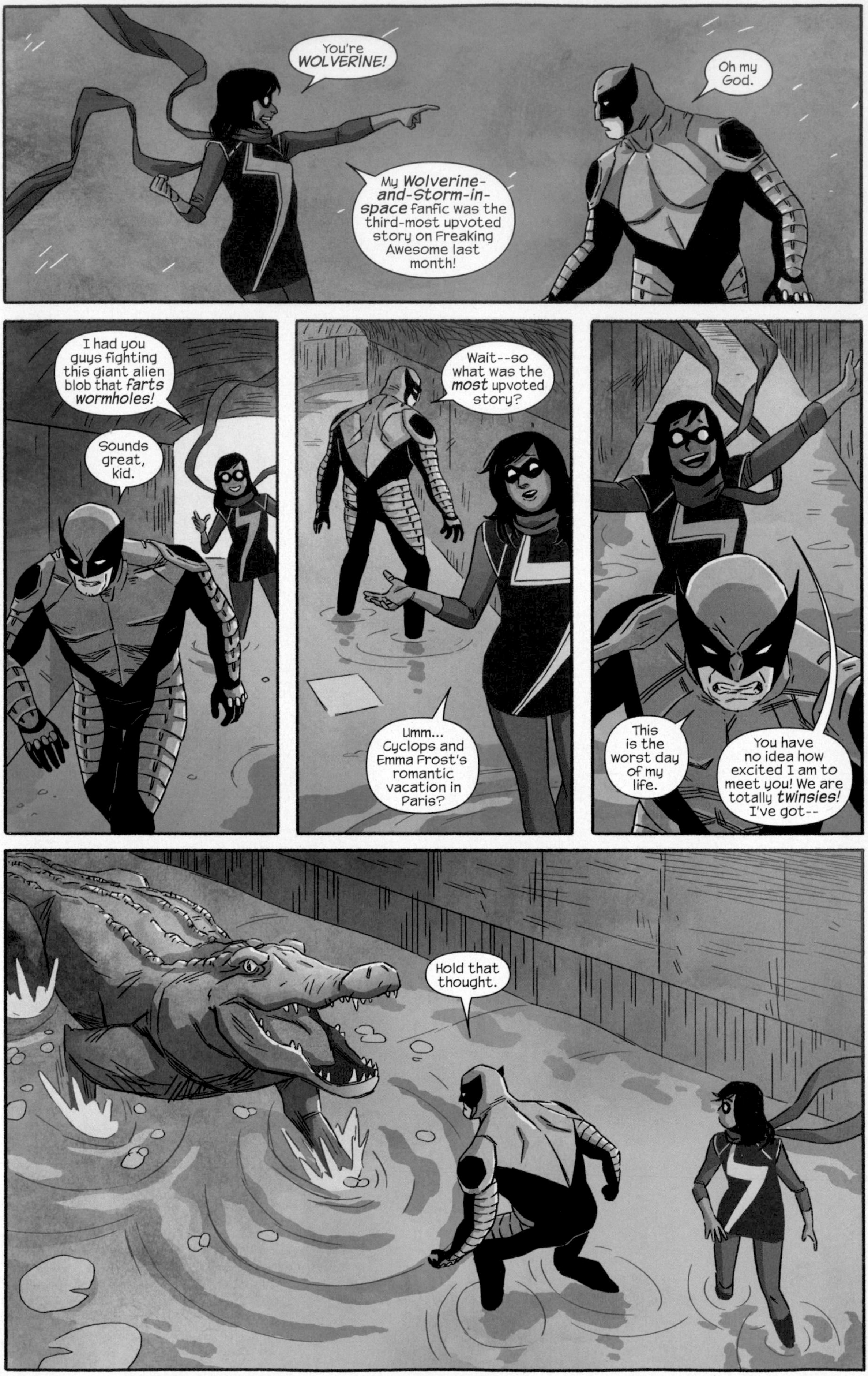
You're WOLVERINE!
Oh my God.
My Wolverine-and-Storm-in-space fanfic was the third-most upvoted story on Freaking Awesome last month!
I had you guys fighting this giant alien blob that farts wormholes!
Sounds great, kid.
Wait--so what was the most upvoted story?
Umm... Cyclops and Emma Frost's romantic vacation in Paris?
You have no idea how excited I am to meet you! We are totally twinsies! I've got--
This is the worst day of my life.
Hold that thought.

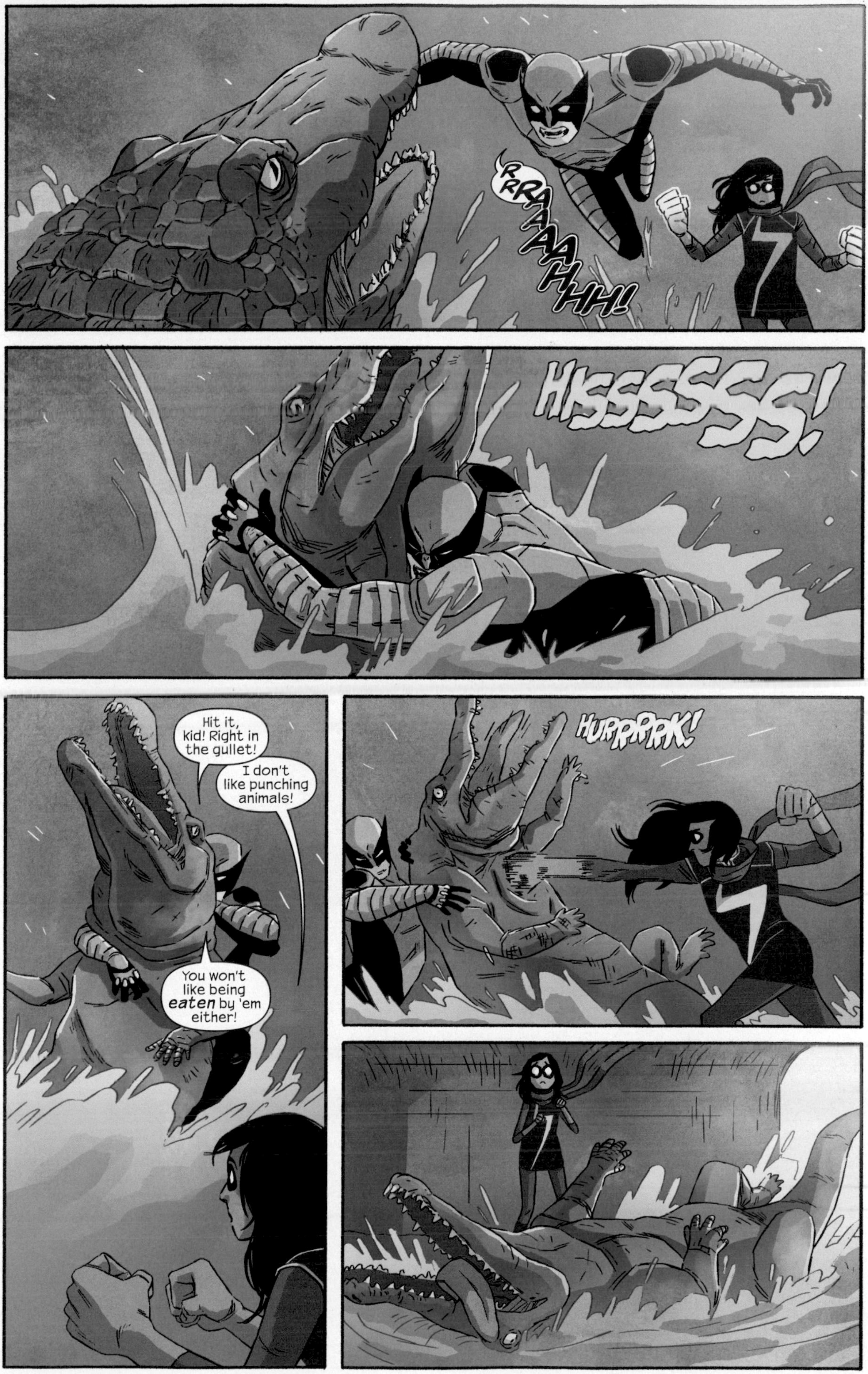

RRRAAAAHHH!
HISSSSSS!
Hit it, kid! Right in the gullet!
I don't like punching animals!
You won't like being *eaten* by 'em either!
HURRRRK!

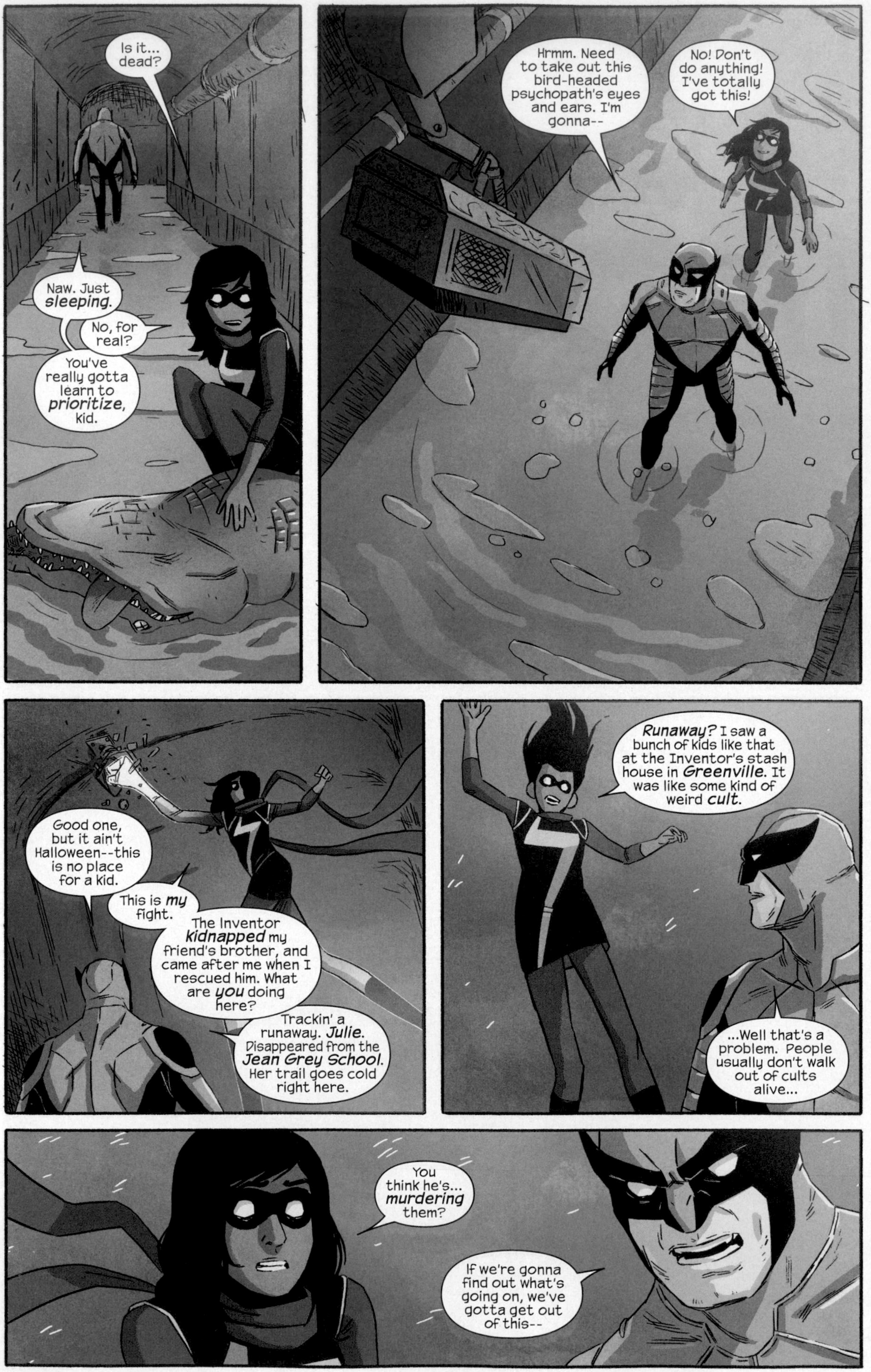

Is it... dead?
Naw. Just *sleeping.*
No, for real?
You've really gotta learn to *prioritize*, kid.
Hrmm. Need to take out this bird-headed psychopath's eyes and ears. I'm gonna--
No! Don't do anything! I've totally got this!
Good one, but it ain't Halloween--this is no place for a kid.
This is *my* fight.
The Inventor *kidnapped* my friend's brother, and came after me when I rescued him. What are *you* doing here?
Trackin' a runaway. *Julie.* Disappeared from the *Jean Grey School.* Her trail goes cold right here.
Runaway? I saw a bunch of kids like that at the Inventor's stash house in *Greenville.* It was like some kind of weird *cult.*
...Well that's a problem. People usually don't walk out of cults alive...
You think he's... *murdering* them?
If we're gonna find out what's going on, we've gotta get out of this--

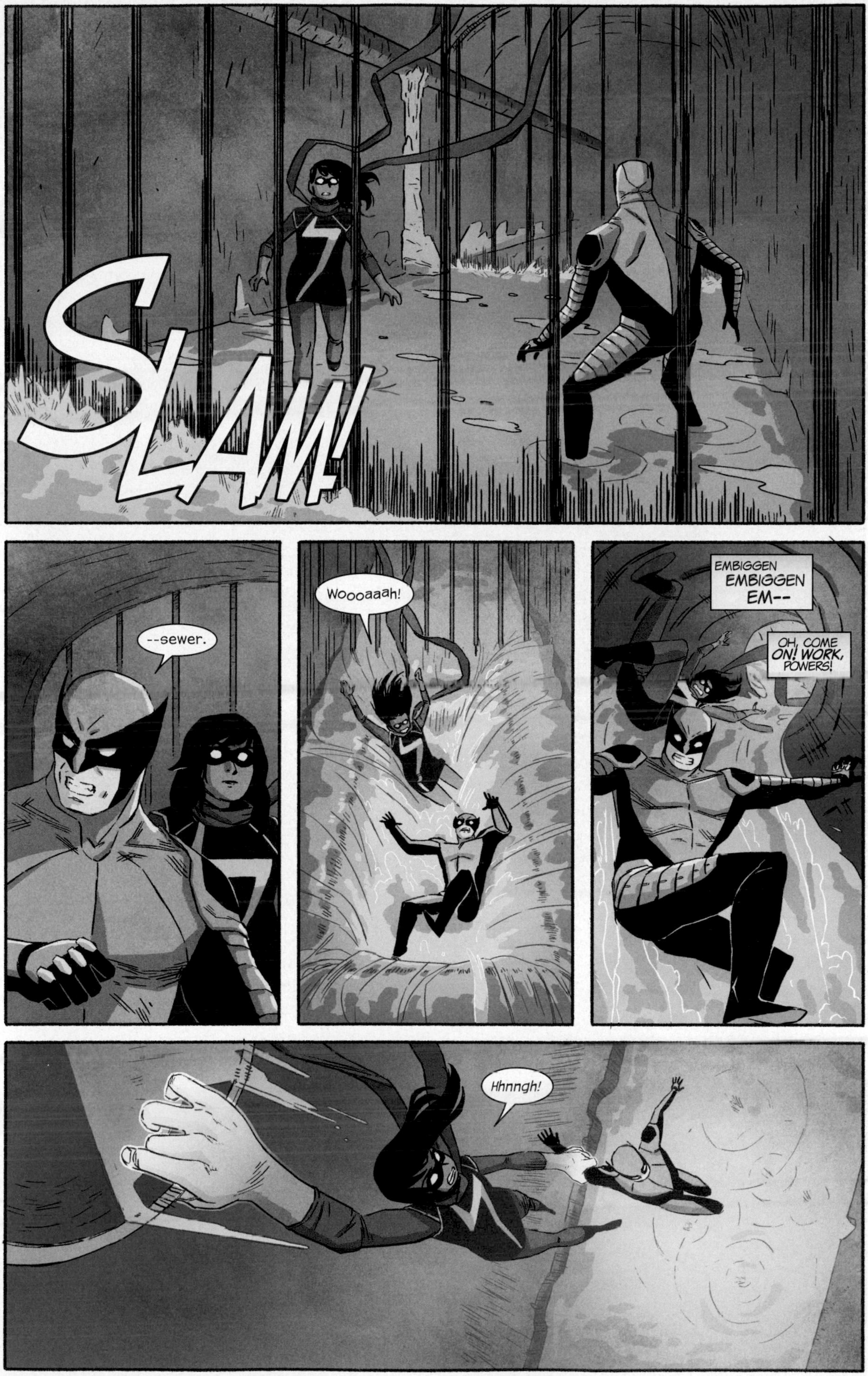
SLAM!
--sewer.
Wooooaaah!
EMBIGGEN EMBIGGEN EM--
OH, COME ON! WORK, POWERS!
Hhnngh!

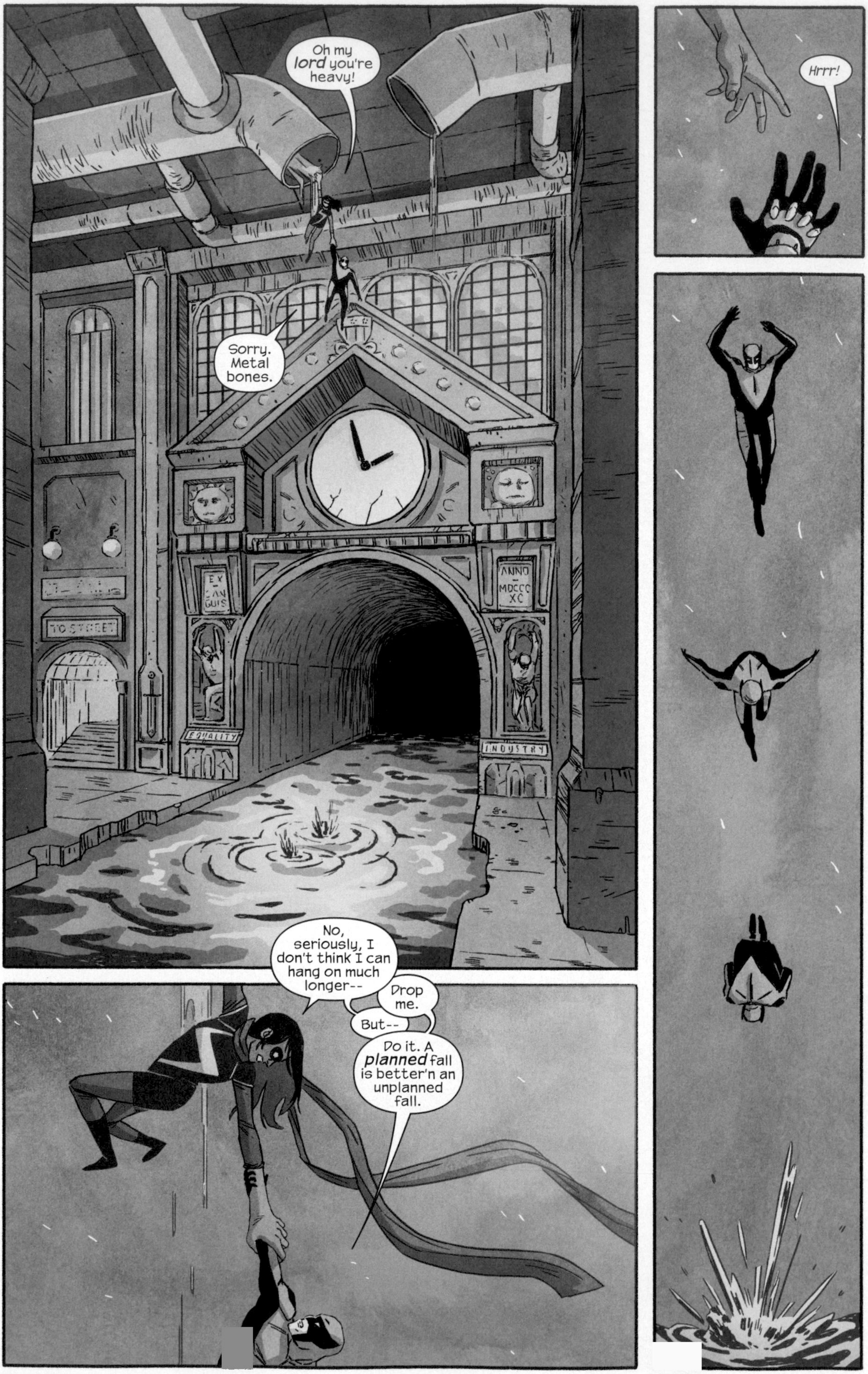
Oh my *lord* you're heavy!
Sorry. Metal bones.
EX SAN GUIS
ANNO MDCCCXC
TO STREET
EQUALITY
INDUSTRY
No, seriously, I don't think I can hang on much longer--
Drop me.
But--
Do it. A *planned* fall is better'n an unplanned fall.
Hrrr!

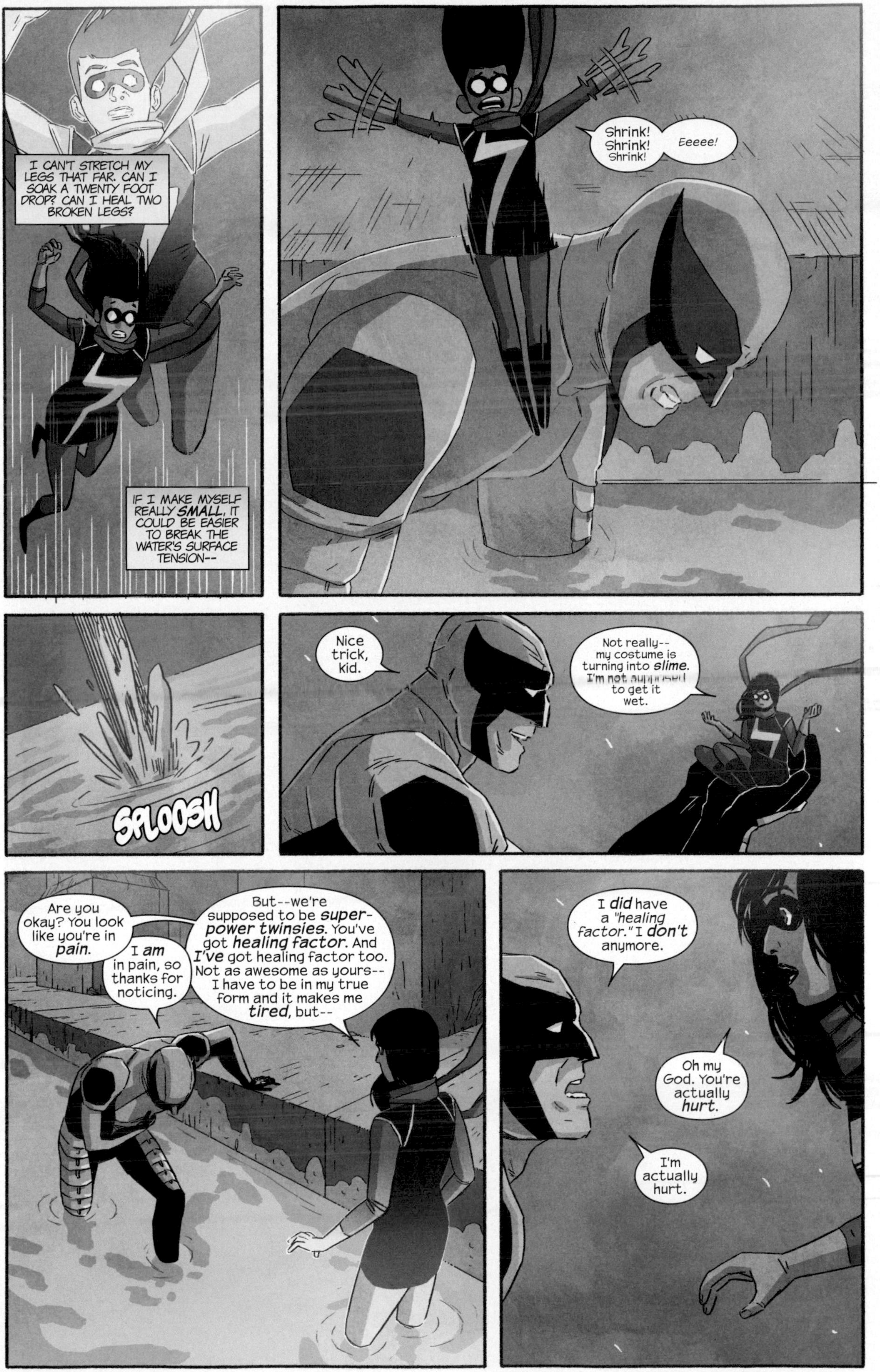
I CAN'T STRETCH MY LEGS THAT FAR. CAN I SOAK A TWENTY FOOT DROP? CAN I HEAL TWO BROKEN LEGS?
IF I MAKE MYSELF REALLY SMALL, IT COULD BE EASIER TO BREAK THE WATER'S SURFACE TENSION--
Shrink! Shrink! Shrink!
Eeeee!
SPLOOSH
Nice trick, kid.
Not really--my costume is turning into slime. I'm not supposed to get it wet.
Are you okay? You look like you're in pain.
I am in pain, so thanks for noticing.
But--we're supposed to be super-power twinsies. You've got healing factor. And I've got healing factor too. Not as awesome as yours--I have to be in my true form and it makes me tired, but--
I did have a "healing factor." I don't anymore.
Oh my God. You're actually hurt.
I'm actually hurt.

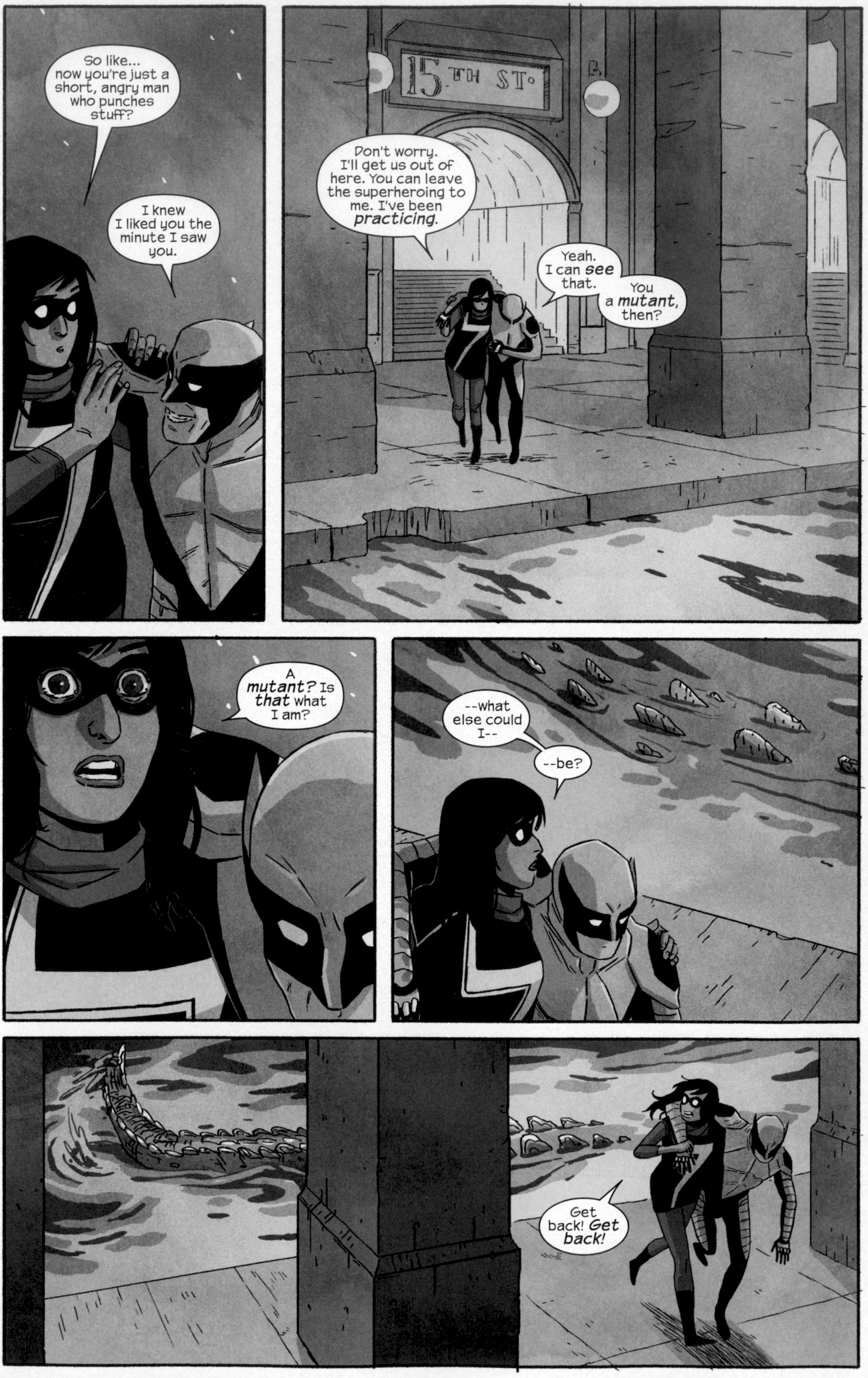
So like... now you're just a short, angry man who punches stuff?
I knew I liked you the minute I saw you.
15TH ST.
Don't worry. I'll get us out of here. You can leave the superheroing to me. I've been *practicing*.
Yeah. I can *see* that.
You a *mutant*, then?
A *mutant*? Is *that* what I am?
--what else could I--
--be?
Get back! *Get back!*

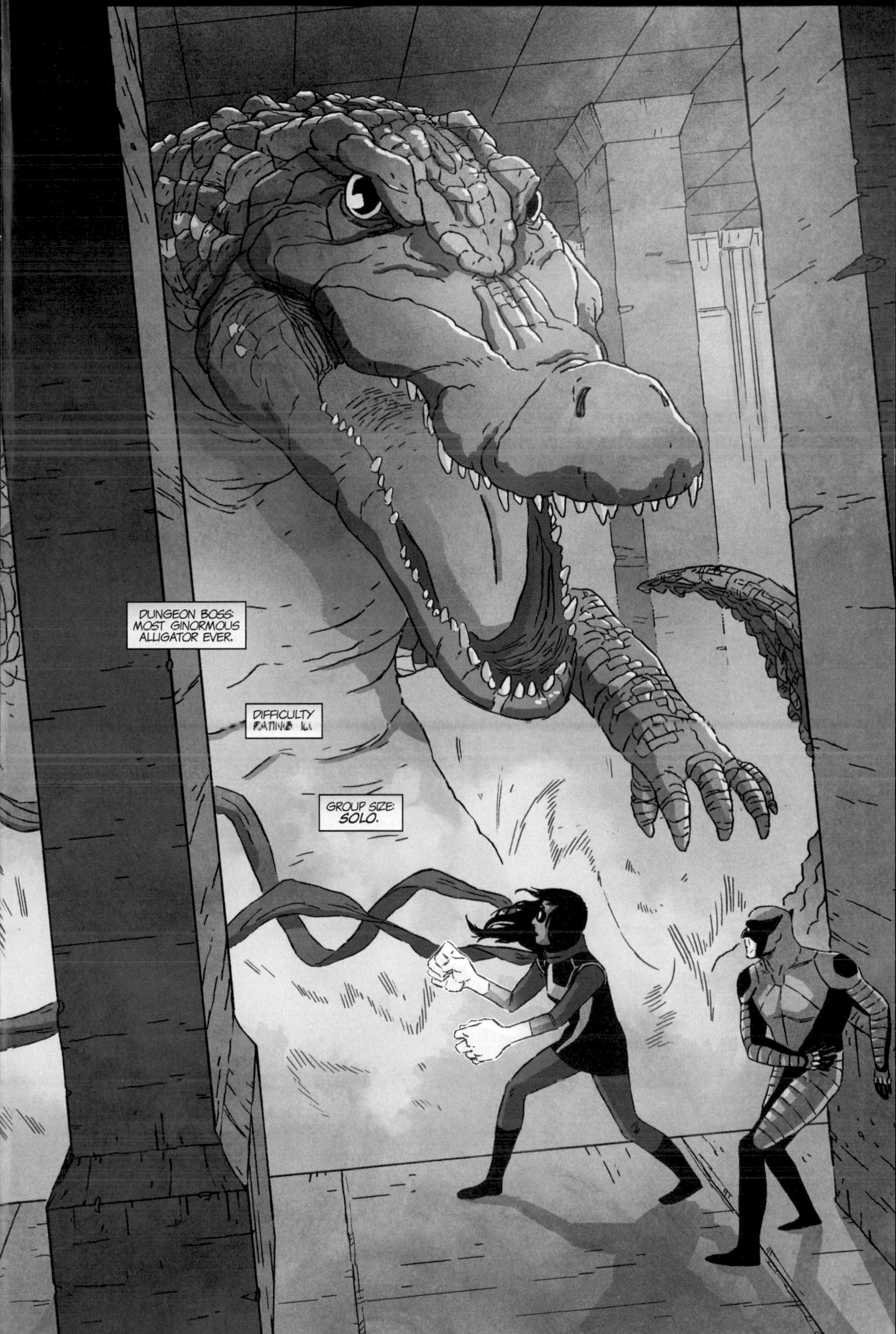
DUNGEON BOSS: MOST GINORMOUS ALLIGATOR EVER.
DIFFICULTY RATING
GROUP SIZE: SOLO.

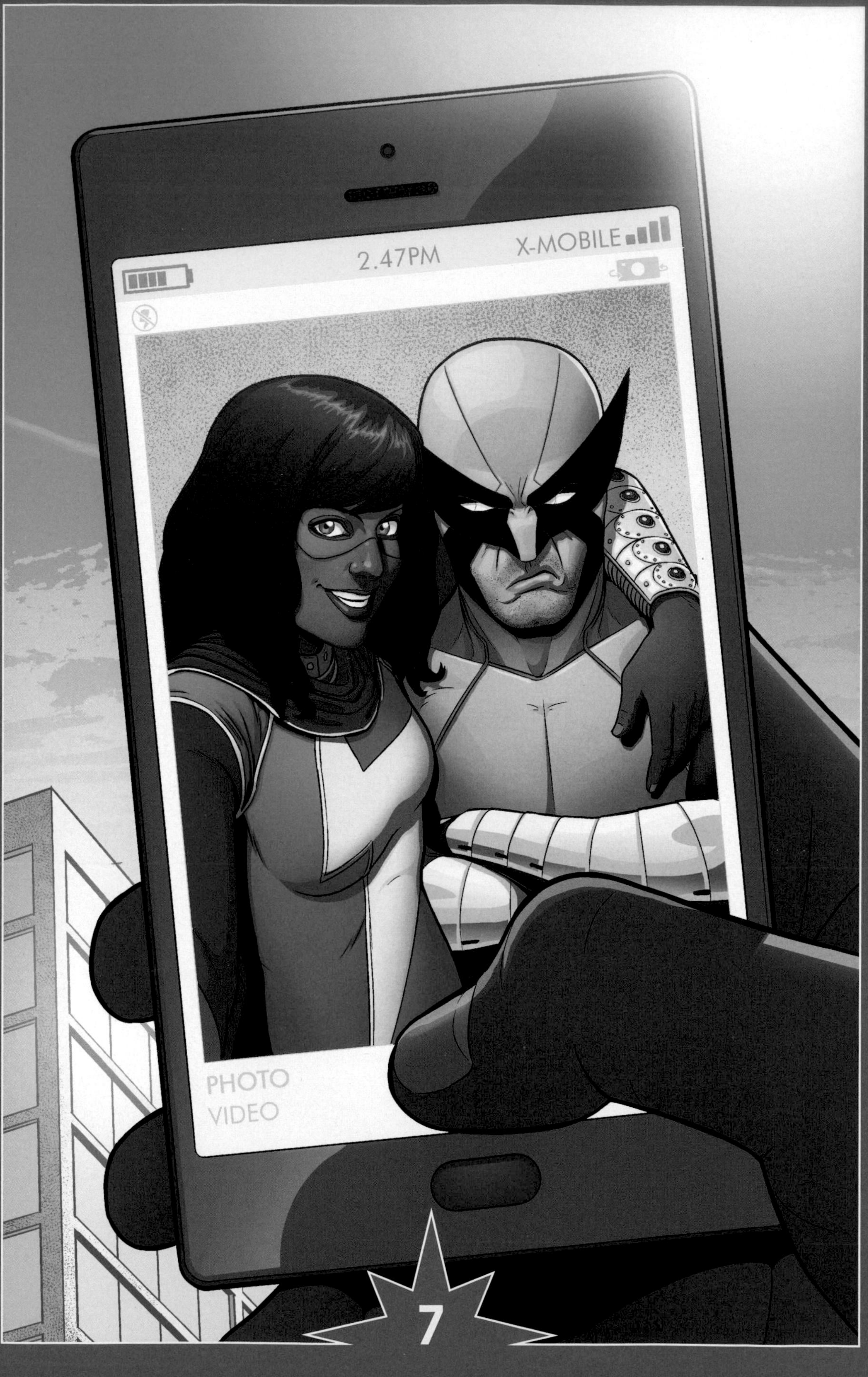
2.47PM
X-MOBILE
PHOTO
VIDEO
7

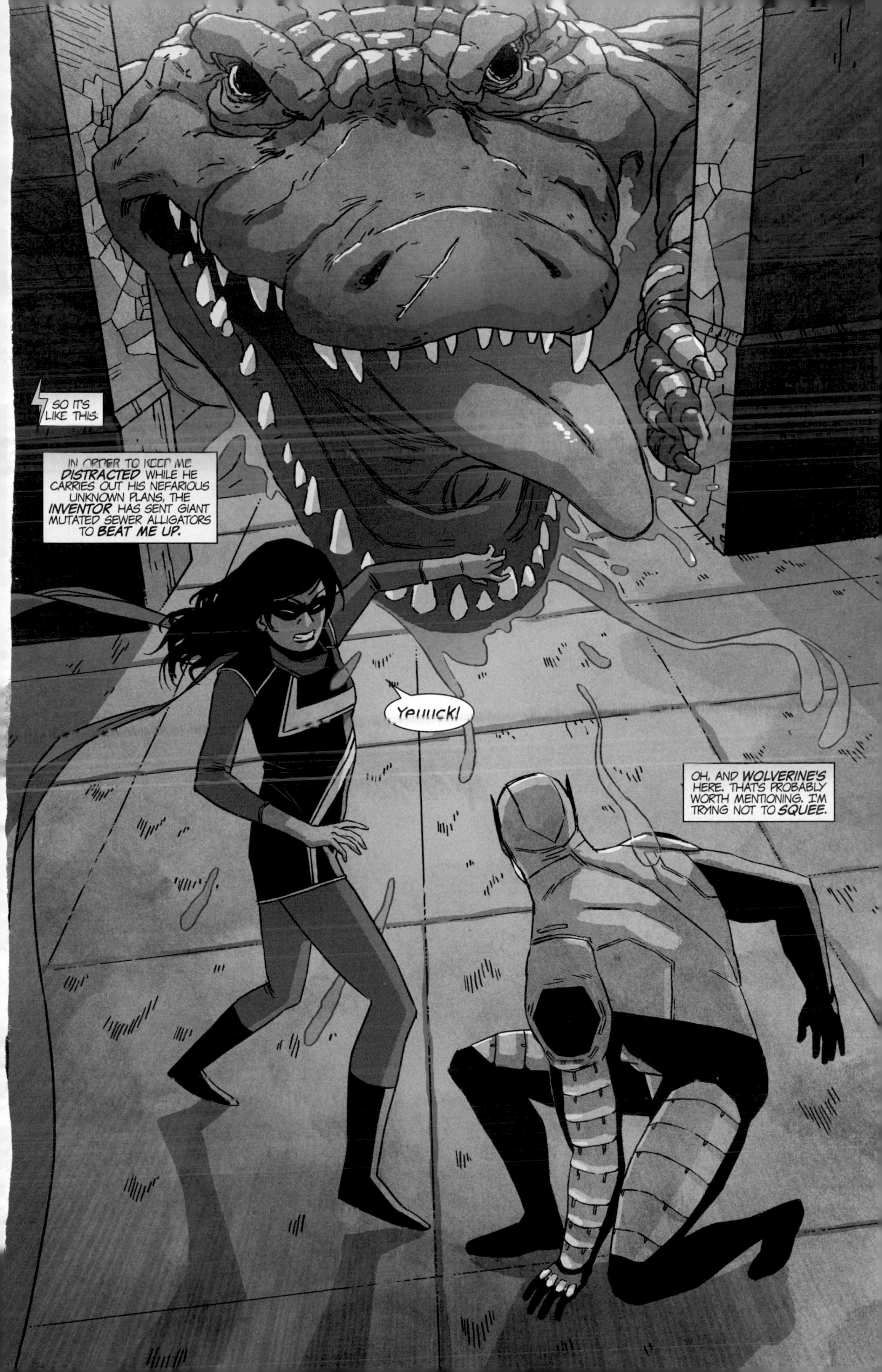
SO IT'S LIKE THIS:
IN ORDER TO KEEP ME DISTRACTED WHILE HE CARRIES OUT HIS NEFARIOUS UNKNOWN PLANS, THE INVENTOR HAS SENT GIANT MUTATED SEWER ALLIGATORS TO BEAT ME UP.
YEUUCK!
OH, AND WOLVERINE'S HERE. THAT'S PROBABLY WORTH MENTIONING. I'M TRYING NOT TO SQUEE.

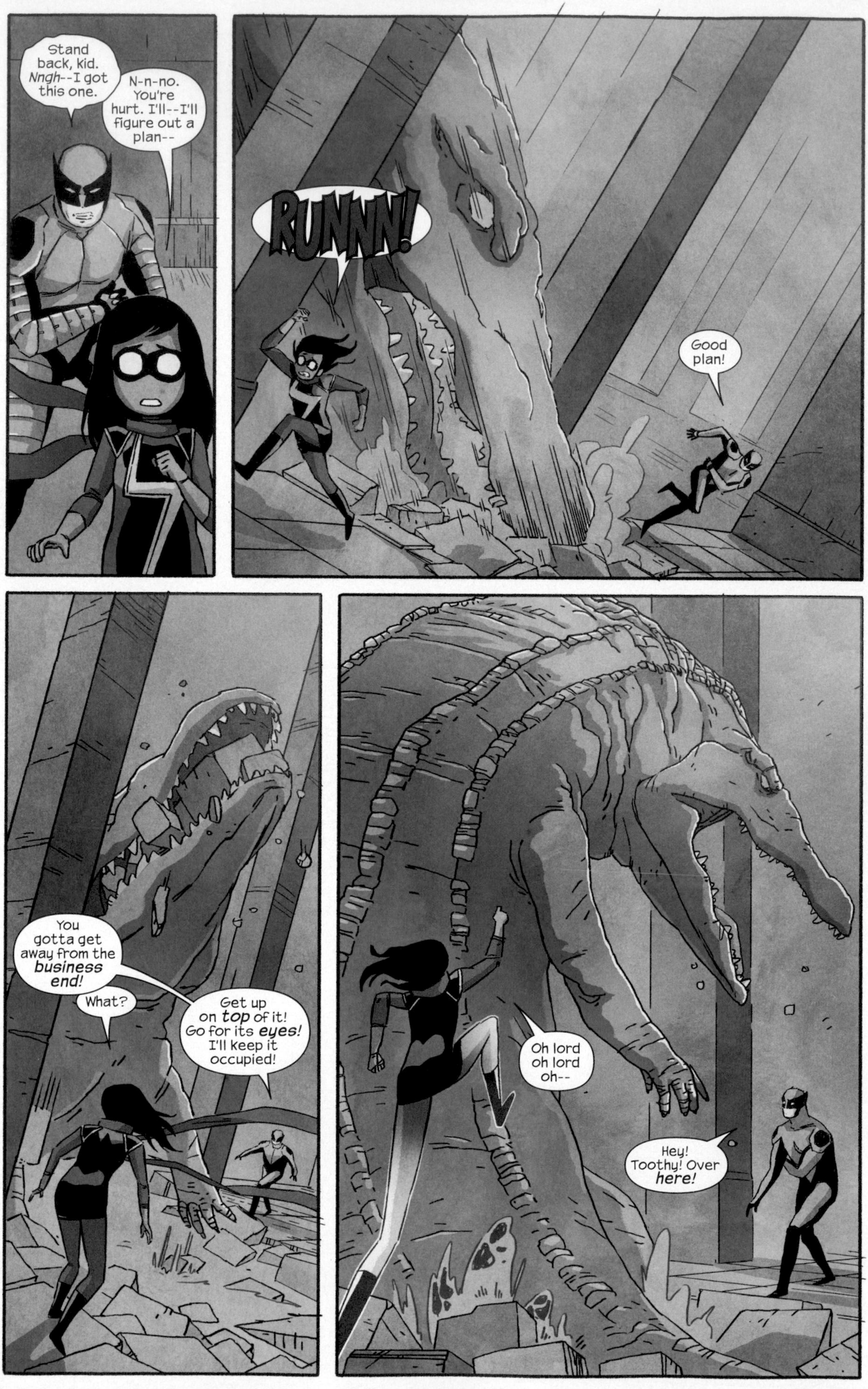
Stand back, kid. *Nngh*--I got this one.
N-n-no. You're hurt. I'll--I'll figure out a plan--
RUNNN!
Good plan!
You gotta get away from the *business end!*
What?
Get up on *top* of it! Go for its *eyes!* I'll keep it occupied!
Oh lord oh lord oh--
Hey! Toothy! Over *here!*

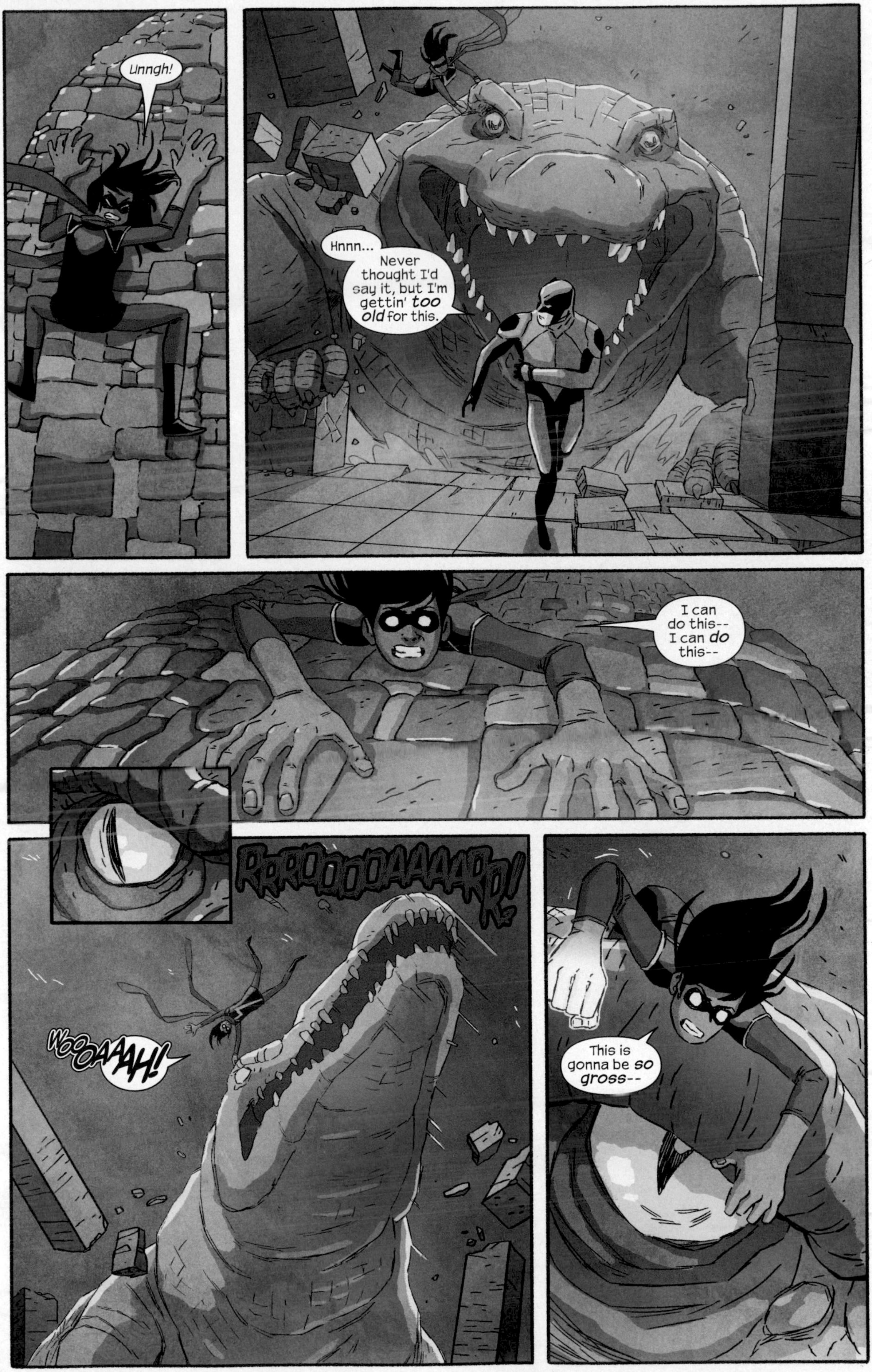
Unngh!
Hnnn...
Never thought I'd say it, but I'm gettin' too old for this.
I can do this-- I can do this--
RRRROOOOAAAARR!
WOOOAAAH!
This is gonna be so gross--

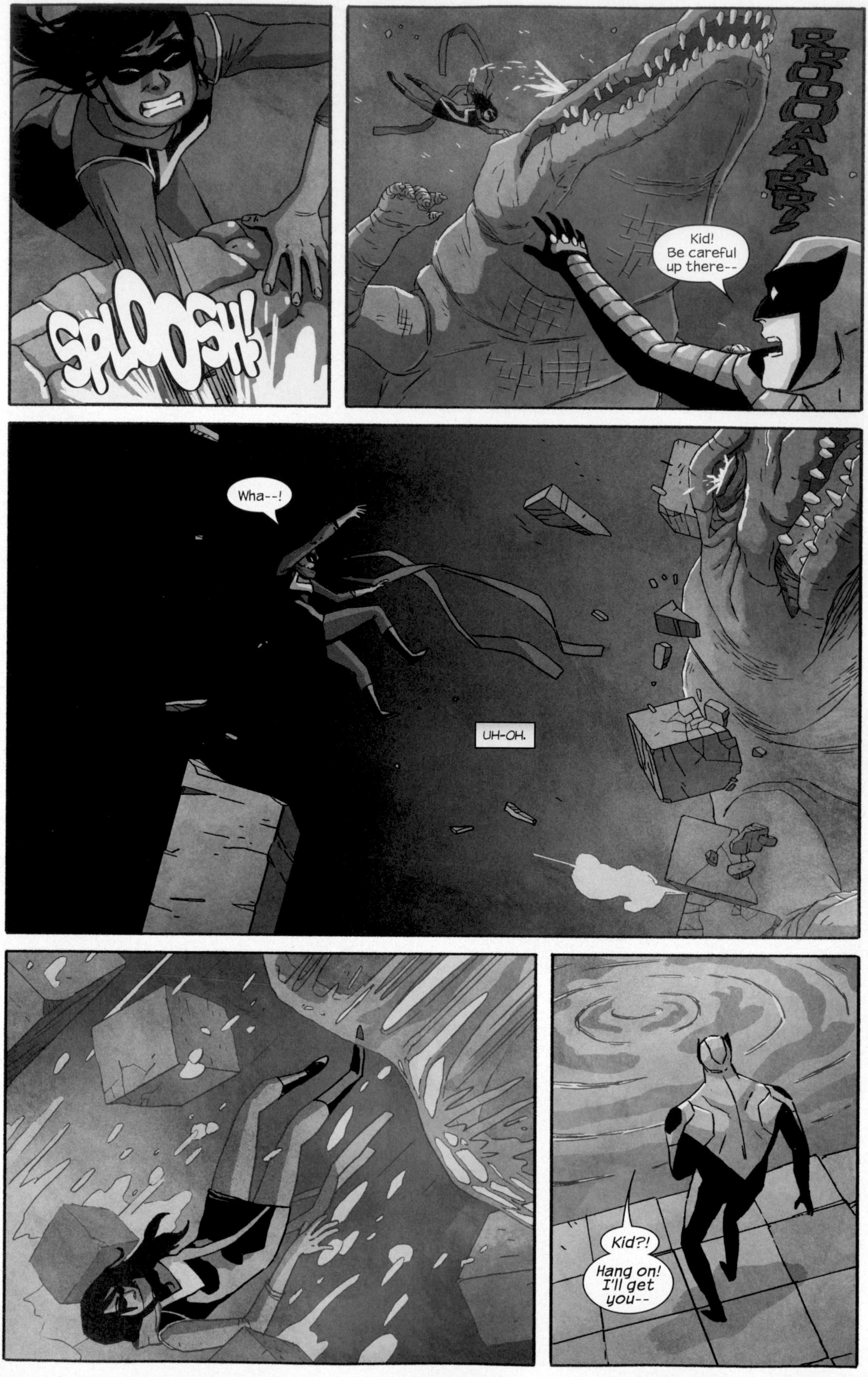
SPLOOSH!
RROOOAAARR!
Kid! Be careful up there--
Wha--!
UH-OH.
Kid?!
Hang on! I'll get you--

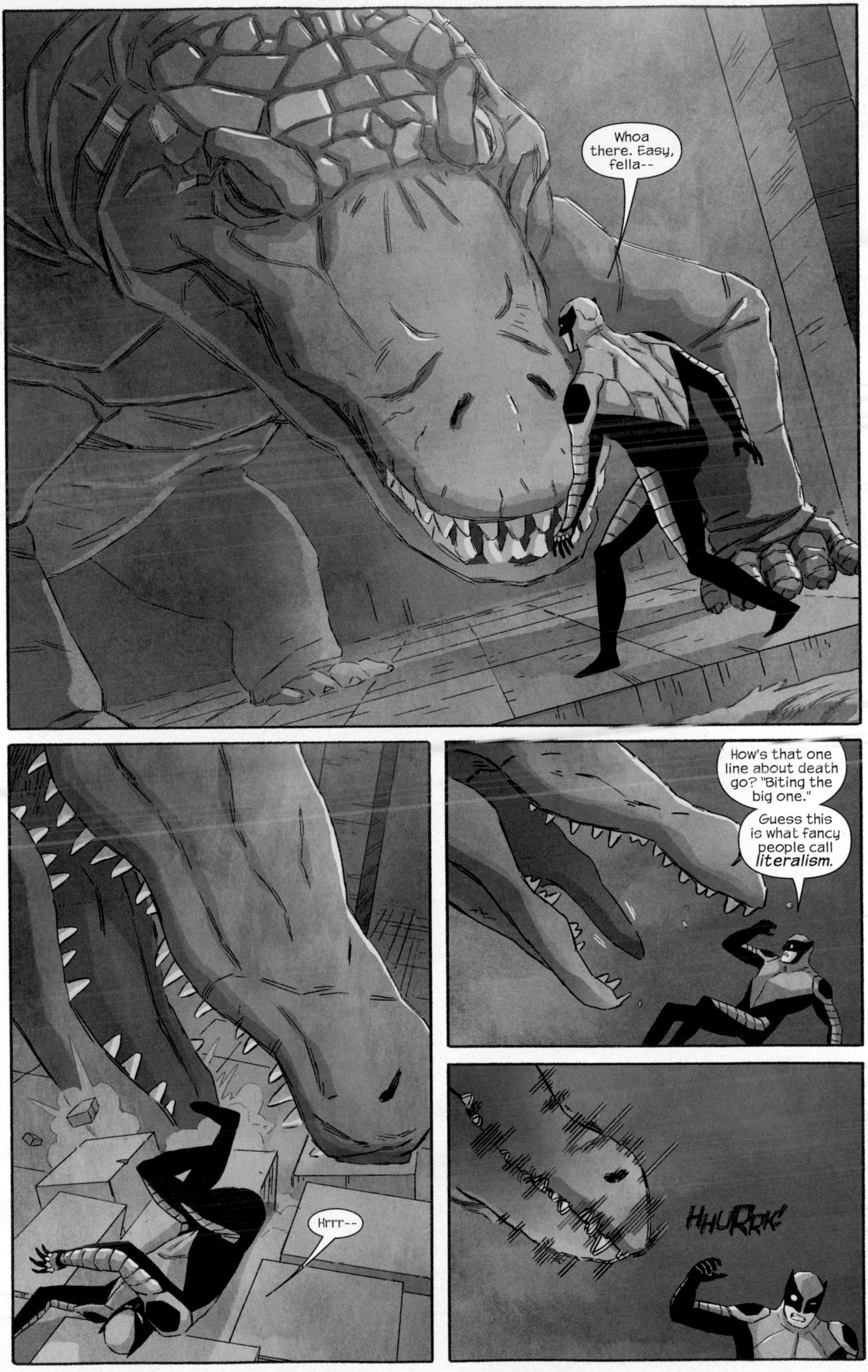
Whoa there. Easy, fella--
Hrrr--
How's that one line about death go? "Biting the big one."
Guess this is what fancy people call *literalism*.
HHURRK!

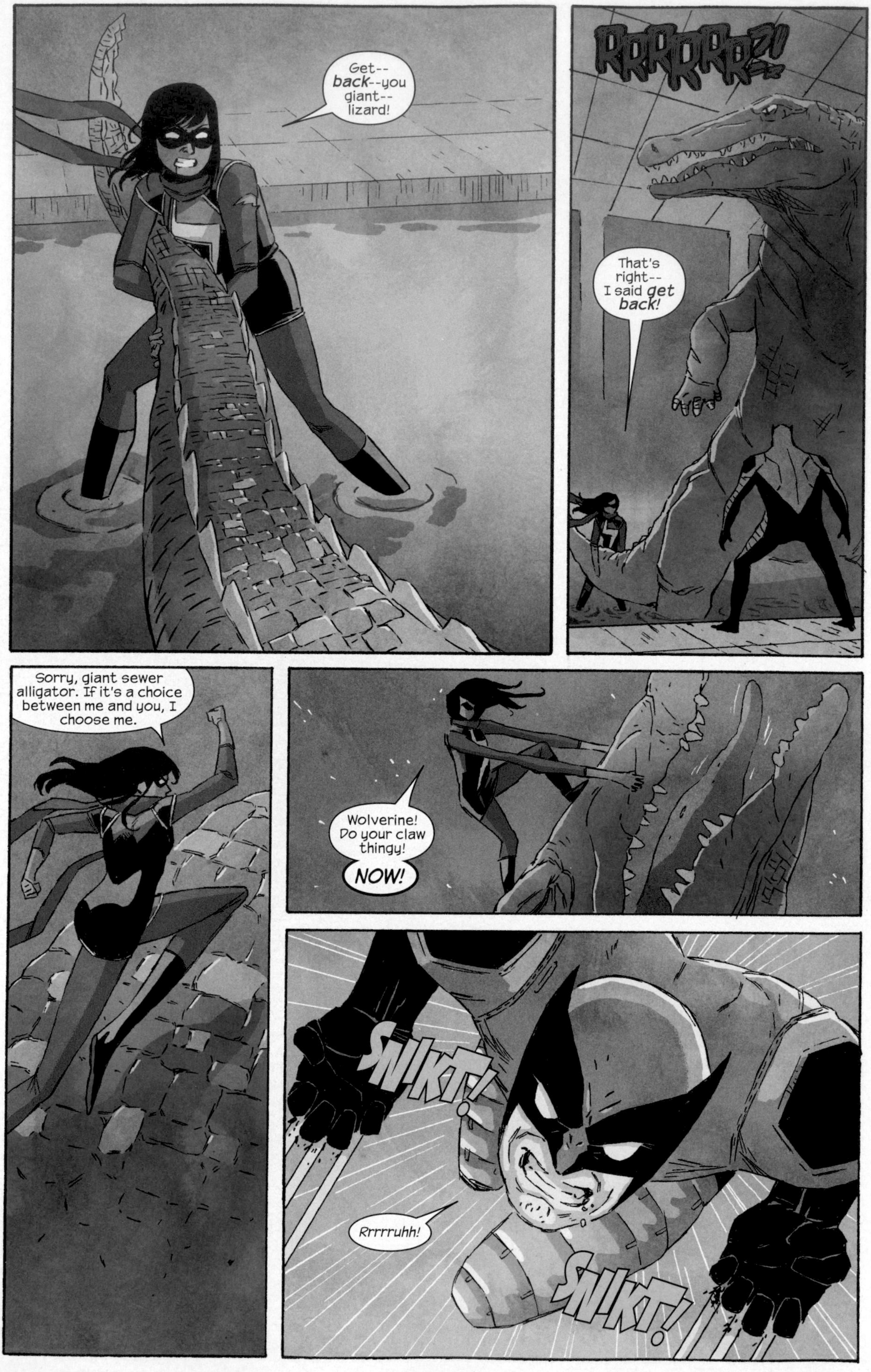
Get--
back--you
giant--
lizard!
RRRRRRZ!
That's
right--
I said get
back!
Sorry, giant sewer
alligator. If it's a choice
between me and you, I
choose me.
Wolverine!
Do your claw
thingy!
NOW!
SNIKT!
Rrrrruhh!
SNIKT!

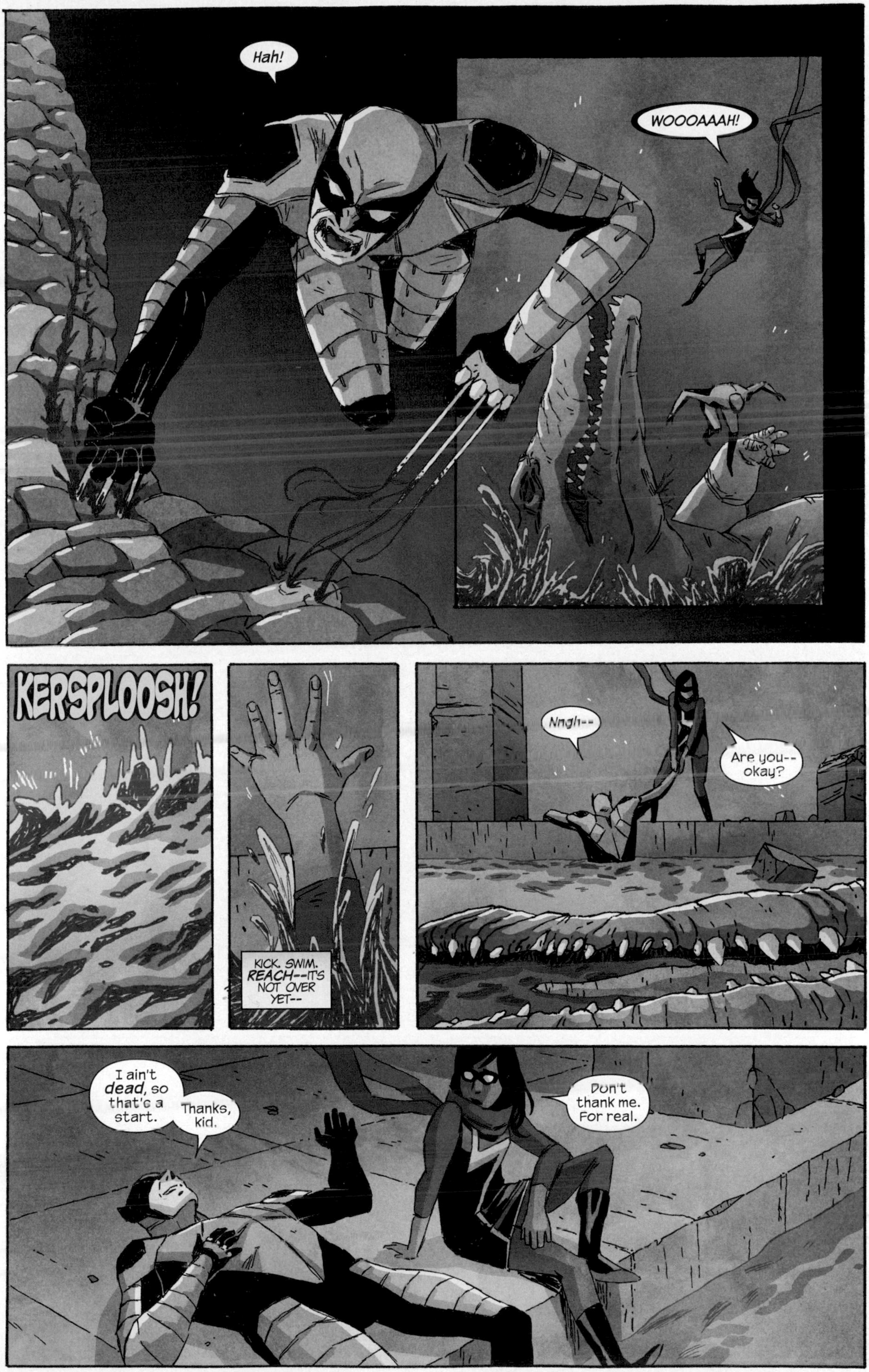
Hah!
WOOOAAAH!
KERSPLOOSH!
KICK. SWIM. REACH--IT'S NOT OVER YET--
Nngh--
Are you--okay?
I ain't dead, so that's a start.
Thanks, kid.
Don't thank me. For real.

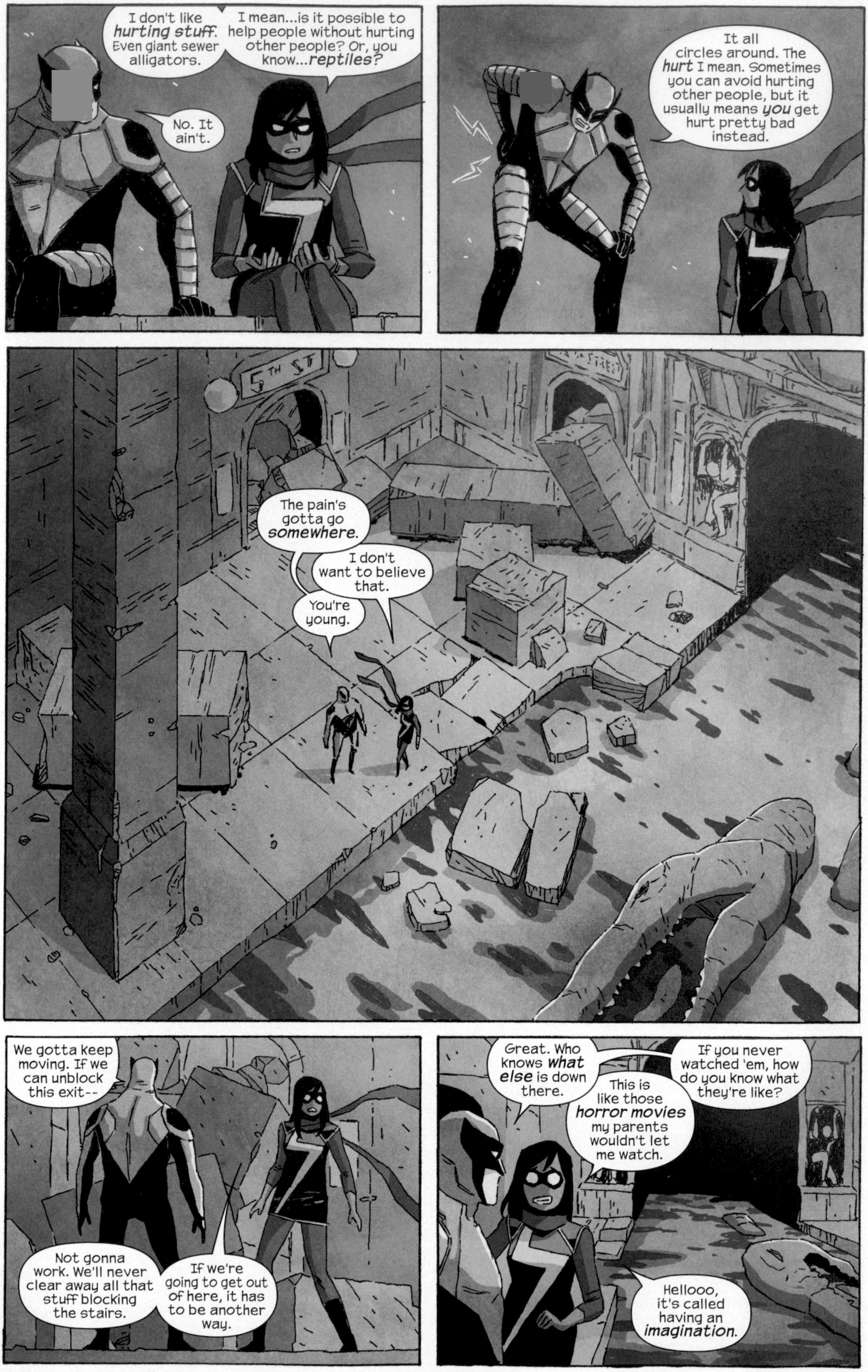
I don't like *hurting stuff*. Even giant sewer alligators.
I mean...is it possible to help people without hurting other people? Or, you know...*reptiles?*
No. It ain't.
It all circles around. The *hurt* I mean. Sometimes you can avoid hurting other people, but it usually means *you* get hurt pretty bad instead.
5TH ST
The pain's gotta go *somewhere*.
I don't want to believe that.
You're young.
We gotta keep moving. If we can unblock this exit--
Not gonna work. We'll never clear away all that stuff blocking the stairs.
If we're going to get out of here, it has to be another way.
Great. Who knows *what else* is down there.
This is like those *horror movies* my parents wouldn't let me watch.
If you never watched 'em, how do you know what they're like?
Hellooo, it's called having an *imagination*.

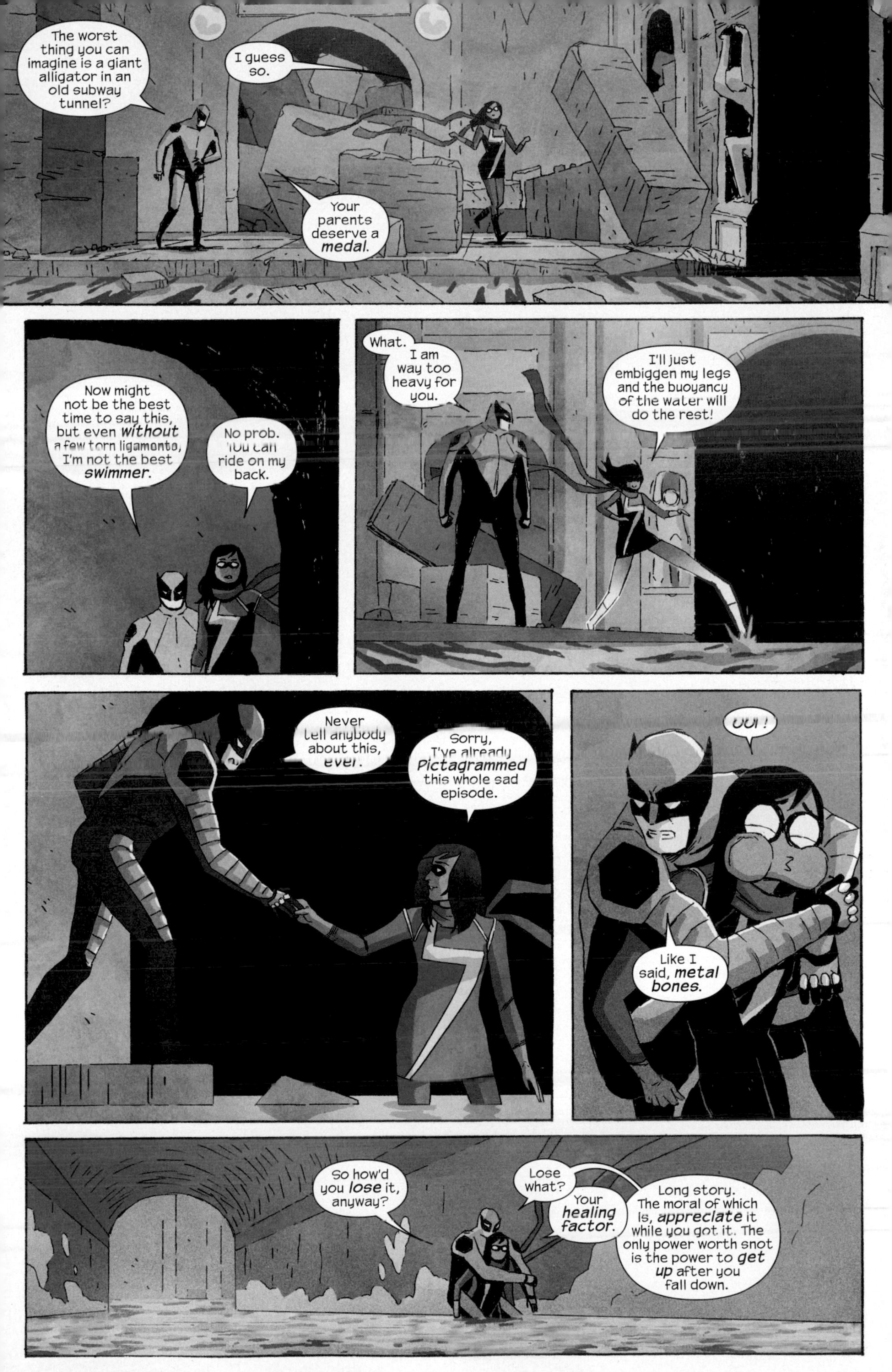

The worst thing you can imagine is a giant alligator in an old subway tunnel?
I guess so.
Your parents deserve a *medal*.
Now might not be the best time to say this, but even *without* a few torn ligaments, I'm not the best *swimmer*.
No prob. You can ride on my back.
What. I am way too heavy for you.
I'll just embiggen my legs and the buoyancy of the water will do the rest!
Never tell anybody about this, *ever*.
Sorry, I've already *Pictagrammed* this whole sad episode.
OOF!
Like I said, *metal bones*.
So how'd you *lose* it, anyway?
Lose what?
Your *healing factor*.
Long story. The moral of which is, *appreciate* it while you got it. The only power worth snot is the power to *get up* after you fall down.

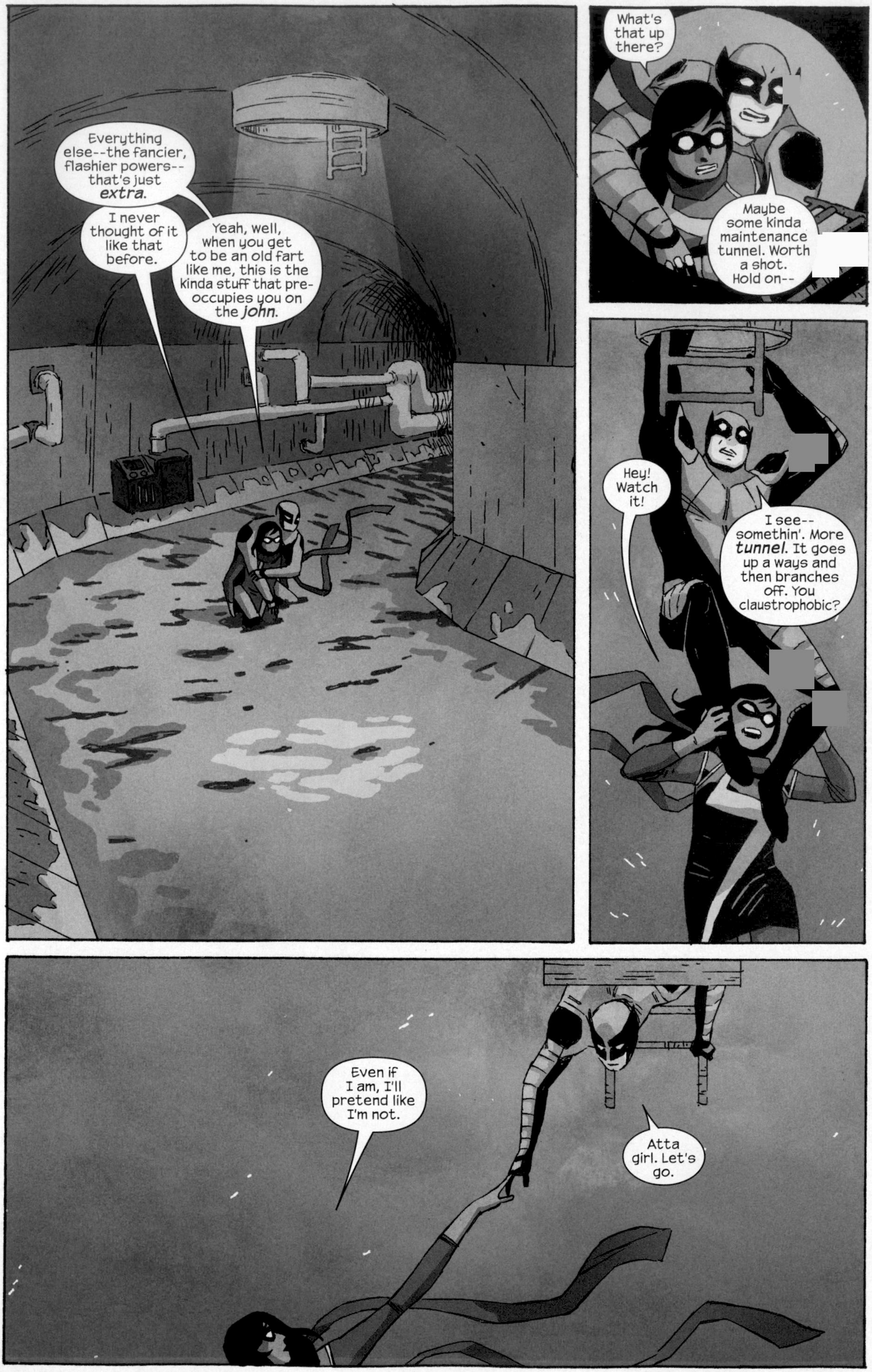

Everything else--the fancier, flashier powers--that's just *extra*.
I never thought of it like that before.
Yeah, well, when you get to be an old fart like me, this is the kinda stuff that pre-occupies you on the *john*.
What's that up there?
Maybe some kinda maintenance tunnel. Worth a shot. Hold on--
Hey! Watch it!
I see--somethin'. More *tunnel*. It goes up a ways and then branches off. You claustrophobic?
Even if I am, I'll pretend like I'm not.
Atta girl. Let's go.

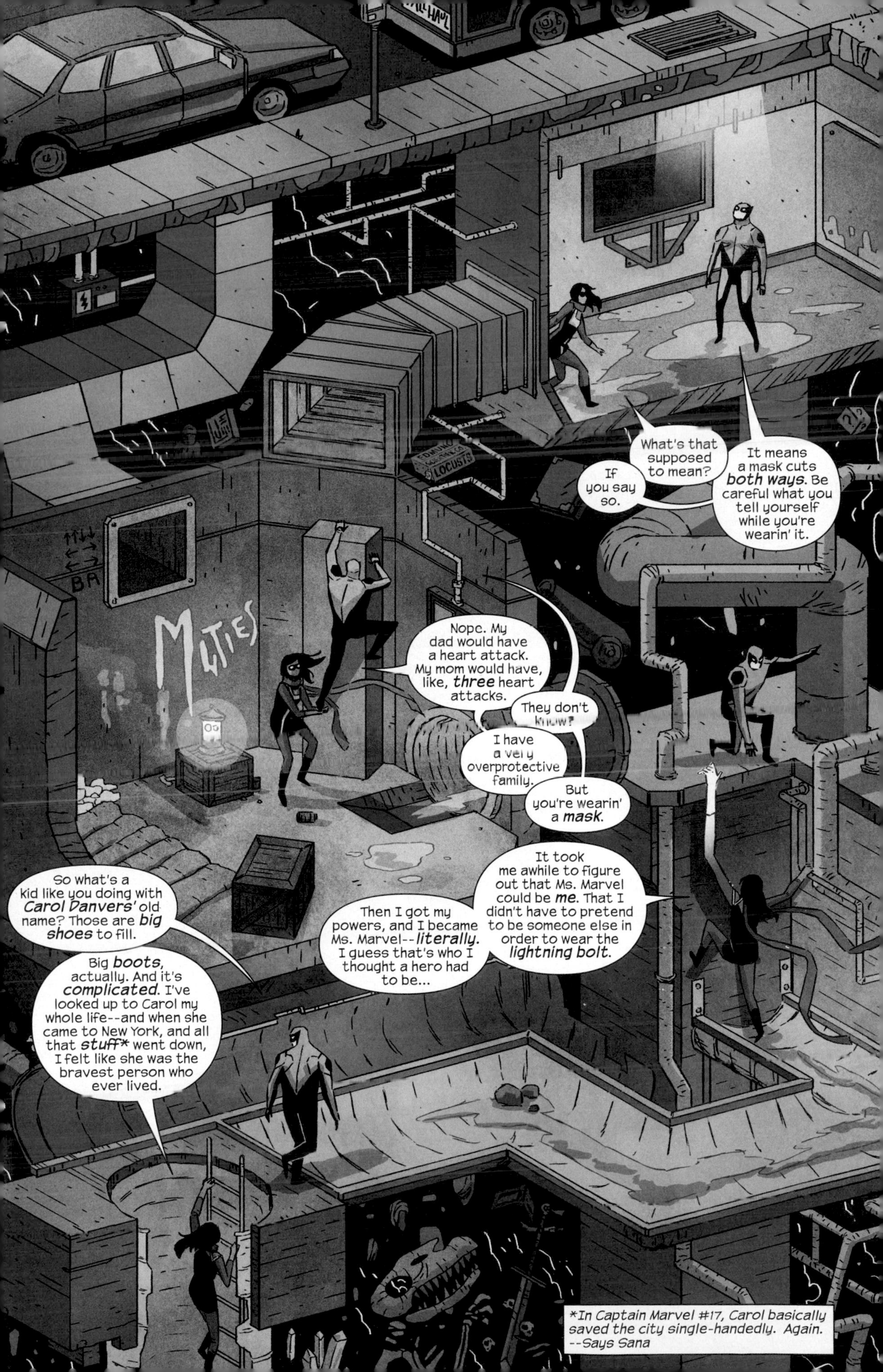

So what's a kid like you doing with Carol Danvers' old name? Those are big shoes to fill.
Big boots, actually. And it's complicated. I've looked up to Carol my whole life--and when she came to New York, and all that stuff* went down, I felt like she was the bravest person who ever lived.
Then I got my powers, and I became Ms. Marvel--literally. I guess that's who I thought a hero had to be...
It took me awhile to figure out that Ms. Marvel could be me. That I didn't have to pretend to be someone else in order to wear the lightning bolt.
Nope. My dad would have a heart attack. My mom would have, like, three heart attacks.
They don't know?
I have a very overprotective family.
But you're wearin' a mask.
What's that supposed to mean?
It means a mask cuts both ways. Be careful what you tell yourself while you're wearin' it.
If you say so.
MUTIES
LOCUSTS
*In Captain Marvel #17, Carol basically saved the city single-handedly. Again. --Says Sana

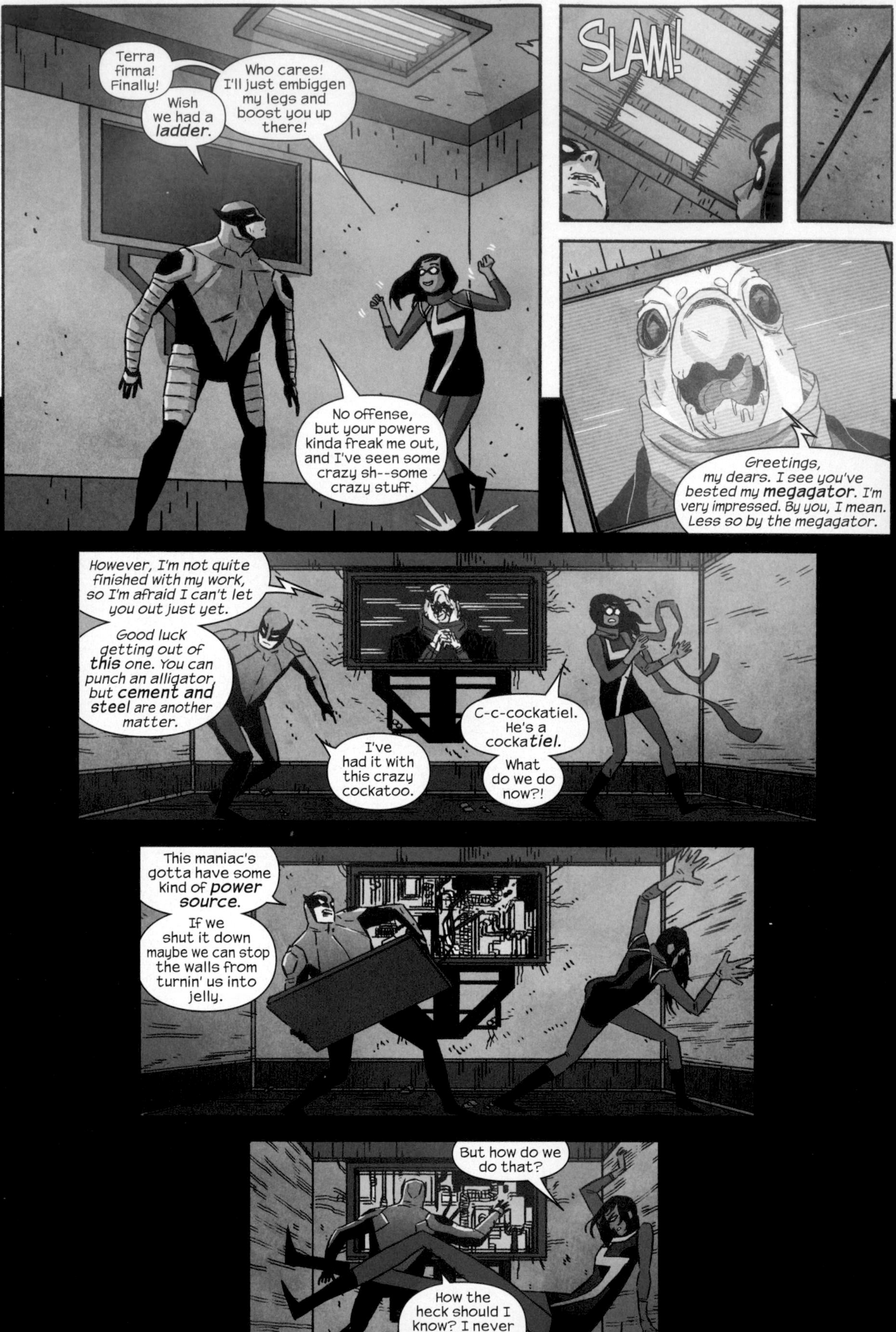
Terra firma! Finally!
Wish we had a ladder.
Who cares! I'll just embiggen my legs and boost you up there!
No offense, but your powers kinda freak me out, and I've seen some crazy sh--some crazy stuff.
SLAM!
Greetings, my dears. I see you've bested my megagator. I'm very impressed. By you, I mean. Less so by the megagator.
However, I'm not quite finished with my work, so I'm afraid I can't let you out just yet.
Good luck getting out of this one. You can punch an alligator, but cement and steel are another matter.
I've had it with this crazy cockatoo.
C-c-cockatiel. He's a cockatiel.
What do we do now?!
This maniac's gotta have some kind of power source.
If we shut it down maybe we can stop the walls from turnin' us into jelly.
But how do we do that?
How the heck should I know? I never made it past high school!
I'm in high school!

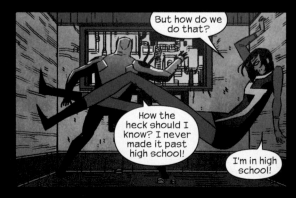

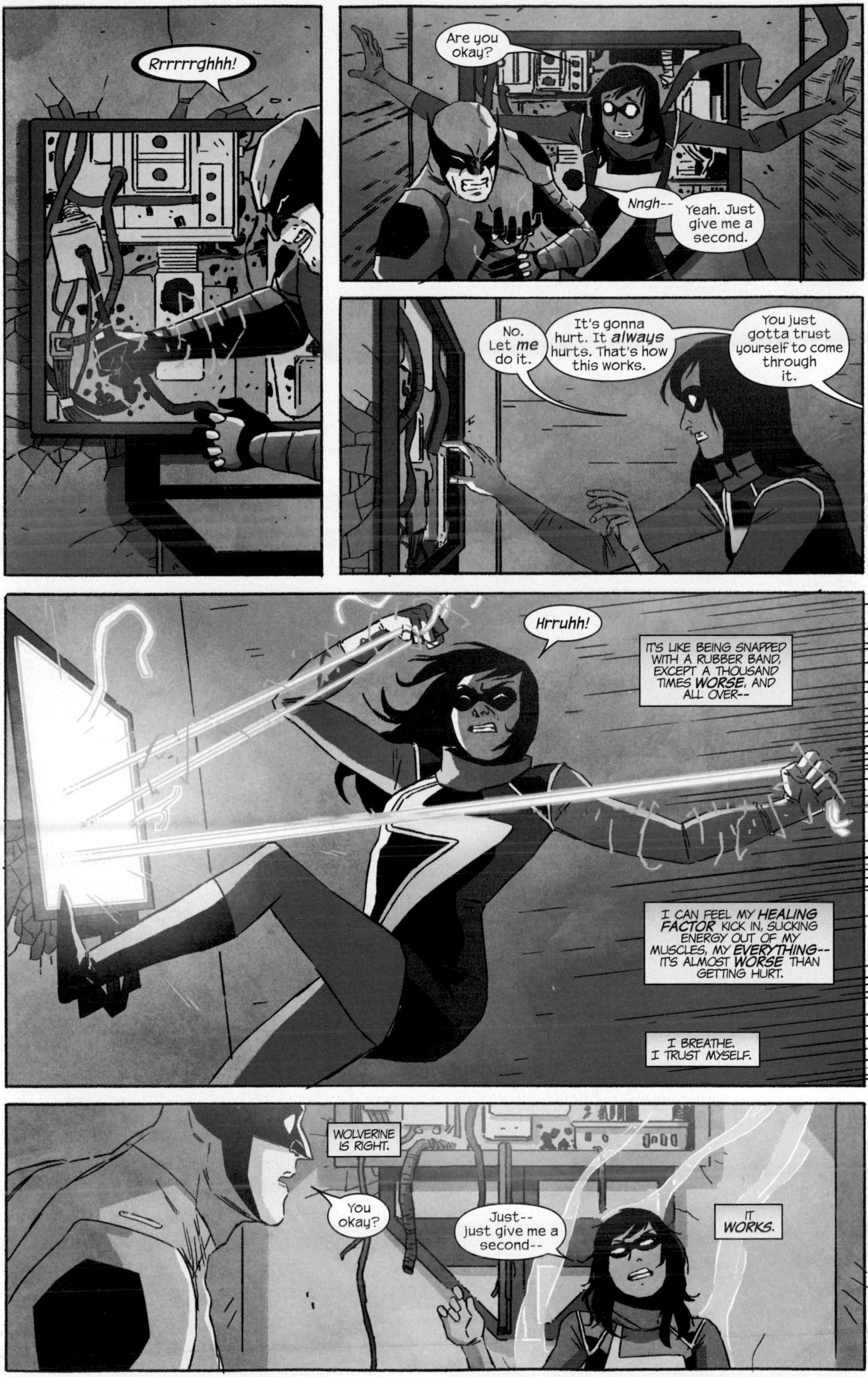

Rrrrrrghhh!
Are you okay?
Nngh--
Yeah. Just give me a second.
No. Let me do it.
It's gonna hurt. It always hurts. That's how this works.
You just gotta trust yourself to come through it.
Hrruhh!
IT'S LIKE BEING SNAPPED WITH A RUBBER BAND, EXCEPT A THOUSAND TIMES WORSE, AND ALL OVER--
I CAN FEEL MY HEALING FACTOR KICK IN, SUCKING ENERGY OUT OF MY MUSCLES, MY EVERYTHING-- IT'S ALMOST WORSE THAN GETTING HURT.
I BREATHE. I TRUST MYSELF.
WOLVERINE IS RIGHT.
You okay?
Just-- just give me a second--
IT WORKS.

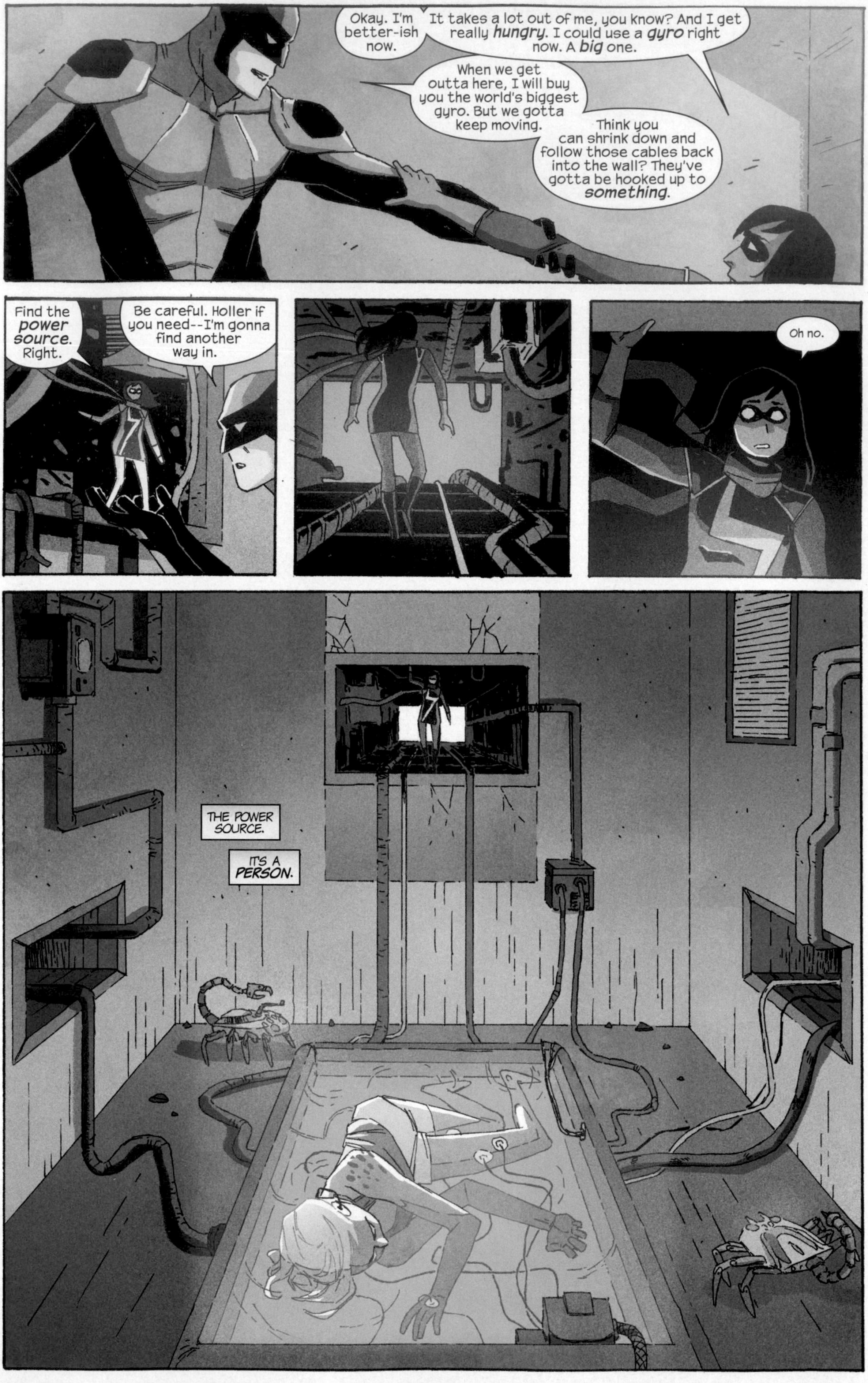
Okay. I'm better-ish now.
It takes a lot out of me, you know? And I get really hungry. I could use a gyro right now. A big one.
When we get outta here, I will buy you the world's biggest gyro. But we gotta keep moving.
Think you can shrink down and follow those cables back into the wall? They've gotta be hooked up to something.
Find the power source. Right.
Be careful. Holler if you need--I'm gonna find another way in.
Oh no.
THE POWER SOURCE.
IT'S A PERSON.

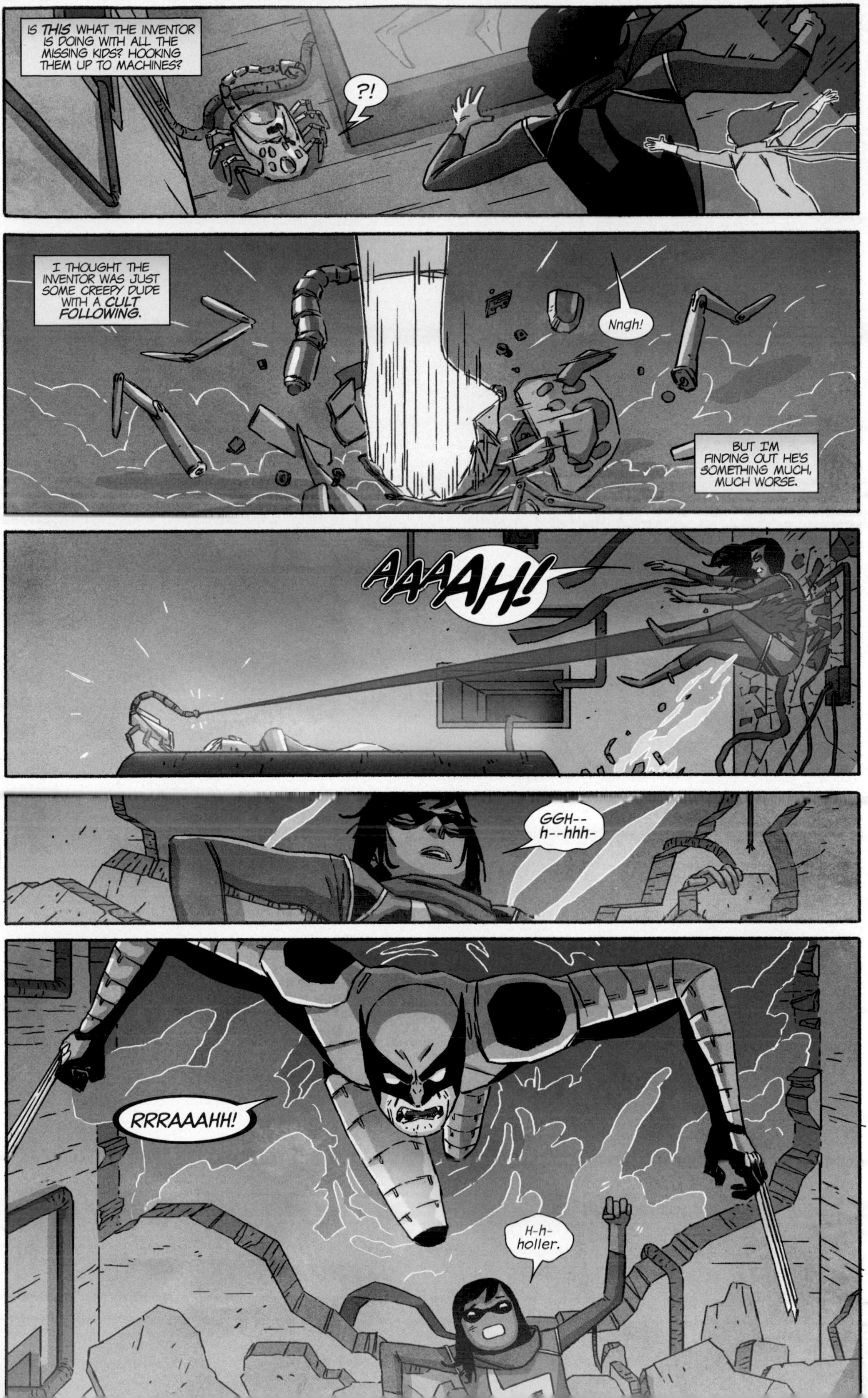
IS THIS WHAT THE INVENTOR IS DOING WITH ALL THE MISSING KIDS? HOOKING THEM UP TO MACHINES?
?!
I THOUGHT THE INVENTOR WAS JUST SOME CREEPY DUDE WITH A CULT FOLLOWING.
Nngh!
BUT I'M FINDING OUT HE'S SOMETHING MUCH, MUCH WORSE.
AAAAH!
GGH-- h--hhh-
RRRAAAHH!
H-h- holler.

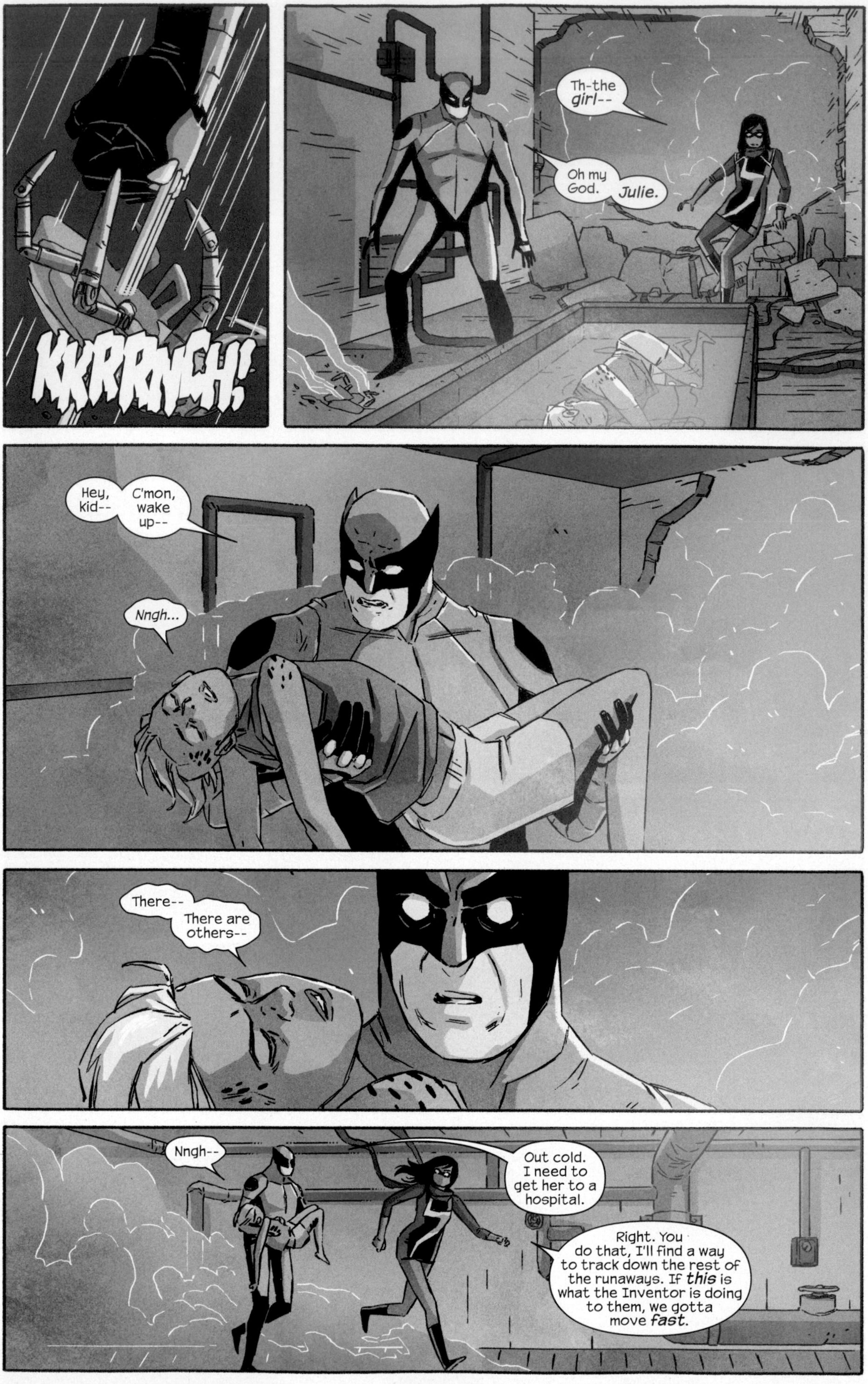
KKRRNGH!
Th-the girl--
Oh my God. Julie.
Hey, kid--
C'mon, wake up--
Nngh...
There--
There are others--
Nngh--
Out cold. I need to get her to a hospital.
Right. You do that, I'll find a way to track down the rest of the runaways. If this is what the Inventor is doing to them, we gotta move fast.

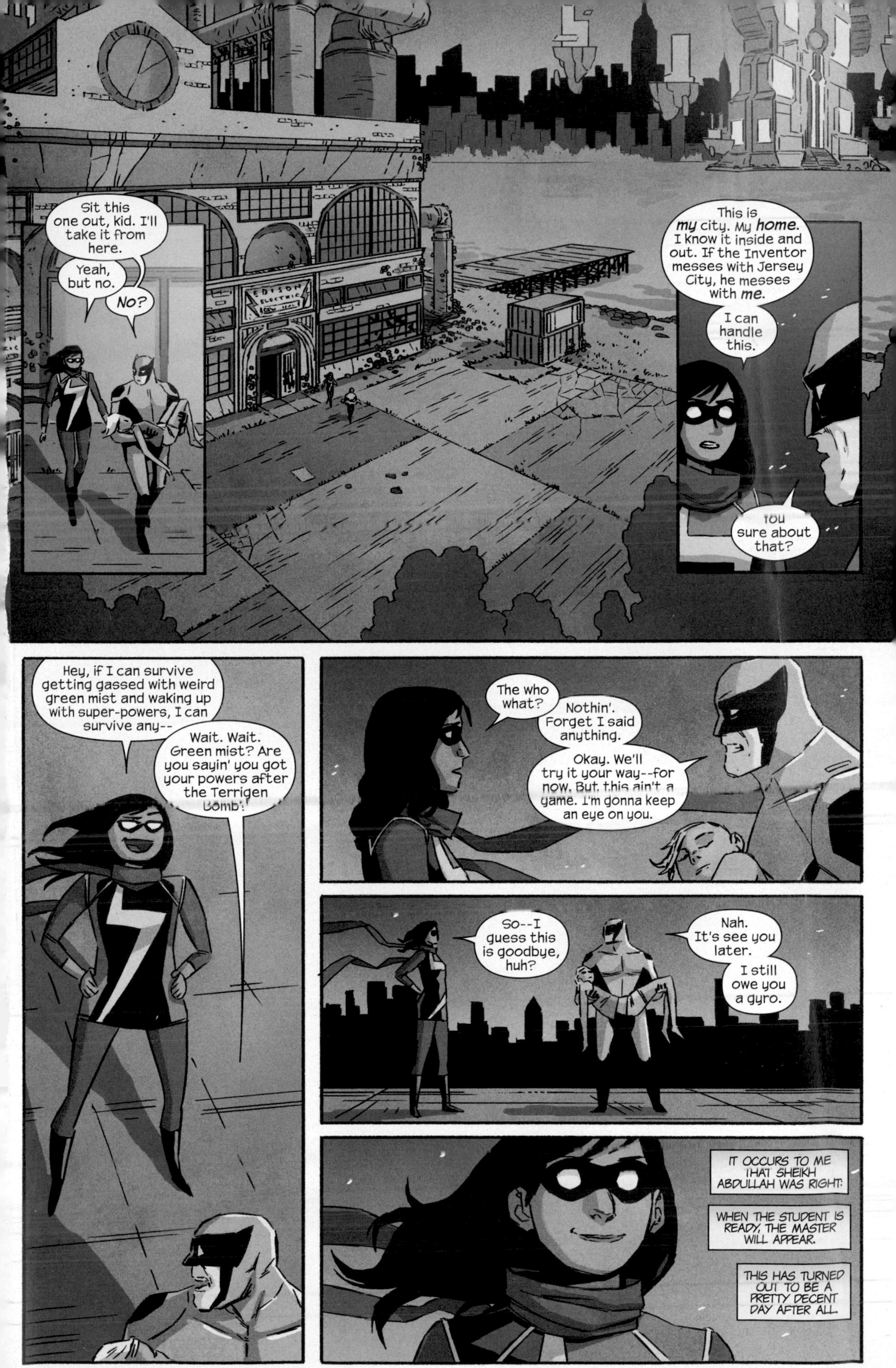
EDISON ELECTRIC
Sit this one out, kid. I'll take it from here.
Yeah, but no.
No?
This is my city. My home. I know it inside and out. If the Inventor messes with Jersey City, he messes with me.
I can handle this.
You sure about that?
Hey, if I can survive getting gassed with weird green mist and waking up with super-powers, I can survive any--
Wait. Wait. Green mist? Are you sayin' you got your powers after the Terrigen Bomb?
The who what?
Nothin'. Forget I said anything.
Okay. We'll try it your way--for now. But this ain't a game. I'm gonna keep an eye on you.
So--I guess this is goodbye, huh?
Nah. It's see you later.
I still owe you a gyro.
IT OCCURS TO ME THAT SHEIKH ABDULLAH WAS RIGHT:
WHEN THE STUDENT IS READY, THE MASTER WILL APPEAR.
THIS HAS TURNED OUT TO BE A PRETTY DECENT DAY AFTER ALL.

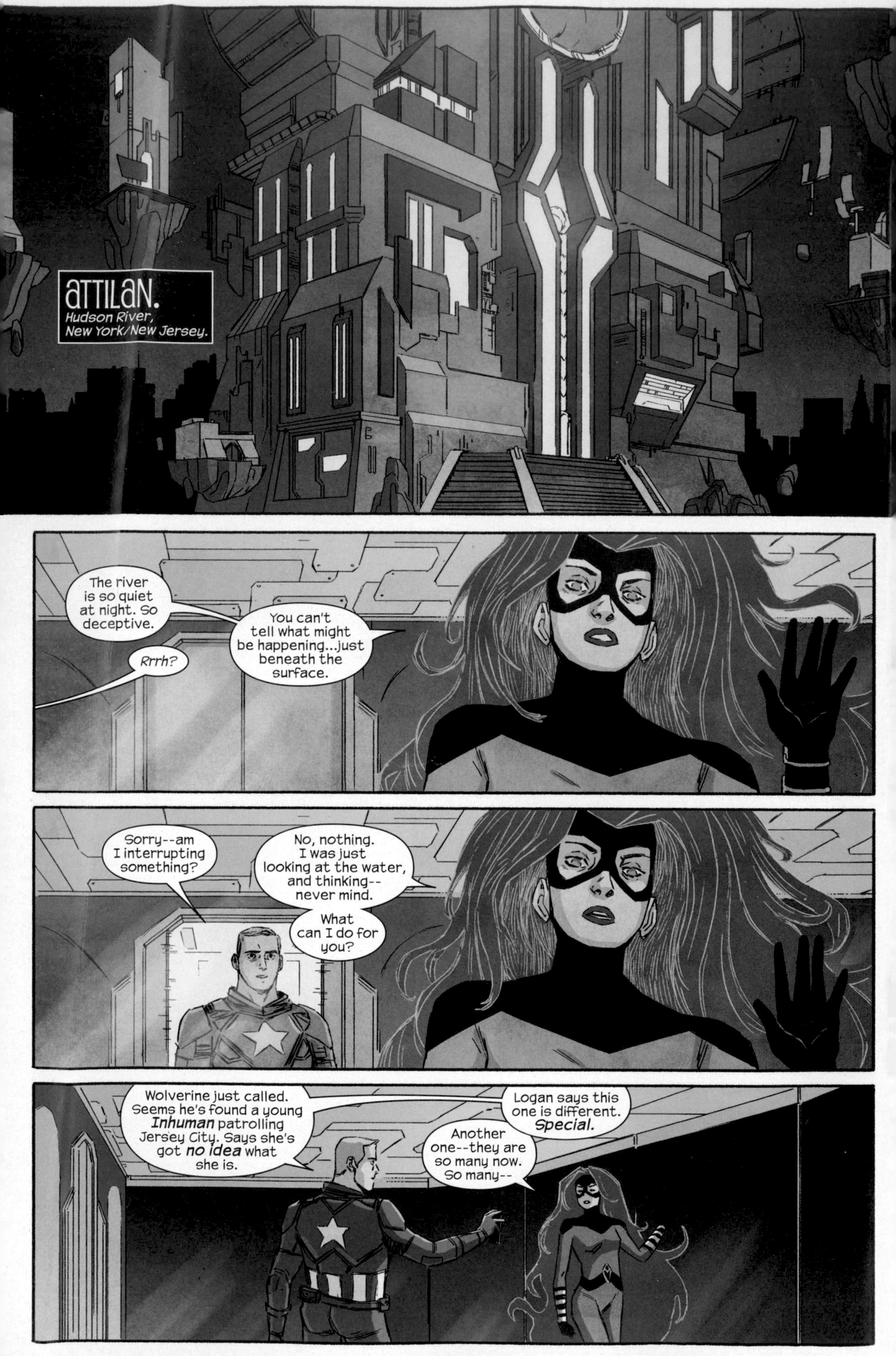

attilan.
Hudson River, New York/New Jersey.
The river is so quiet at night. So deceptive.
You can't tell what might be happening...just beneath the surface.
Rrrh?
Sorry--am I interrupting something?
No, nothing. I was just looking at the water, and thinking--never mind.
What can I do for you?
Wolverine just called. Seems he's found a young Inhuman patrolling Jersey City. Says she's got no idea what she is.
Logan says this one is different. Special.
Another one--they are so many now. So many--

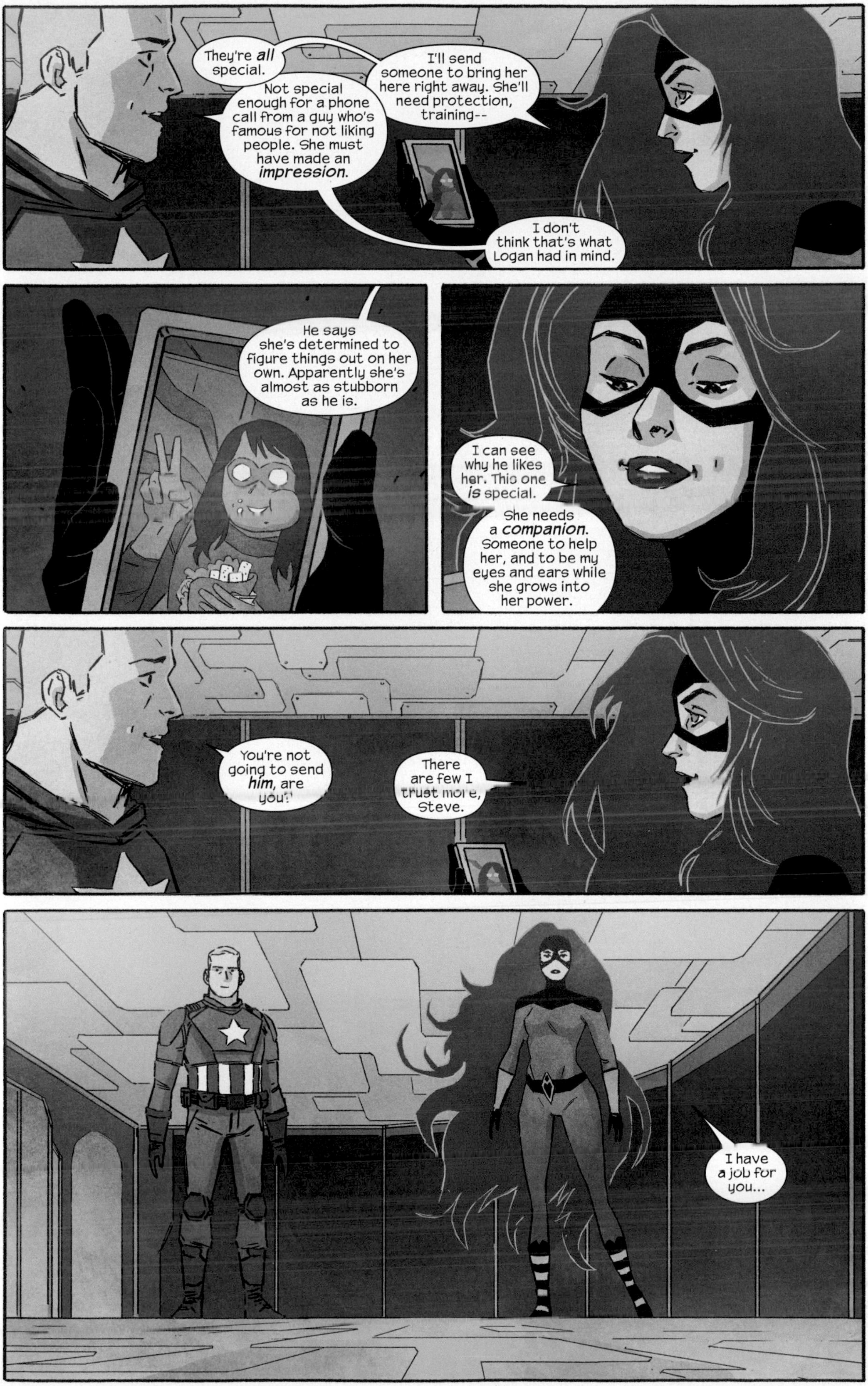
They're all special.
Not special enough for a phone call from a guy who's famous for not liking people. She must have made an impression.
I'll send someone to bring her here right away. She'll need protection, training--
I don't think that's what Logan had in mind.
He says she's determined to figure things out on her own. Apparently she's almost as stubborn as he is.
I can see why he likes her. This one is special.
She needs a companion. Someone to help her, and to be my eyes and ears while she grows into her power.
You're not going to send him, are you?
There are few I trust more, Steve.
I have a job for you...

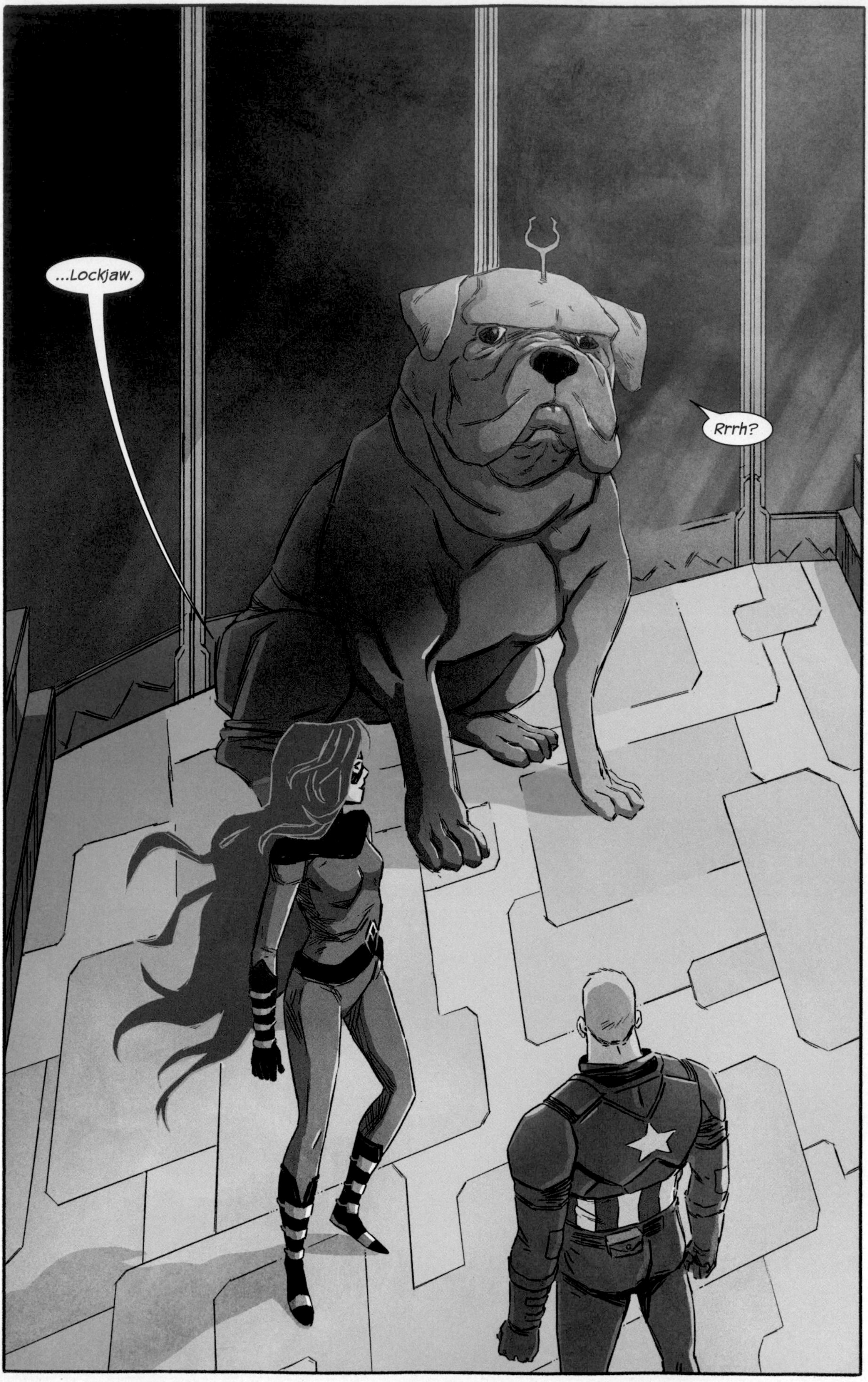
...Lockjaw.
Rrrh?

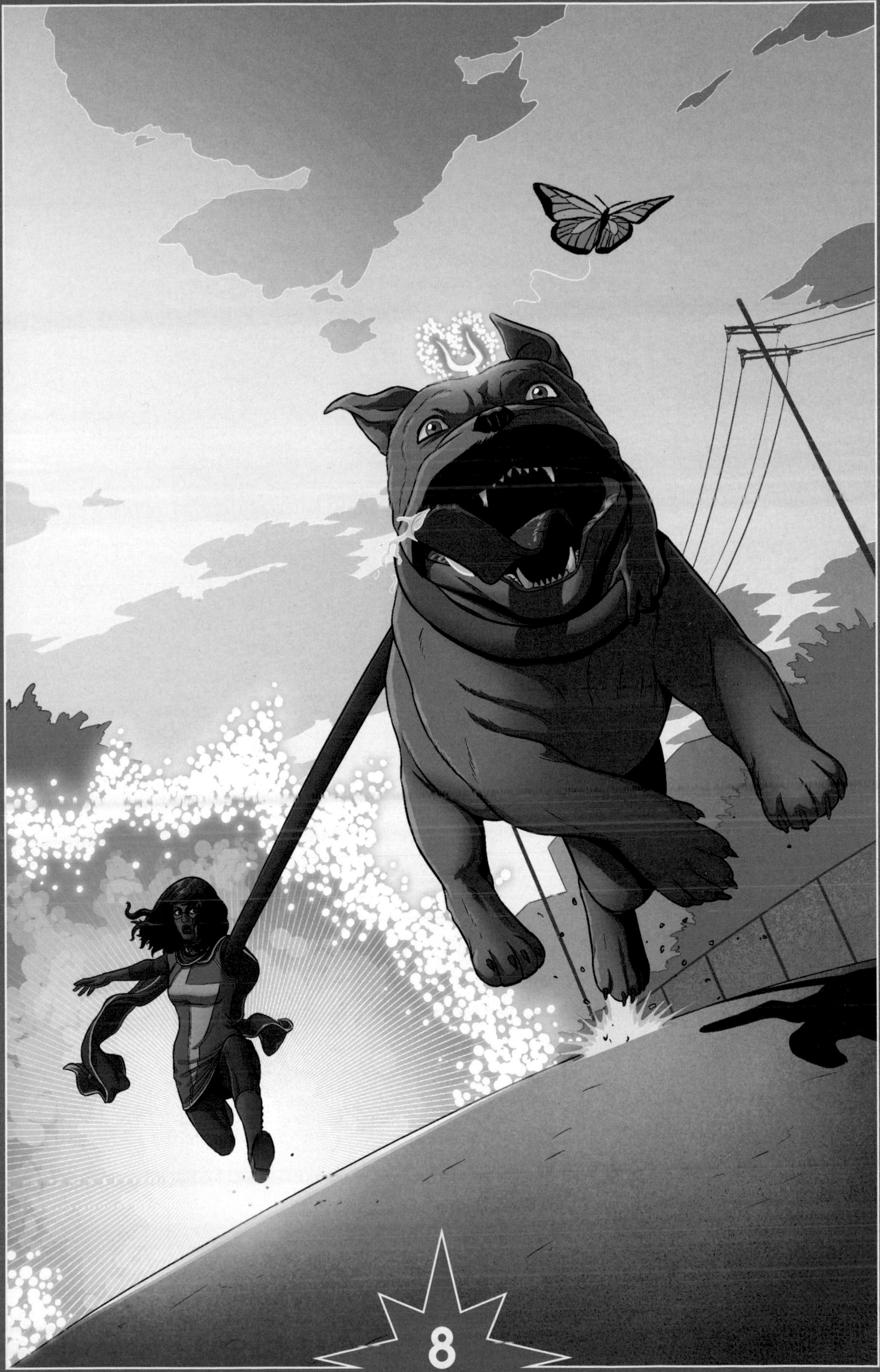
8

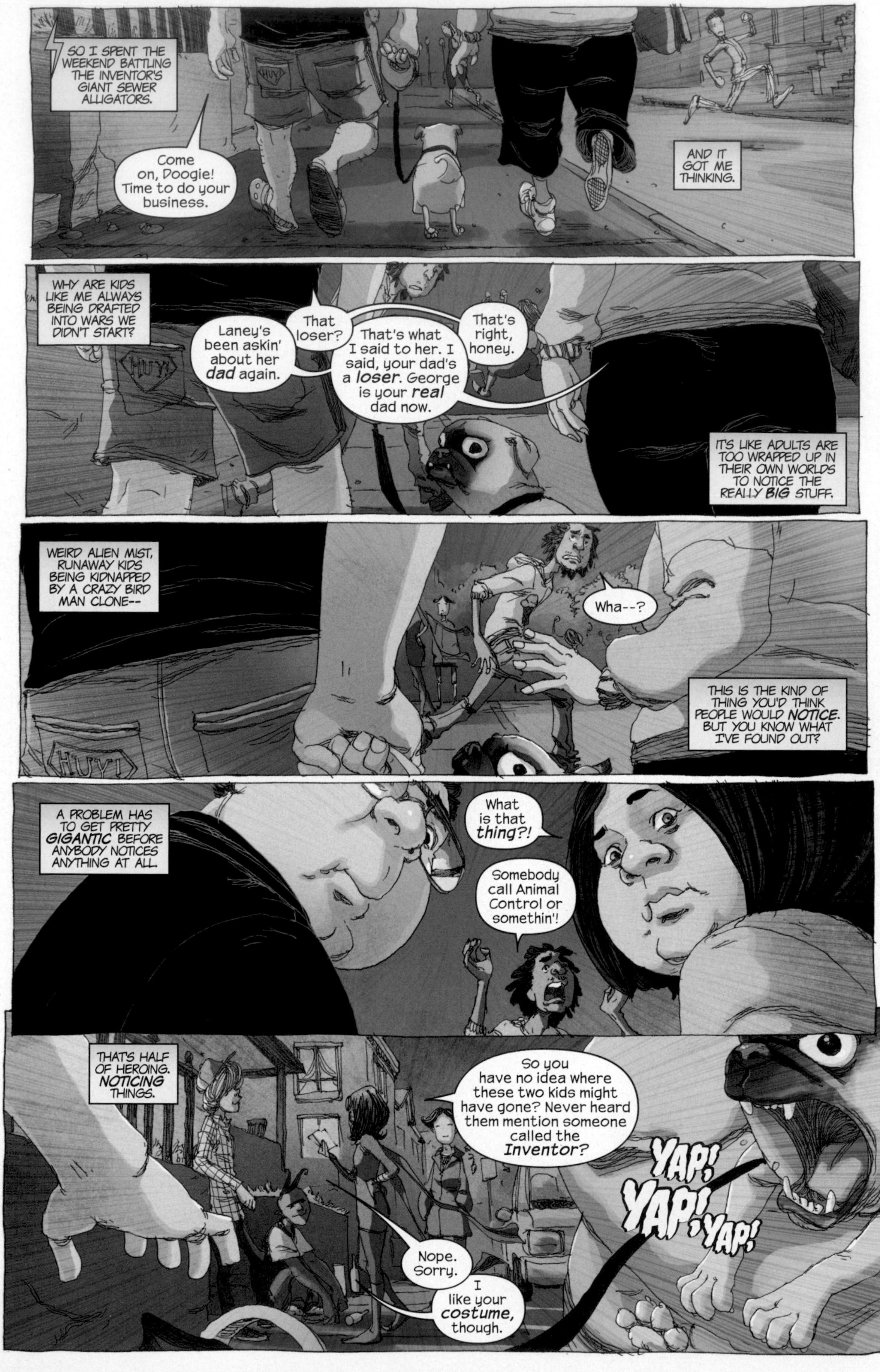
SO I SPENT THE WEEKEND BATTLING THE INVENTOR'S GIANT SEWER ALLIGATORS.
Come on, Doogie! Time to do your business.
AND IT GOT ME THINKING.
WHY ARE KIDS LIKE ME ALWAYS BEING DRAFTED INTO WARS WE DIDN'T START?
Laney's been askin' about her dad again.
That loser?
That's what I said to her. I said, your dad's a loser. George is your real dad now.
That's right, honey.
IT'S LIKE ADULTS ARE TOO WRAPPED UP IN THEIR OWN WORLDS TO NOTICE THE REALLY BIG STUFF.
WEIRD ALIEN MIST, RUNAWAY KIDS BEING KIDNAPPED BY A CRAZY BIRD MAN CLONE--
Wha--?
THIS IS THE KIND OF THING YOU'D THINK PEOPLE WOULD NOTICE. BUT YOU KNOW WHAT I'VE FOUND OUT?
A PROBLEM HAS TO GET PRETTY GIGANTIC BEFORE ANYBODY NOTICES ANYTHING AT ALL.
What is that thing?!
Somebody call Animal Control or somethin'!
THAT'S HALF OF HEROING. NOTICING THINGS.
So you have no idea where these two kids might have gone? Never heard them mention someone called the Inventor?
YAP! YAP! YAP!
Nope. Sorry.
I like your costume, though.

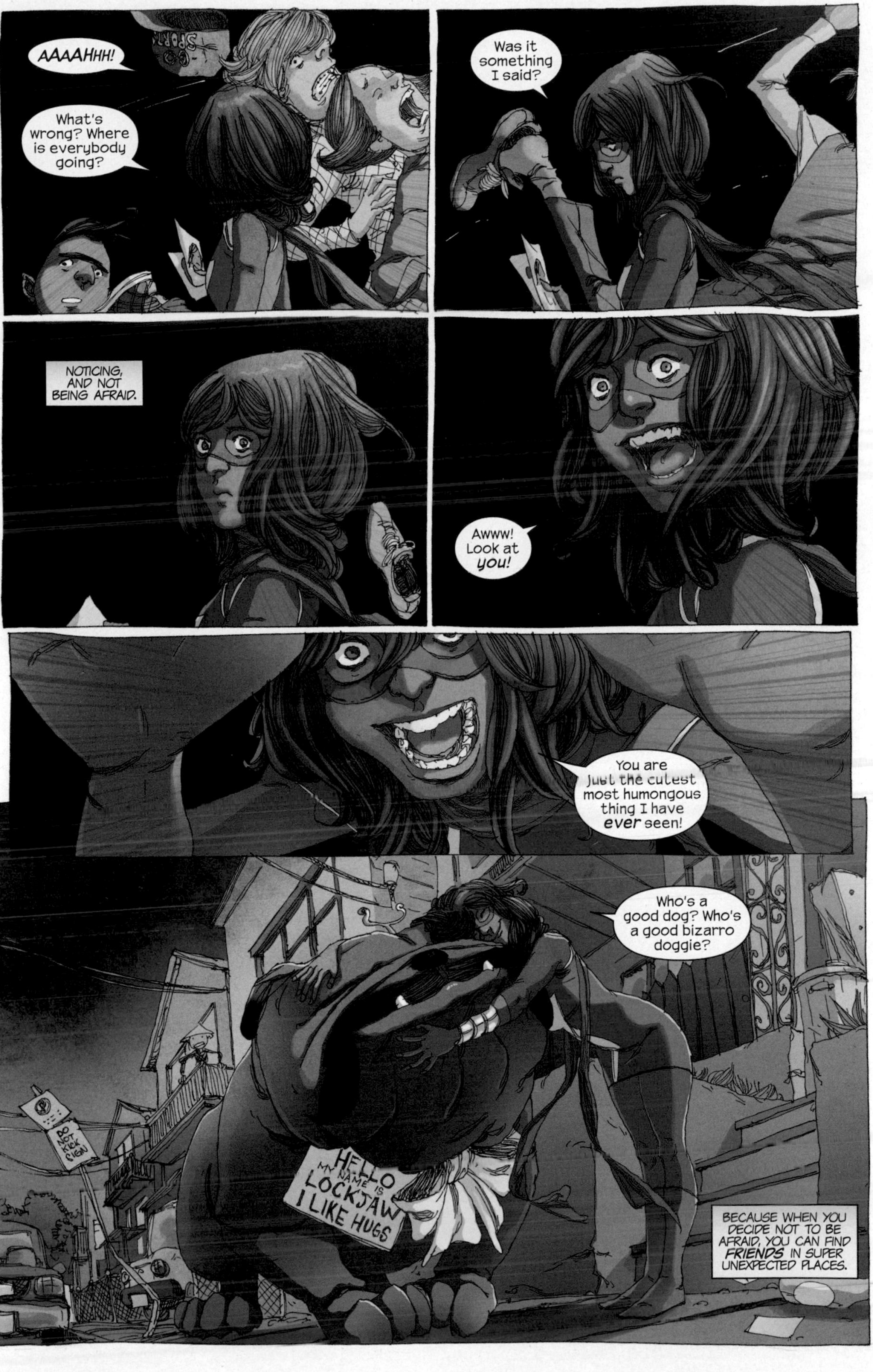
AAAAHHH!
What's wrong? Where is everybody going?
Was it something I said?
NOTICING, AND NOT BEING AFRAID.
Awww! Look at *you!*
You are just the cutest most humongous thing I have *ever* seen!
Who's a good dog? Who's a good bizarro doggie?
DO NOT KICK SIGN
HELLO MY NAME IS LOCKJAW I LIKE HUGS
BECAUSE WHEN YOU DECIDE NOT TO BE AFRAID, YOU CAN FIND *FRIENDS* IN SUPER UNEXPECTED PLACES.

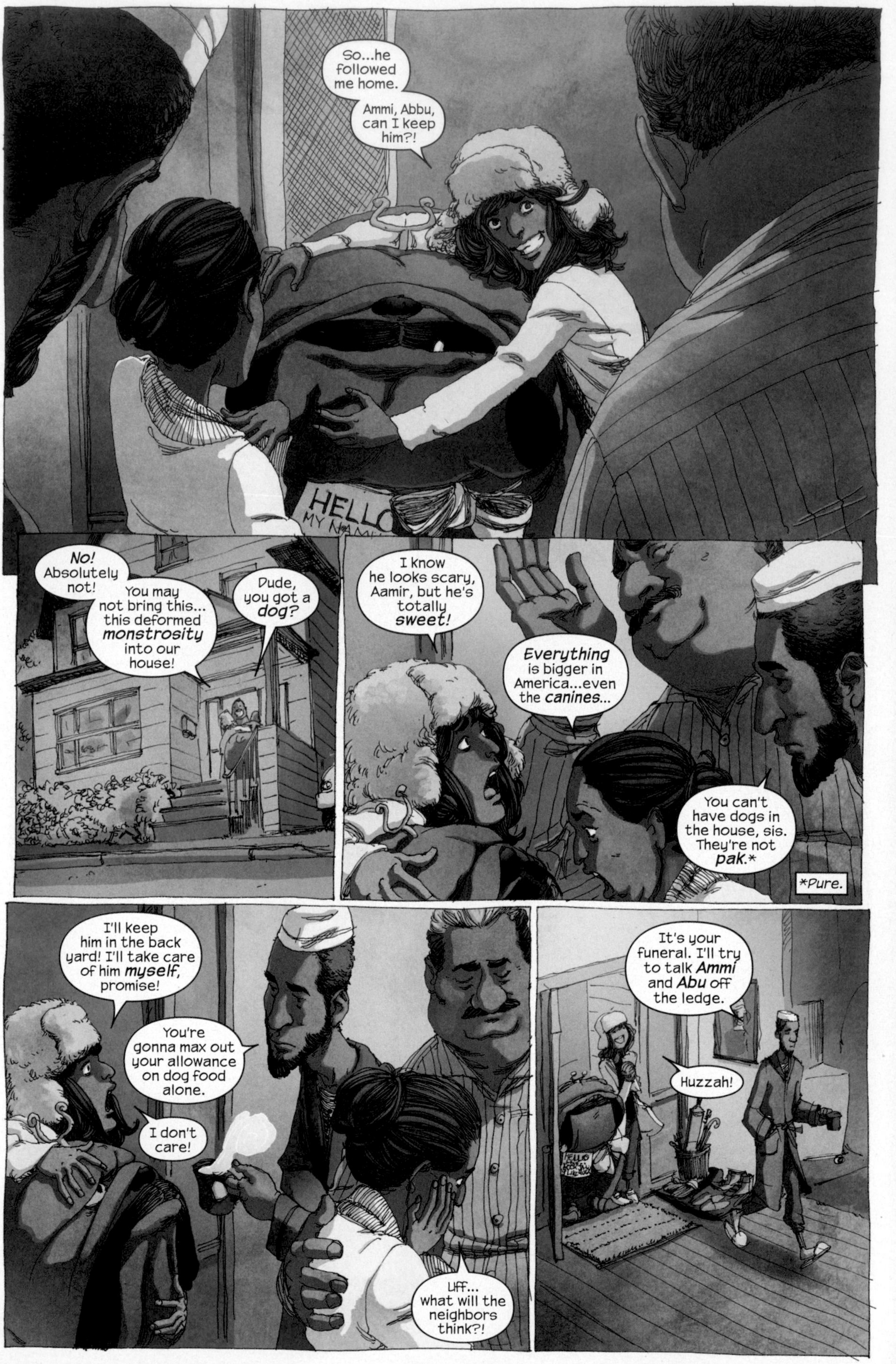
So...he followed me home.
Ammi, Abbu, can I keep him?!
HELLO MY NAM
No! Absolutely not!
You may not bring this... this deformed *monstrosity* into our house!
Dude, you got a *dog?*
I know he looks scary, Aamir, but he's totally *sweet!*
Everything is bigger in America...even the *canines*...
You can't have dogs in the house, sis. They're not *pak*.*
*Pure.
I'll keep him in the back yard! I'll take care of him *myself*, promise!
You're gonna max out your allowance on dog food alone.
I don't care!
Uff... what will the neighbors think?!
It's your funeral. I'll try to talk *Ammi* and *Abu* off the ledge.
Huzzah!

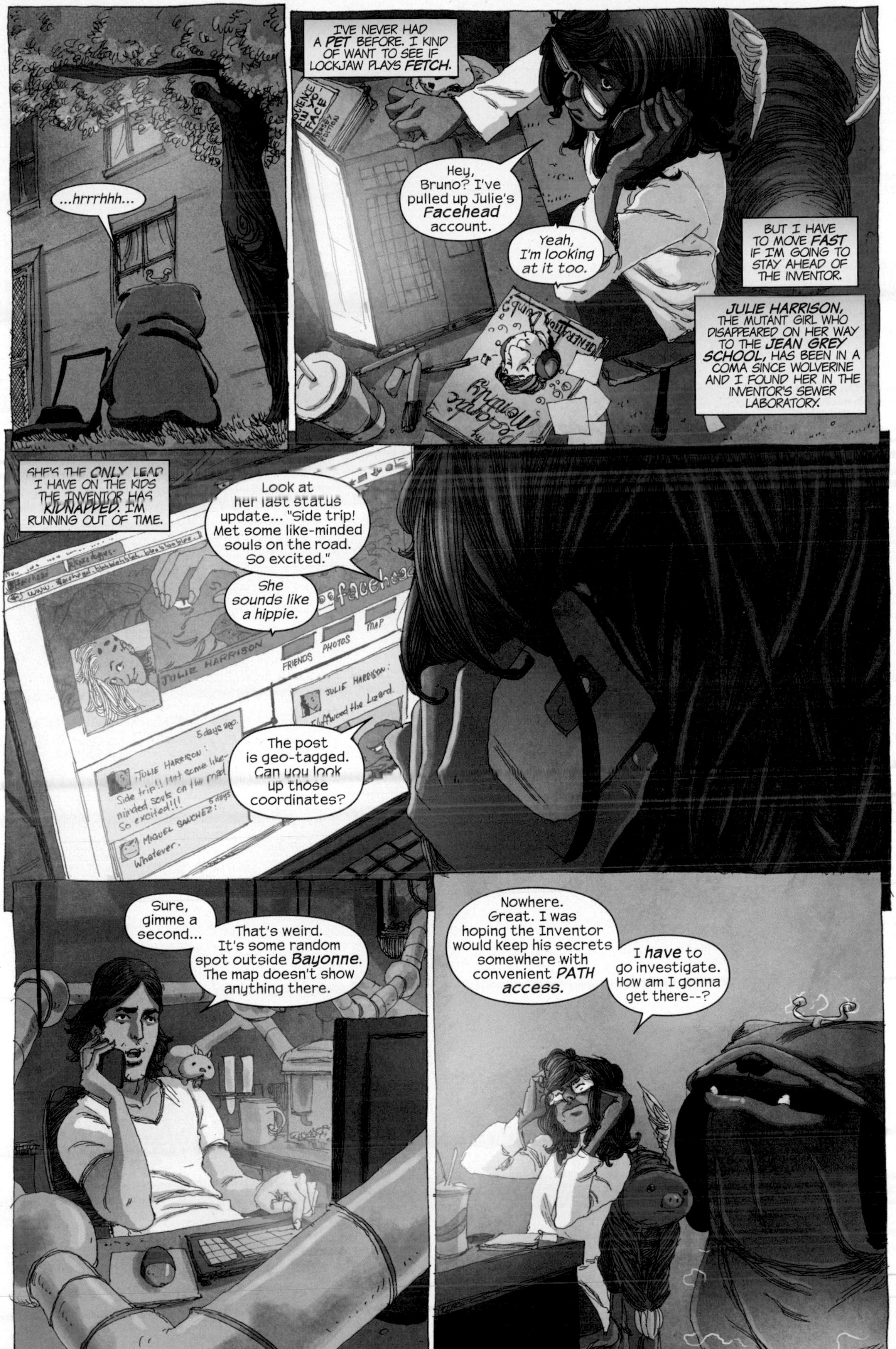
...hrrrhhh...
I'VE NEVER HAD A PET BEFORE. I KIND OF WANT TO SEE IF LOCKJAW PLAYS FETCH.
Hey, Bruno? I've pulled up Julie's Facehead account.
Yeah, I'm looking at it too.
BUT I HAVE TO MOVE FAST IF I'M GOING TO STAY AHEAD OF THE INVENTOR.
JULIE HARRISON, THE MUTANT GIRL WHO DISAPPEARED ON HER WAY TO THE JEAN GREY SCHOOL, HAS BEEN IN A COMA SINCE WOLVERINE AND I FOUND HER IN THE INVENTOR'S SEWER LABORATORY.
SHE'S THE ONLY LEAD I HAVE ON THE KIDS THE INVENTOR HAS KIDNAPPED. I'M RUNNING OUT OF TIME.
Look at her last status update... "Side trip! Met some like-minded souls on the road. So excited."
She sounds like a hippie.
JULIE HARRISON
FRIENDS
PHOTOS
MAP
The post is geo-tagged. Can you look up those coordinates?
Sure, gimme a second...
That's weird. It's some random spot outside Bayonne. The map doesn't show anything there.
Nowhere. Great. I was hoping the Inventor would keep his secrets somewhere with convenient PATH access.
I have to go investigate. How am I gonna get there--?

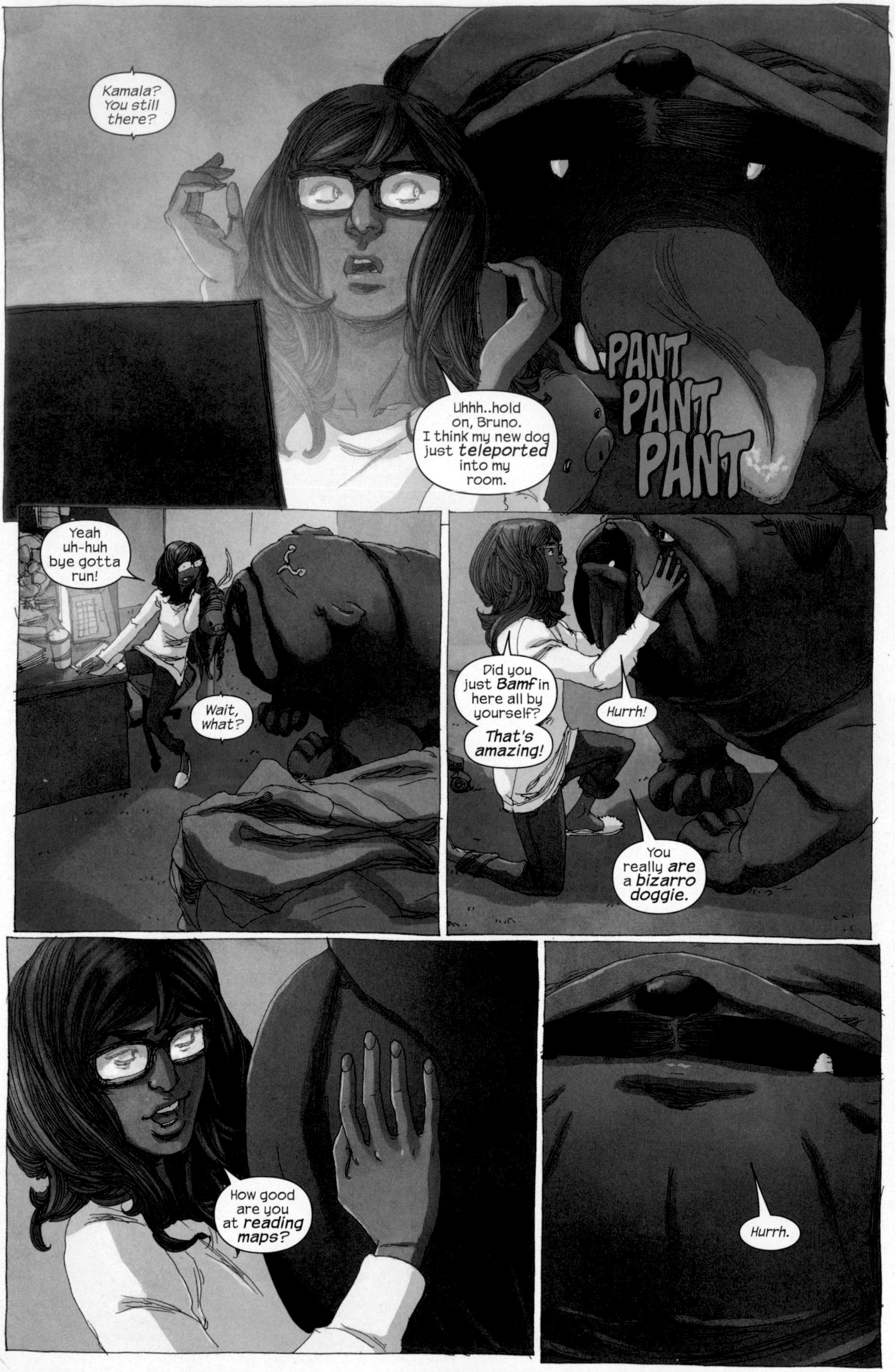
Kamala? You still there?
Uhhh..hold on, Bruno. I think my new dog just teleported into my room.
PANT PANT PANT
Yeah uh-huh bye gotta run!
Wait, what?
Did you just Bamf in here all by yourself? That's amazing!
Hurrh!
You really are a bizarro doggie.
How good are you at reading maps?
Hurrh.

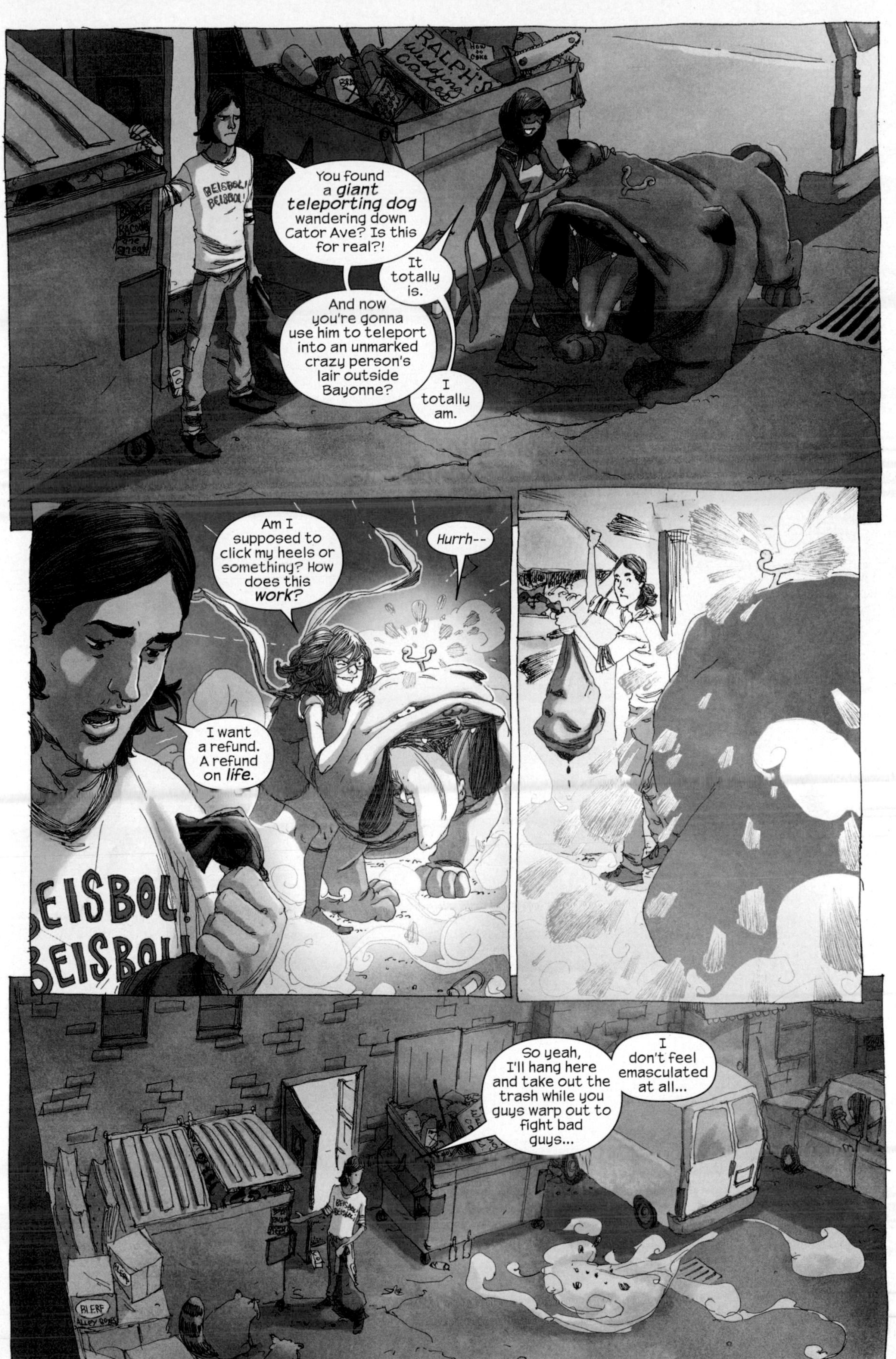
RALPH'S Wedding Cakes
BEISBOL! BEISBOL!
You found a **giant teleporting dog** wandering down Cator Ave? Is this for real?!
It totally is.
And now you're gonna use him to teleport into an unmarked crazy person's lair outside Bayonne?
I totally am.
Am I supposed to click my heels or something? How does this **work?**
Hurrh--
I want a refund. A refund on *life.*
BEISBOL! BEISBOL!
So yeah, I'll hang here and take out the trash while you guys warp out to fight bad guys...
I don't feel emasculated at all...
BLERF ALLEY BOYS

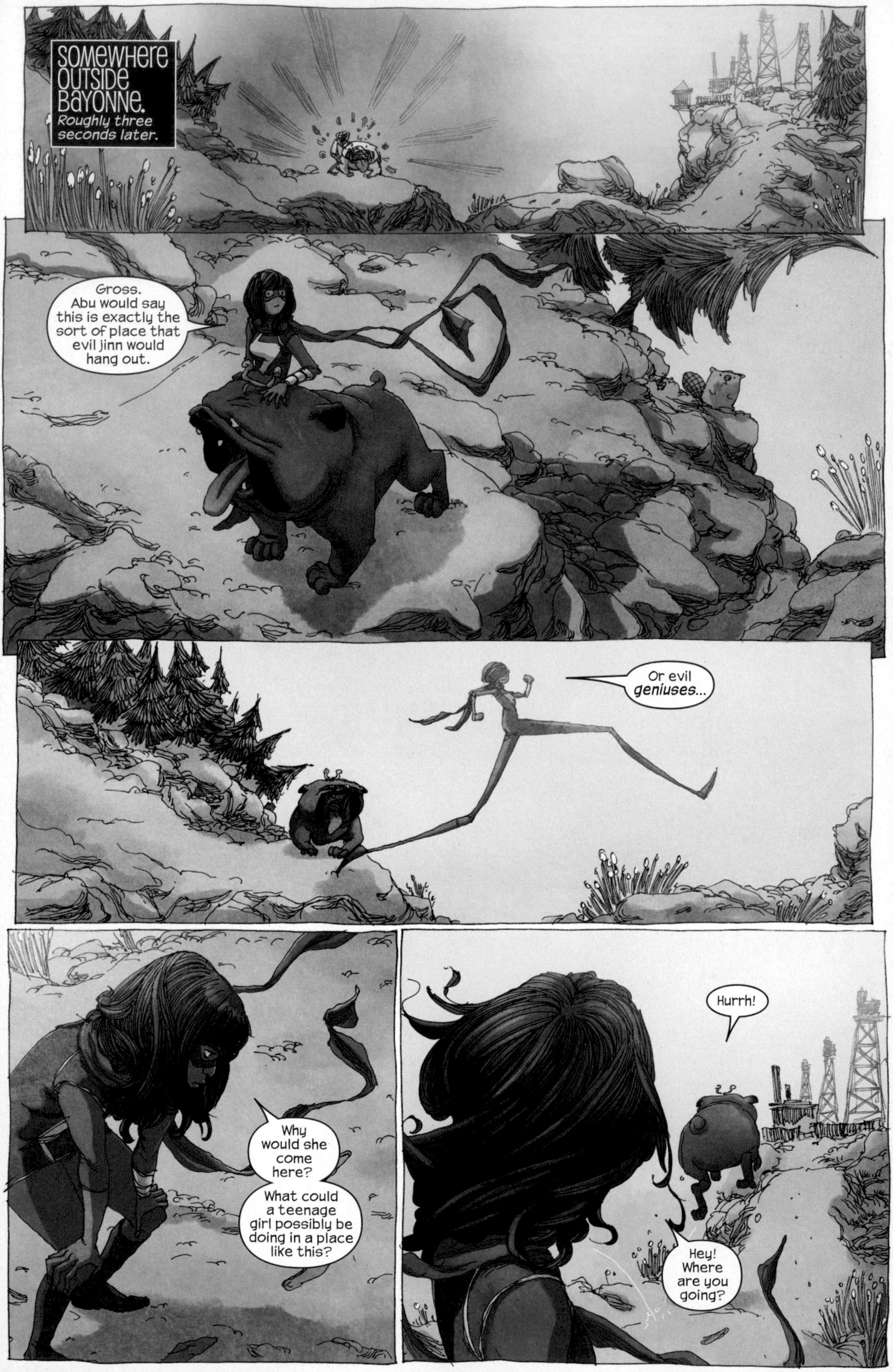
SOMEWHERE OUTSIDE BAYONNE.
Roughly three seconds later.
Gross. Abu would say this is exactly the sort of place that evil jinn would hang out.
Or evil geniuses...
Why would she come here?
What could a teenage girl possibly be doing in a place like this?
Hurrh!
Hey! Where are you going?

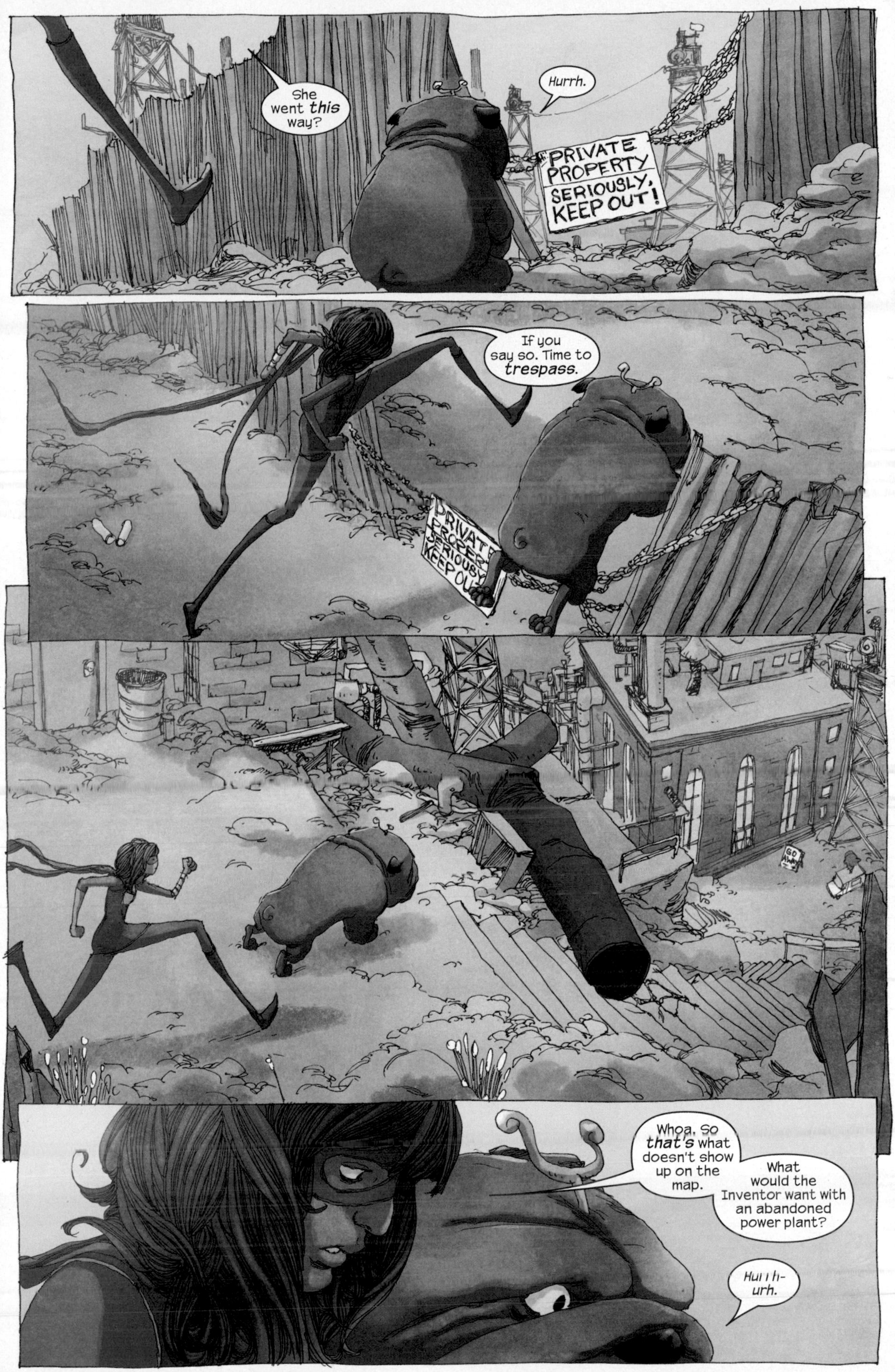
She went this way?
Hurrh.
PRIVATE PROPERTY
SERIOUSLY, KEEP OUT!
If you say so. Time to trespass.
GO AWAY
Whoa. So that's what doesn't show up on the map.
What would the Inventor want with an abandoned power plant?
Hurrh-urh.

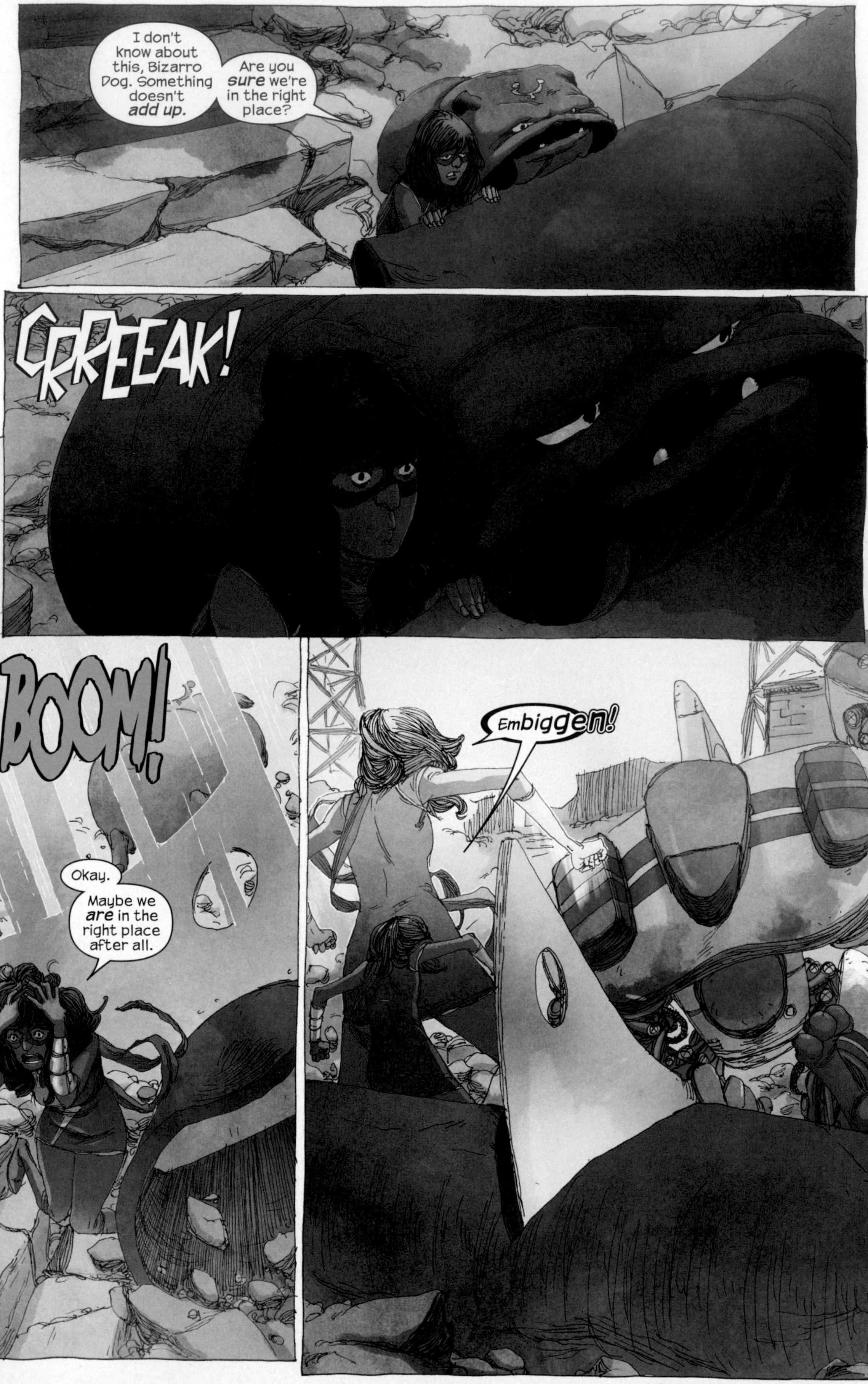
I don't know about this, Bizarro Dog. Something doesn't add up.
Are you sure we're in the right place?
CRREEAK!
BOOM!
Okay.
Maybe we are in the right place after all.
Embiggen!

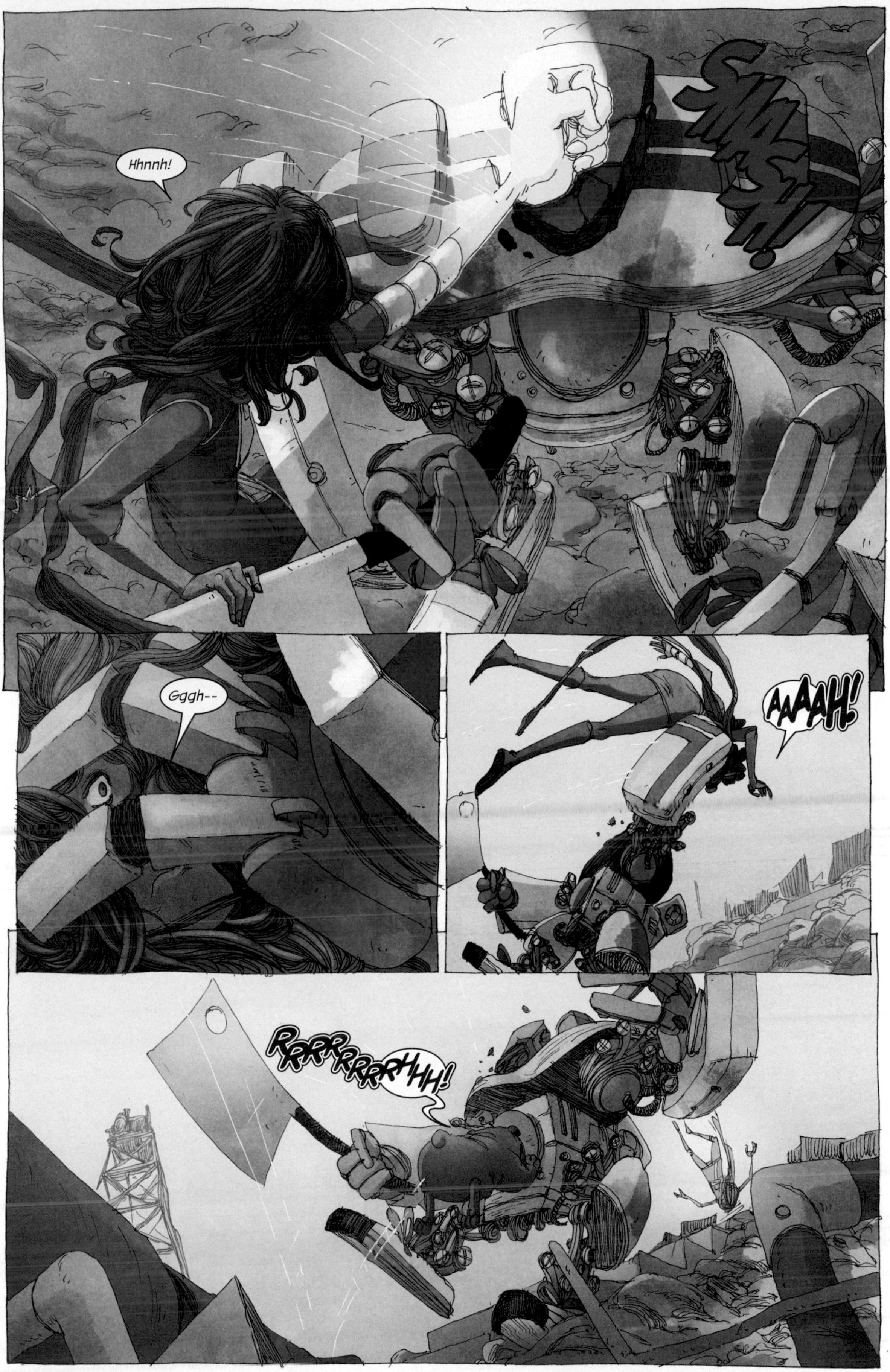

Hhnnh!
SMASH!
Gggh--
AAAAH!
RRRRRRRRHHH!

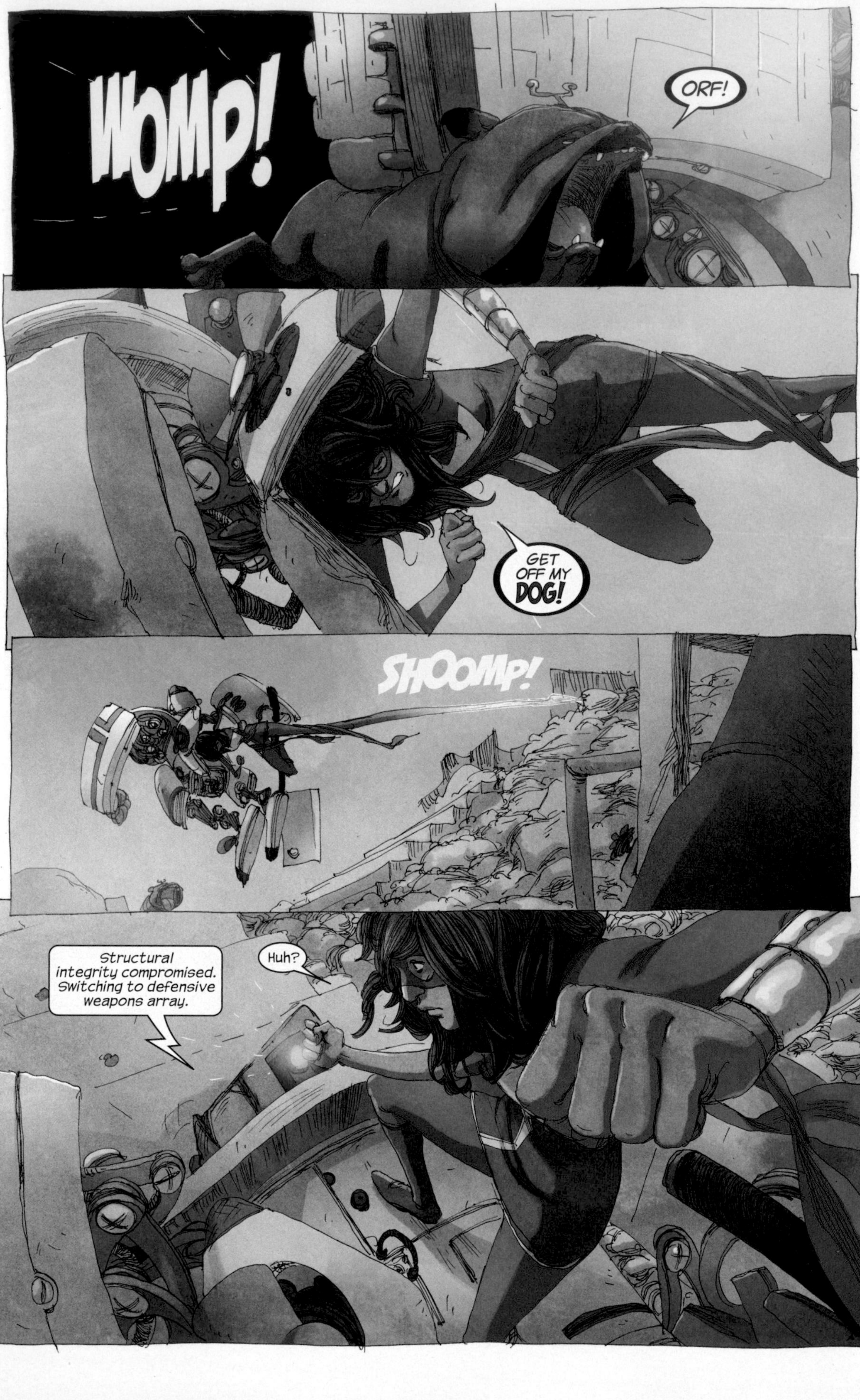
WOMP!
ORF!
GET OFF MY DOG!
SHOOMP!
Structural integrity compromised. Switching to defensive weapons array.
Huh?

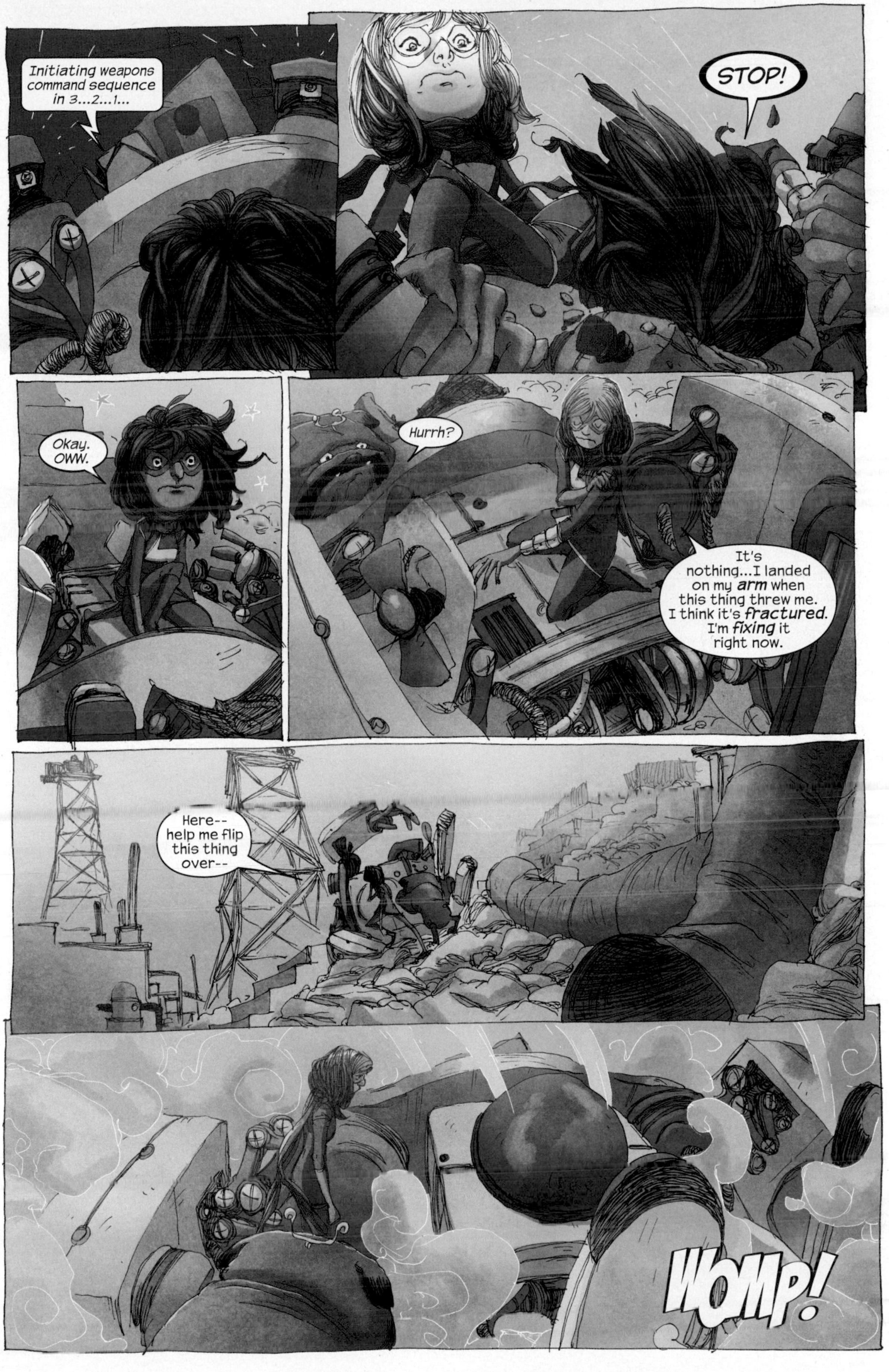

Initiating weapons command sequence in 3...2...1...
STOP!
Okay. OWW.
Hurrh?
It's nothing...I landed on my *arm* when this thing threw me. I think it's *fractured*. I'm *fixing* it right now.
Here-- help me flip this thing over--
WOMP!

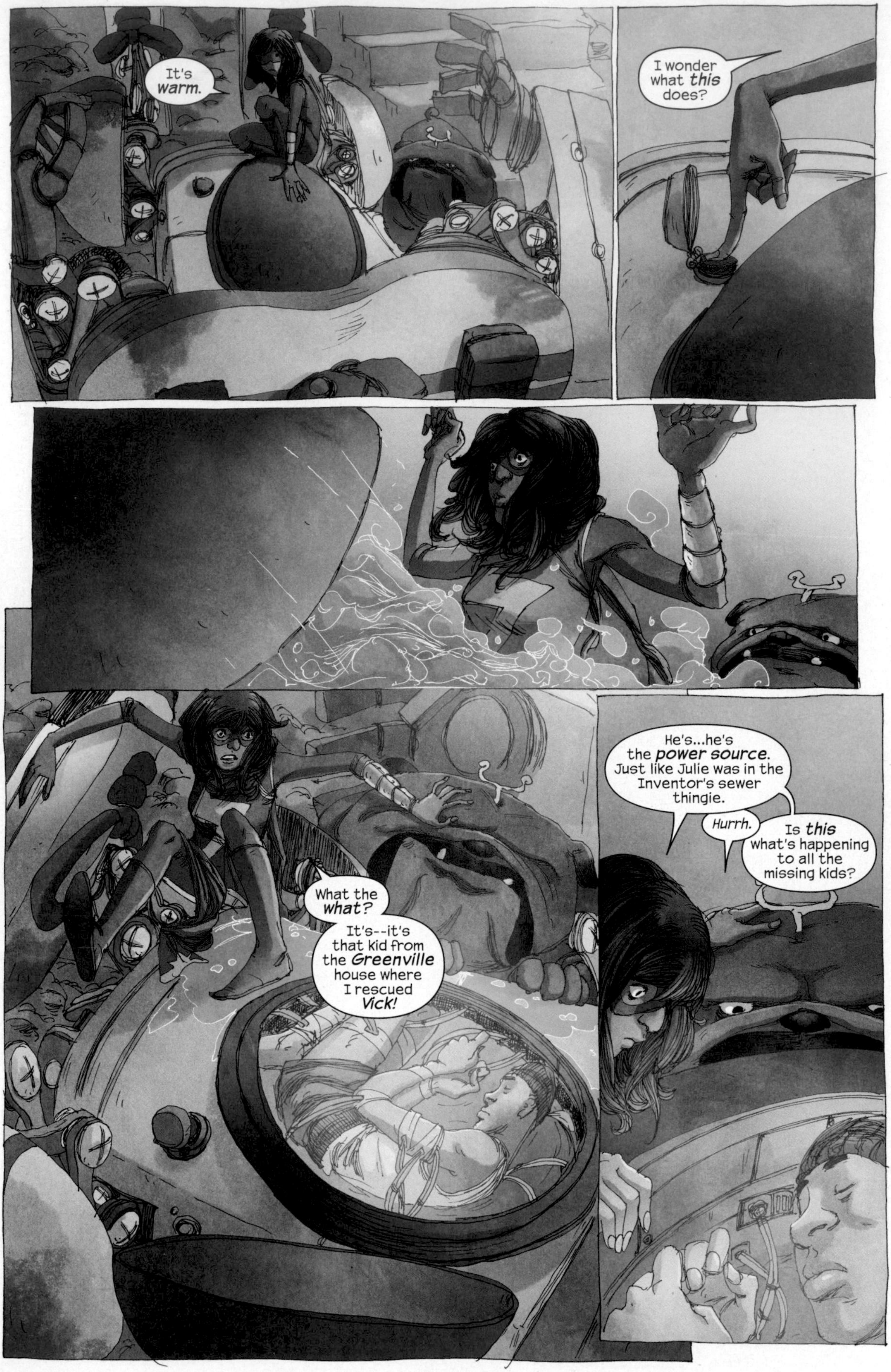

It's *warm.*
I wonder what *this* does?
He's...he's the *power source.* Just like Julie was in the Inventor's sewer thingie.
Hurrh.
Is *this* what's happening to all the missing kids?
What the *what?*
It's--it's that kid from the *Greenville* house where I rescued *Vick!*

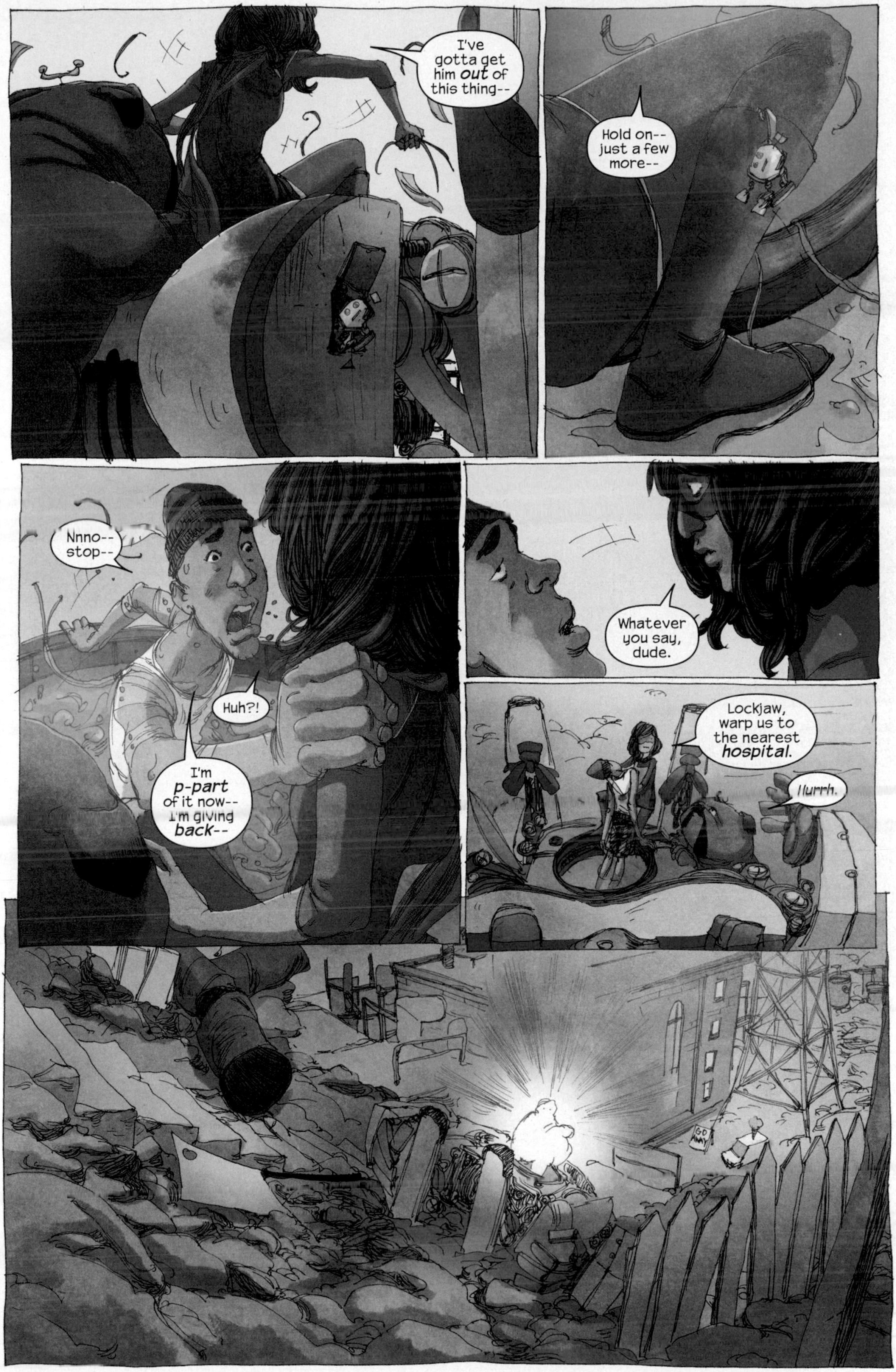

I've gotta get him *out* of this thing--
Hold on-- just a few more--
Nnno-- stop--
Huh?!
I'm *p-part* of it now-- I'm giving *back*--
Whatever you say, dude.
Lockjaw, warp us to the nearest *hospital*.
Hurrh.
GO AWAY

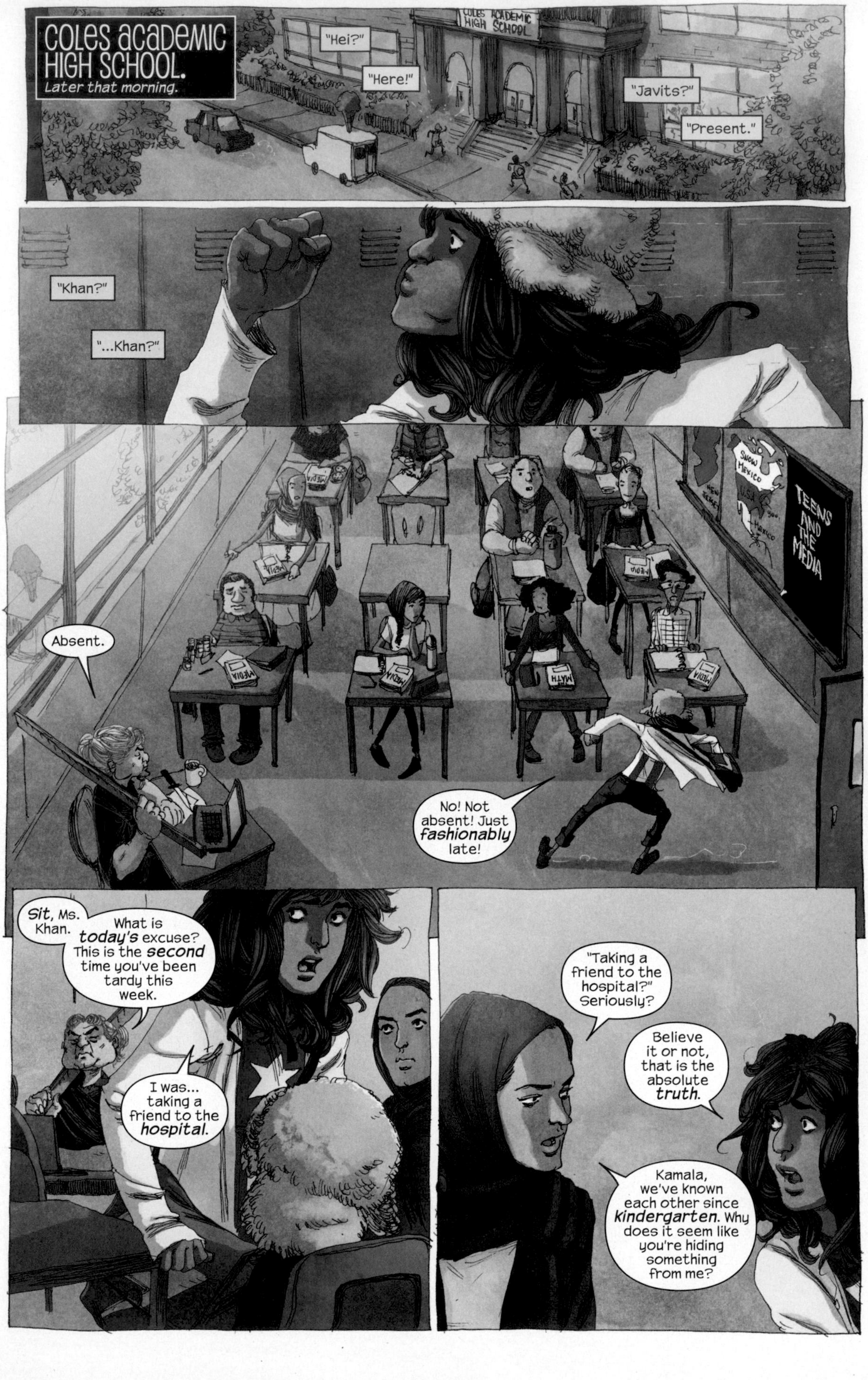
COLES ACADEMIC HIGH SCHOOL.
Later that morning.
COLES ACADEMIC HIGH SCHOOL
"Hei?"
"Here!"
"Javits?"
"Present."
"Khan?"
"...Khan?"
Absent.
TEENS AND THE MEDIA
No! Not absent! Just fashionably late!
Sit, Ms. Khan.
What is today's excuse? This is the second time you've been tardy this week.
I was... taking a friend to the hospital.
"Taking a friend to the hospital?" Seriously?
Believe it or not, that is the absolute truth.
Kamala, we've known each other since kindergarten. Why does it seem like you're hiding something from me?

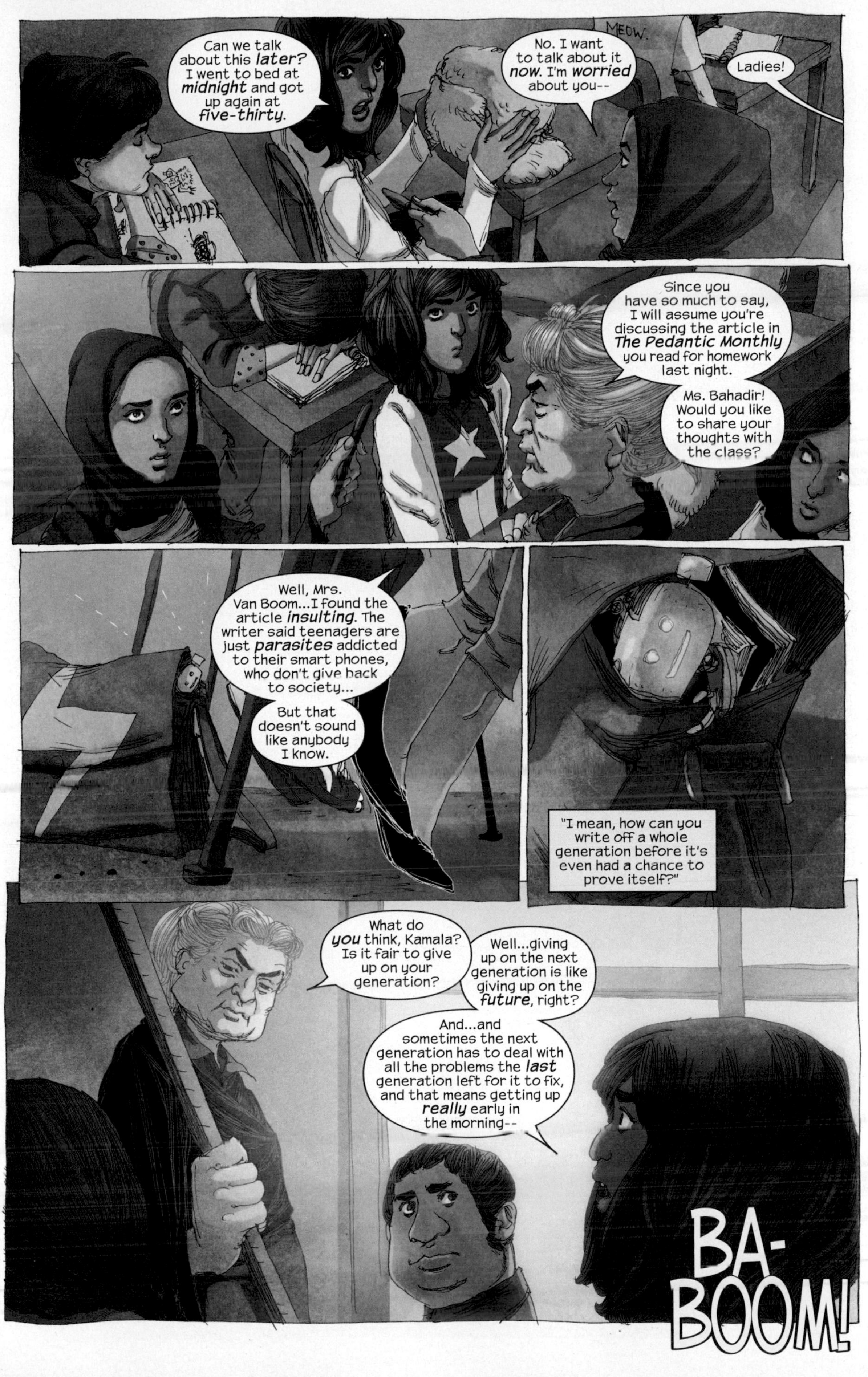
Can we talk about this later? I went to bed at midnight and got up again at five-thirty.
MEOW.
No. I want to talk about it now. I'm worried about you--
Ladies!
Since you have so much to say, I will assume you're discussing the article in The Pedantic Monthly you read for homework last night.
Ms. Bahadir! Would you like to share your thoughts with the class?
Well, Mrs. Van Boom...I found the article insulting. The writer said teenagers are just parasites addicted to their smart phones, who don't give back to society...
But that doesn't sound like anybody I know.
"I mean, how can you write off a whole generation before it's even had a chance to prove itself?"
What do you think, Kamala? Is it fair to give up on your generation?
Well...giving up on the next generation is like giving up on the future, right?
And...and sometimes the next generation has to deal with all the problems the last generation left for it to fix, and that means getting up really early in the morning--
BA-BOOM!

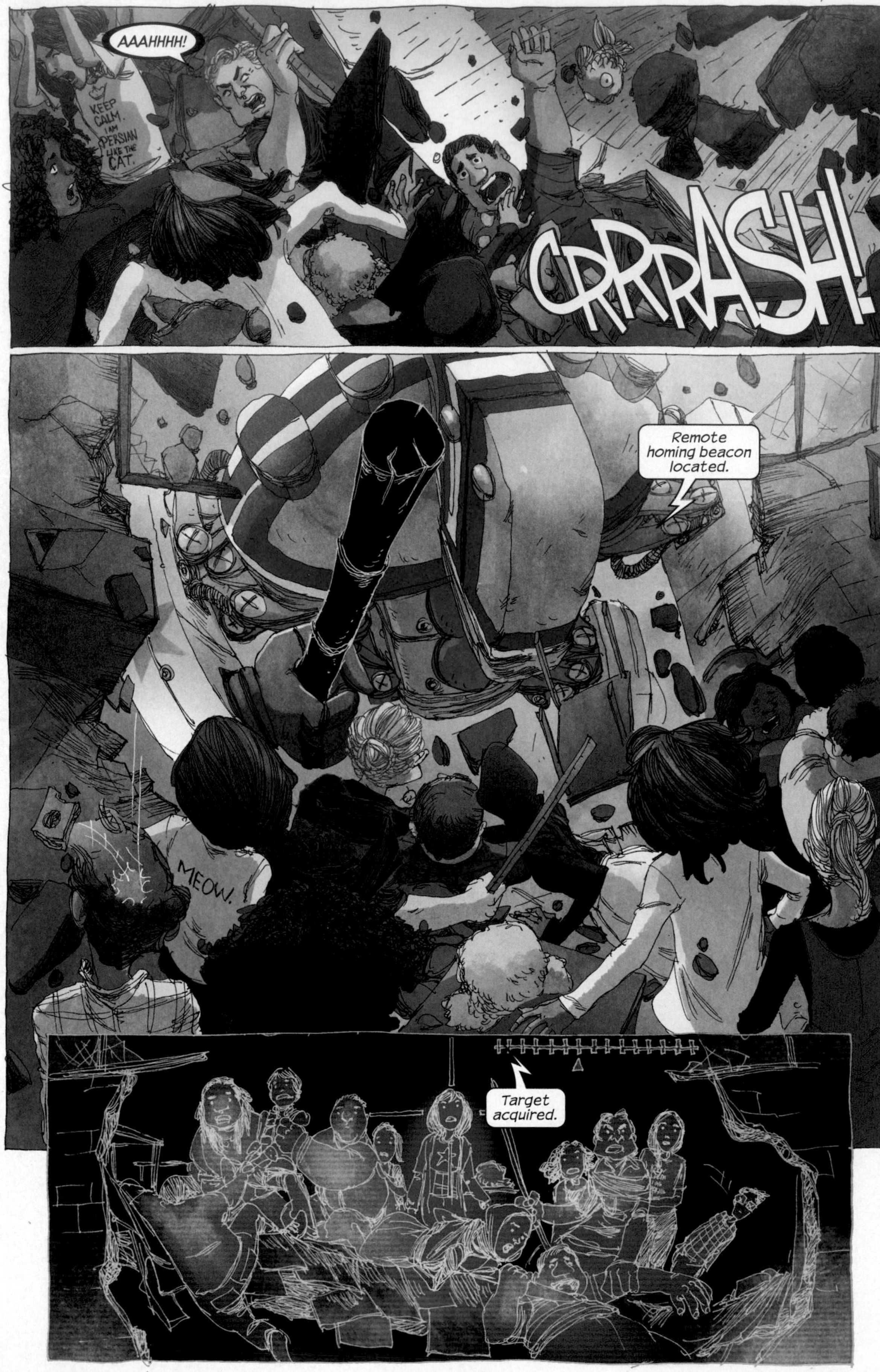
AAAHHHH!
KEEP CALM. I AM PERSIAN LIKE THE CAT.
CRRRASH!
Remote homing beacon located.
MEOW.
Target acquired.

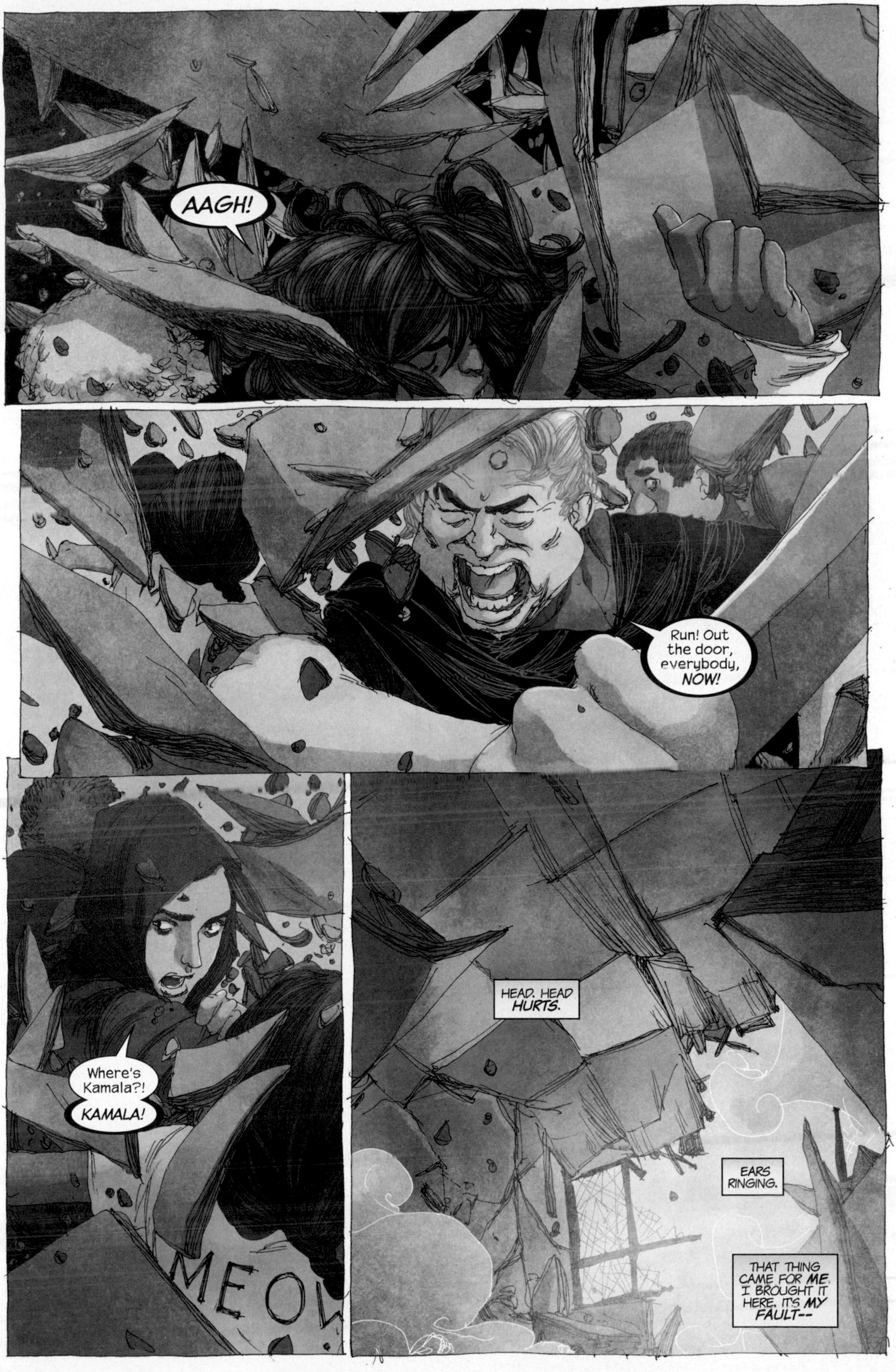
AAGH!
Run! Out the door, everybody, NOW!
Where's Kamala?!
KAMALA!
MEO
HEAD. HEAD HURTS.
EARS RINGING.
THAT THING CAME FOR ME. I BROUGHT IT HERE. IT'S MY FAULT--

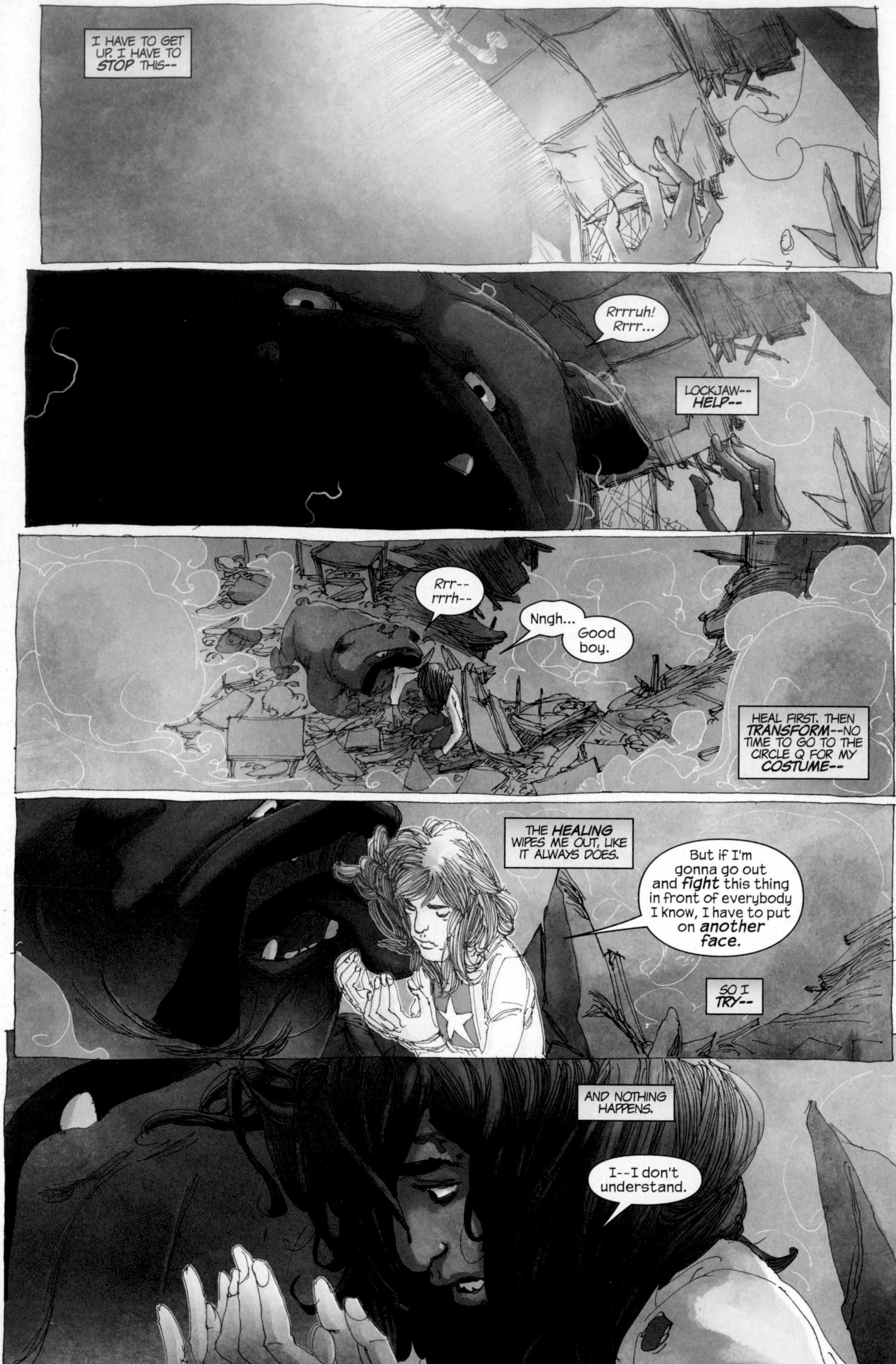
I HAVE TO GET UP. I HAVE TO STOP THIS--
Rrrruh! Rrrr...
LOCKJAW-- HELP--
Rrr-- rrrh--
Nngh... Good boy.
HEAL FIRST. THEN TRANSFORM--NO TIME TO GO TO THE CIRCLE Q FOR MY COSTUME--
THE HEALING WIPES ME OUT, LIKE IT ALWAYS DOES.
But if I'm gonna go out and fight this thing in front of everybody I know, I have to put on another face.
SO I TRY--
AND NOTHING HAPPENS.
I--I don't understand.

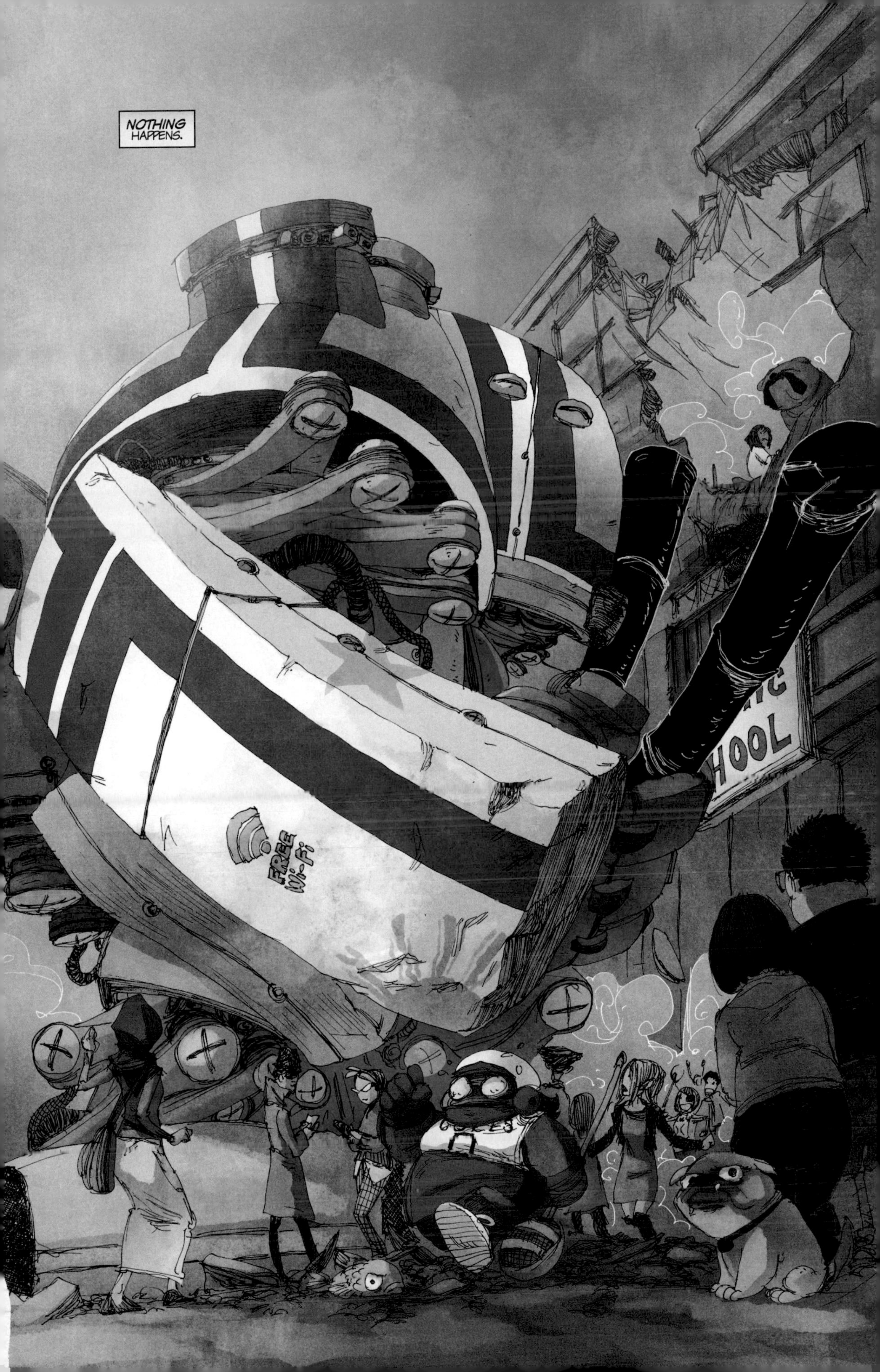
NOTHING HAPPENS.
FREE Wi-Fi
HOOL

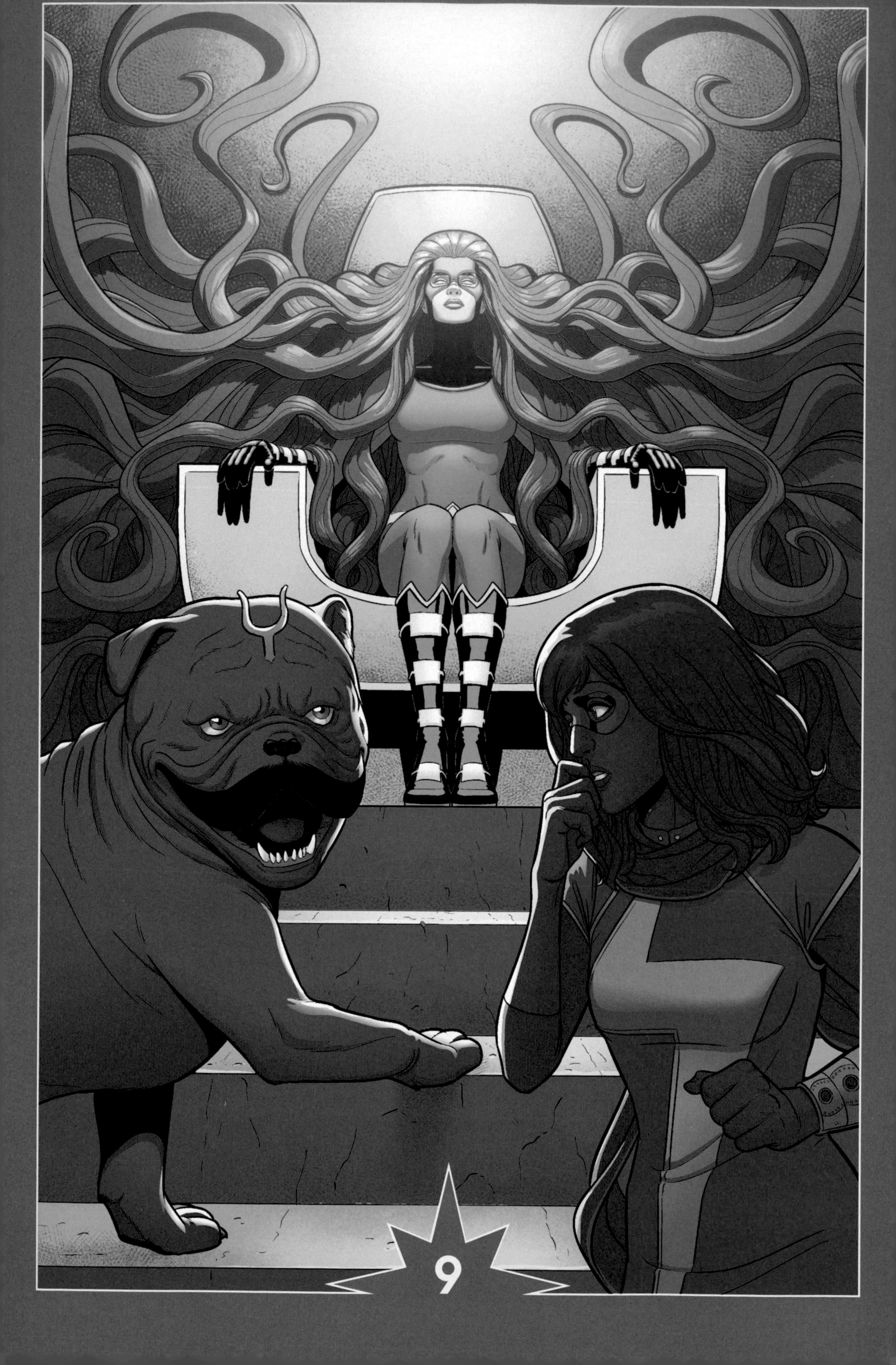
9

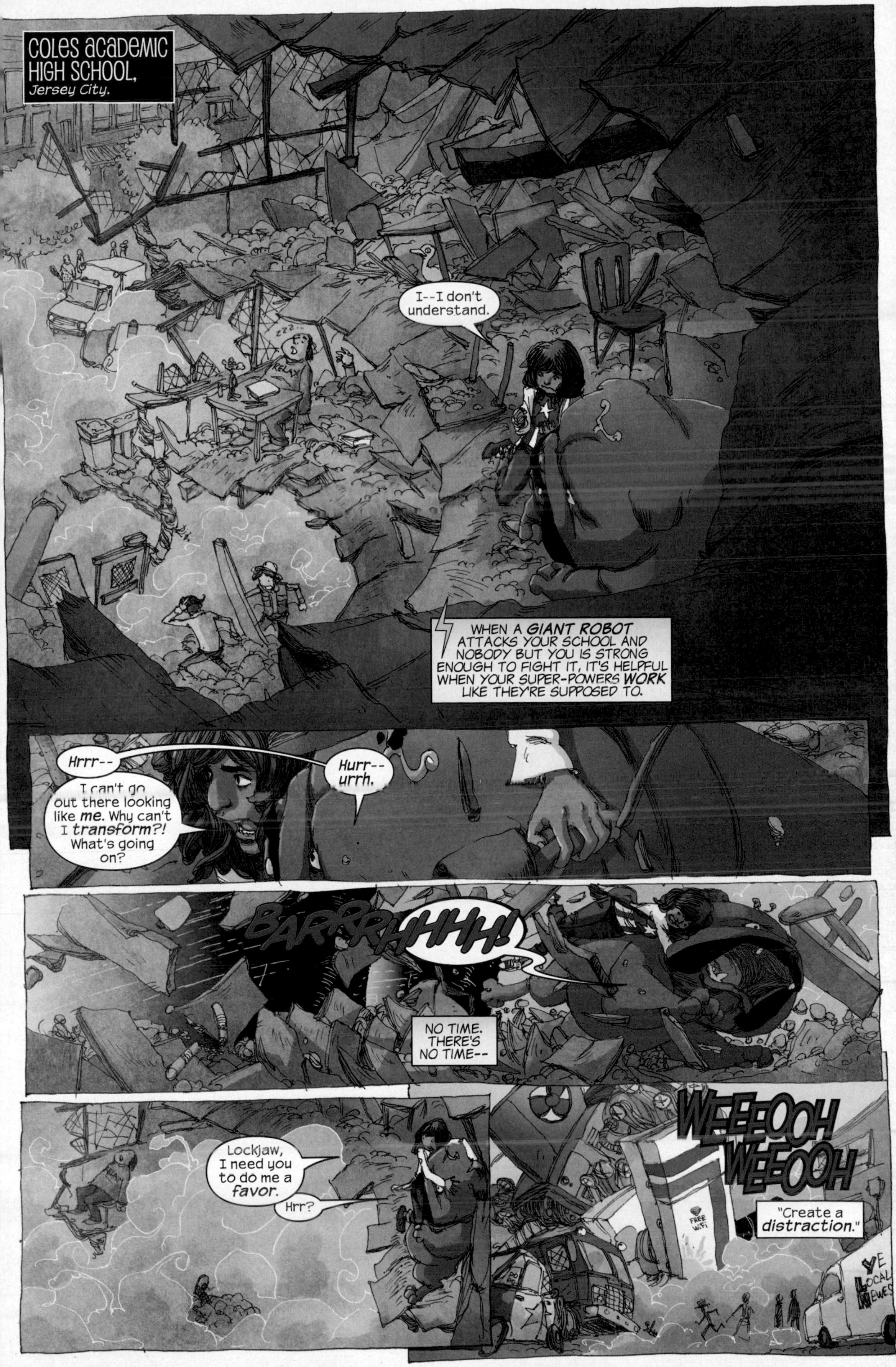

COLES ACADEMIC HIGH SCHOOL,
Jersey City.
I--I don't understand.
WHEN A GIANT ROBOT ATTACKS YOUR SCHOOL AND NOBODY BUT YOU IS STRONG ENOUGH TO FIGHT IT, IT'S HELPFUL WHEN YOUR SUPER-POWERS WORK LIKE THEY'RE SUPPOSED TO.
Hrrr--
I can't go out there looking like me. Why can't I transform?! What's going on?
Hurr--urrh.
BARRRHHHH!
NO TIME. THERE'S NO TIME--
Lockjaw, I need you to do me a favor.
Hrr?
WEEEOOH WEEOOH
"Create a distraction."

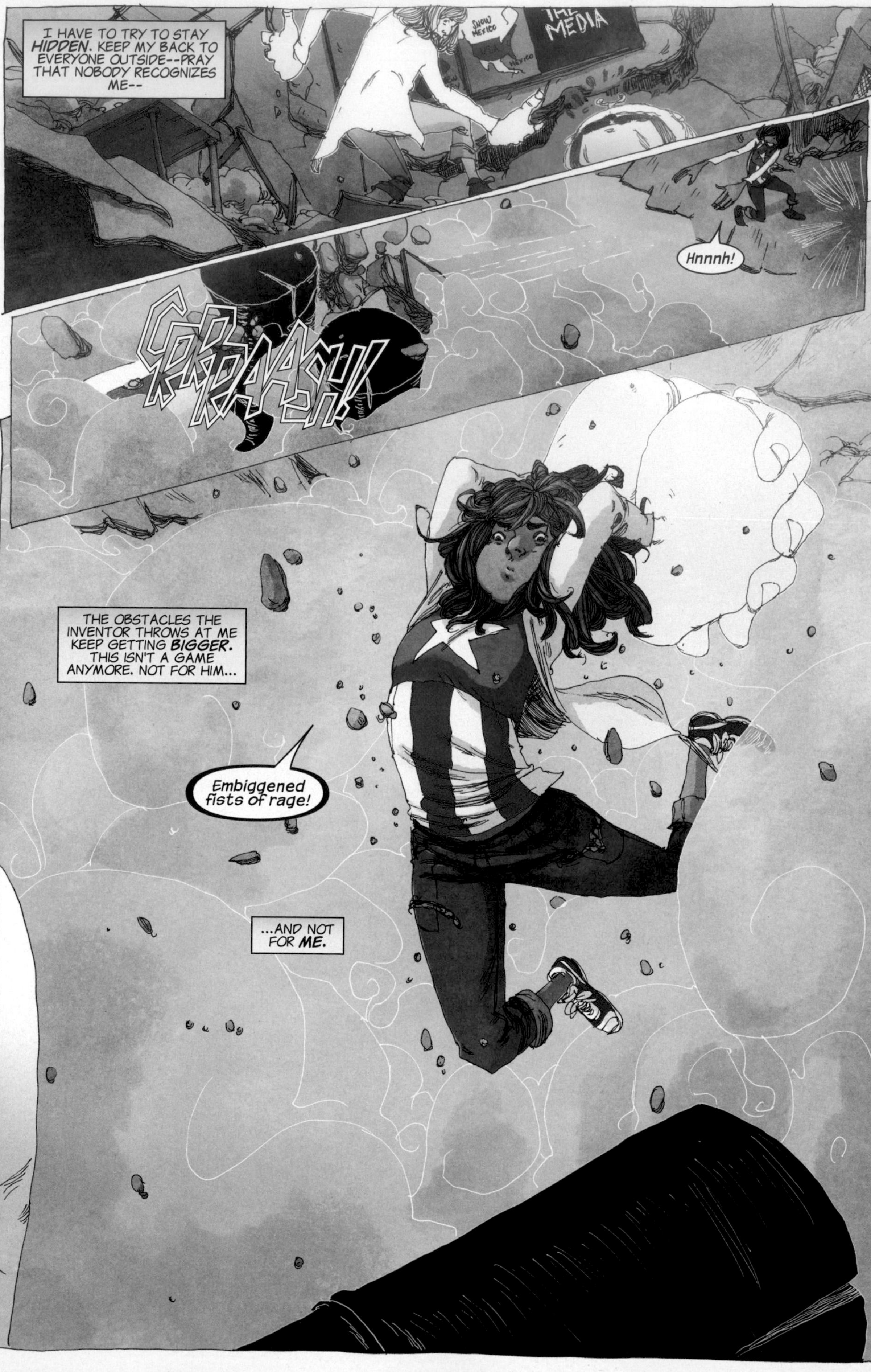
I HAVE TO TRY TO STAY HIDDEN. KEEP MY BACK TO EVERYONE OUTSIDE--PRAY THAT NOBODY RECOGNIZES ME--
THE MEDIA
Hnnnh!
THE OBSTACLES THE INVENTOR THROWS AT ME KEEP GETTING BIGGER. THIS ISN'T A GAME ANYMORE. NOT FOR HIM...
Embiggened fists of rage!
...AND NOT FOR ME.

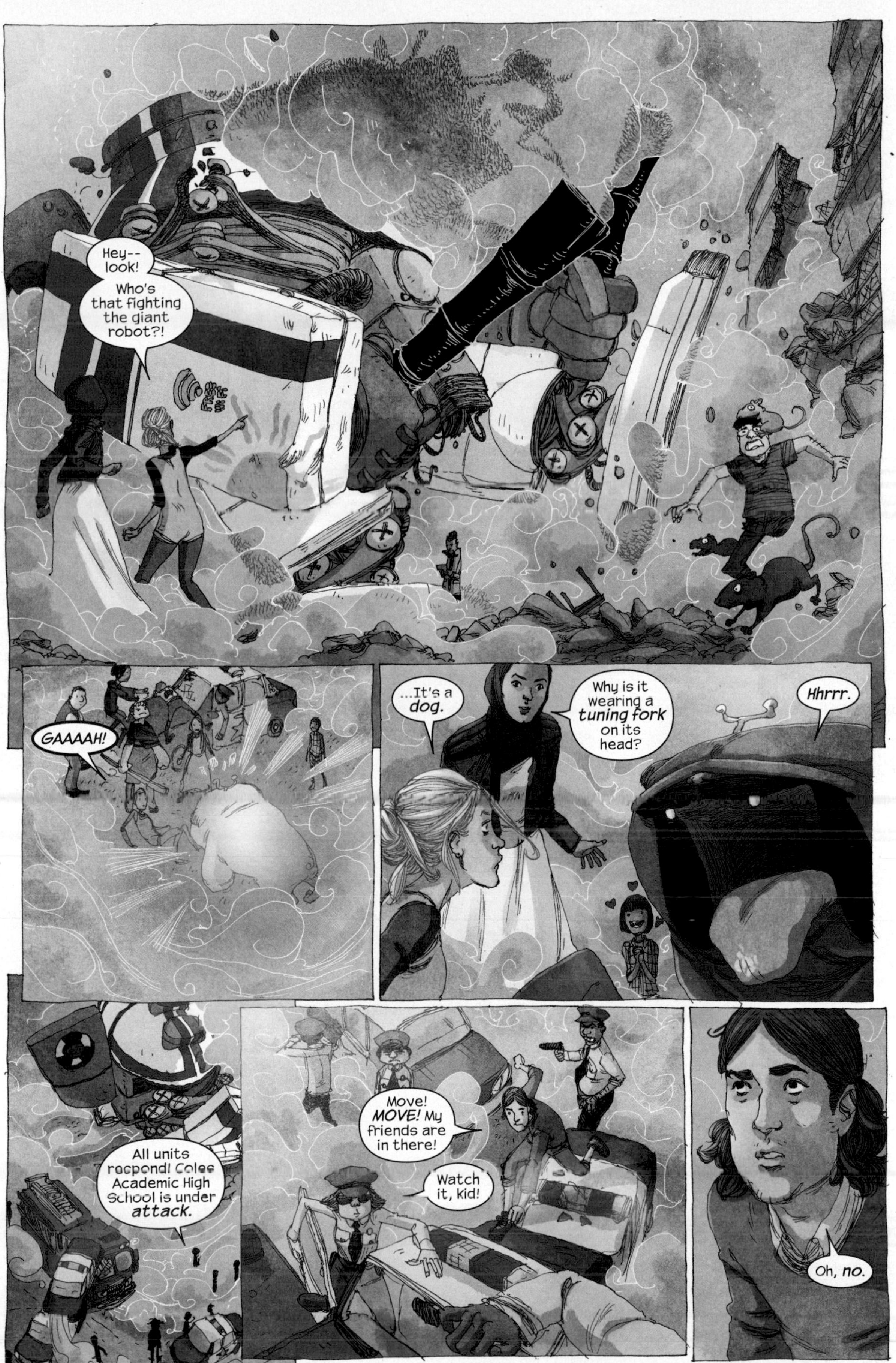
Hey--
look!
Who's that fighting the giant robot?!
GAAAAH!
...It's a dog.
Why is it wearing a tuning fork on its head?
Hhrrr.
All units respond! Coles Academic High School is under attack.
Move! MOVE! My friends are in there!
Watch it, kid!
Oh, no.

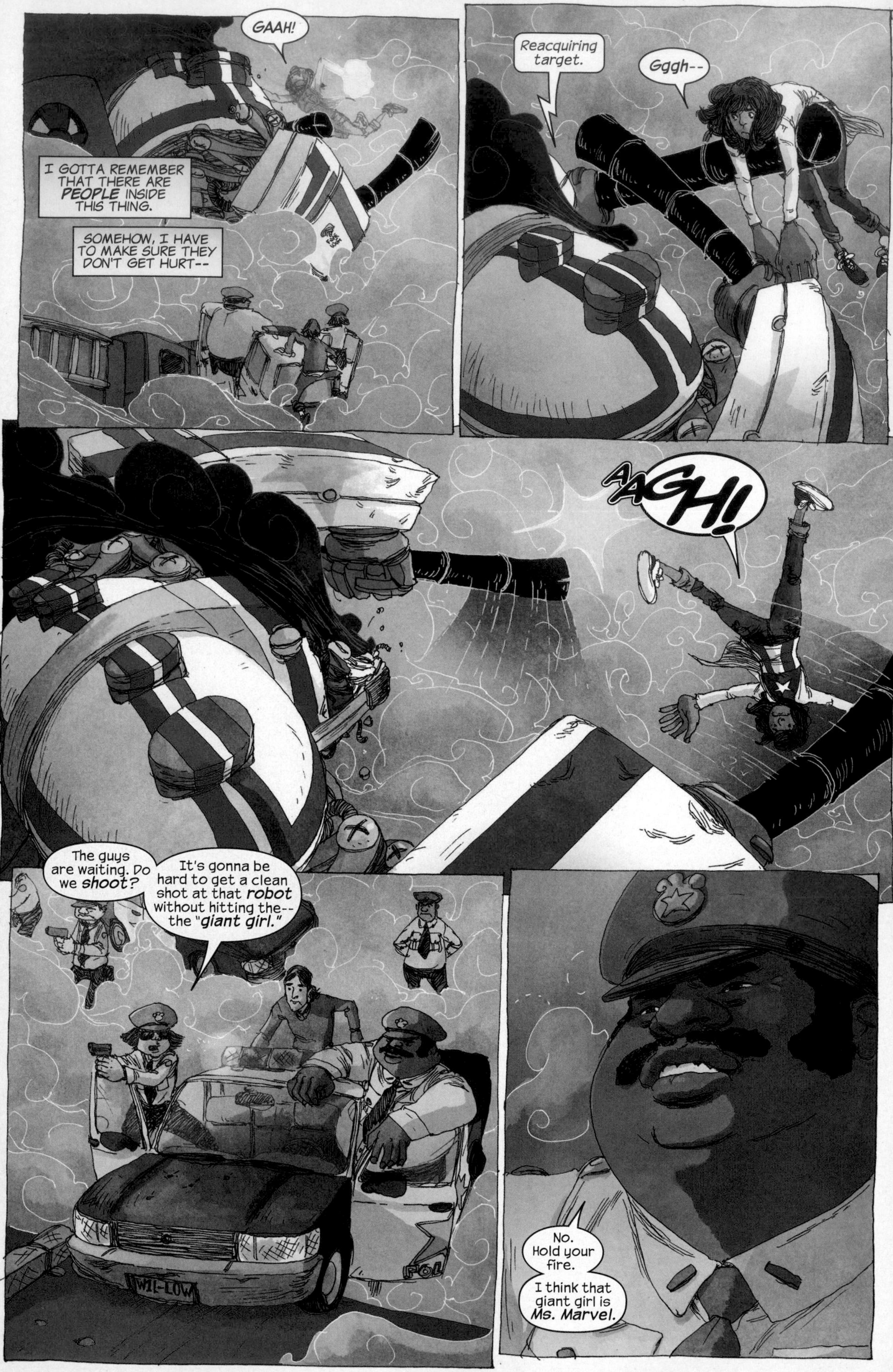
GAAH!
I GOTTA REMEMBER THAT THERE ARE PEOPLE INSIDE THIS THING.
SOMEHOW, I HAVE TO MAKE SURE THEY DON'T GET HURT--
Reacquiring target.
Gggh--
AAGH!
The guys are waiting. Do we shoot?
It's gonna be hard to get a clean shot at that robot without hitting the-- the "giant girl."
No. Hold your fire.
I think that giant girl is Ms. Marvel.

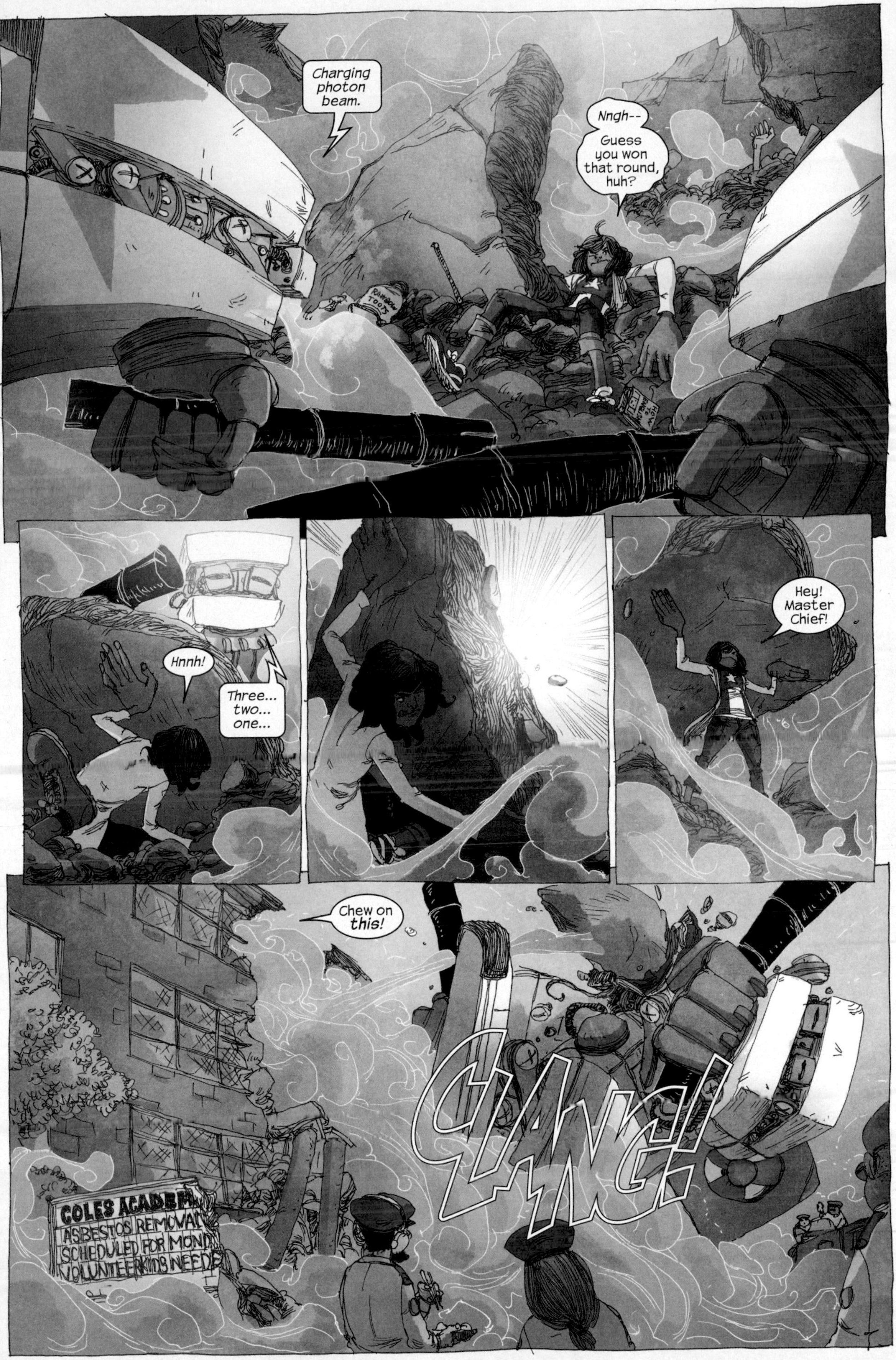

Charging photon beam.
Nngh--
Guess you won that round, huh?
RAINBOW TOOTS
Hnnh!
Three... two... one...
Hey! Master Chief!
Chew on this!
CLANG!
COLES ACADEM
ASBESTOS REMOVAL
SCHEDULED FOR MOND
VOLUNTEER KIDS NEED

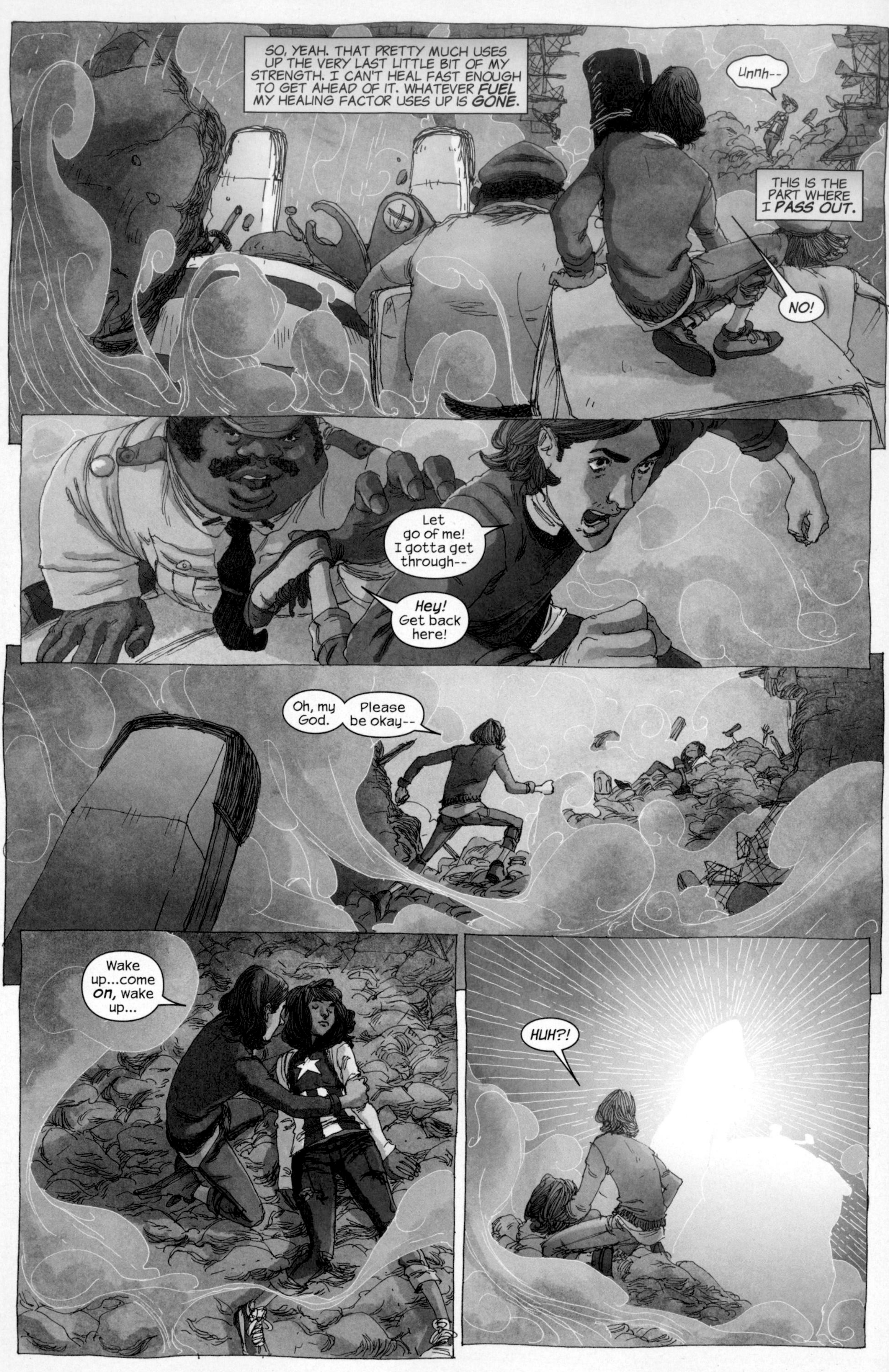
SO, YEAH. THAT PRETTY MUCH USES UP THE VERY LAST LITTLE BIT OF MY STRENGTH. I CAN'T HEAL FAST ENOUGH TO GET AHEAD OF IT. WHATEVER FUEL MY HEALING FACTOR USES UP IS GONE.
Unnh--
THIS IS THE PART WHERE I PASS OUT.
NO!
Let go of me! I gotta get through--
Hey! Get back here!
Oh, my God.
Please be okay--
Wake up...come on, wake up...
HUH?!

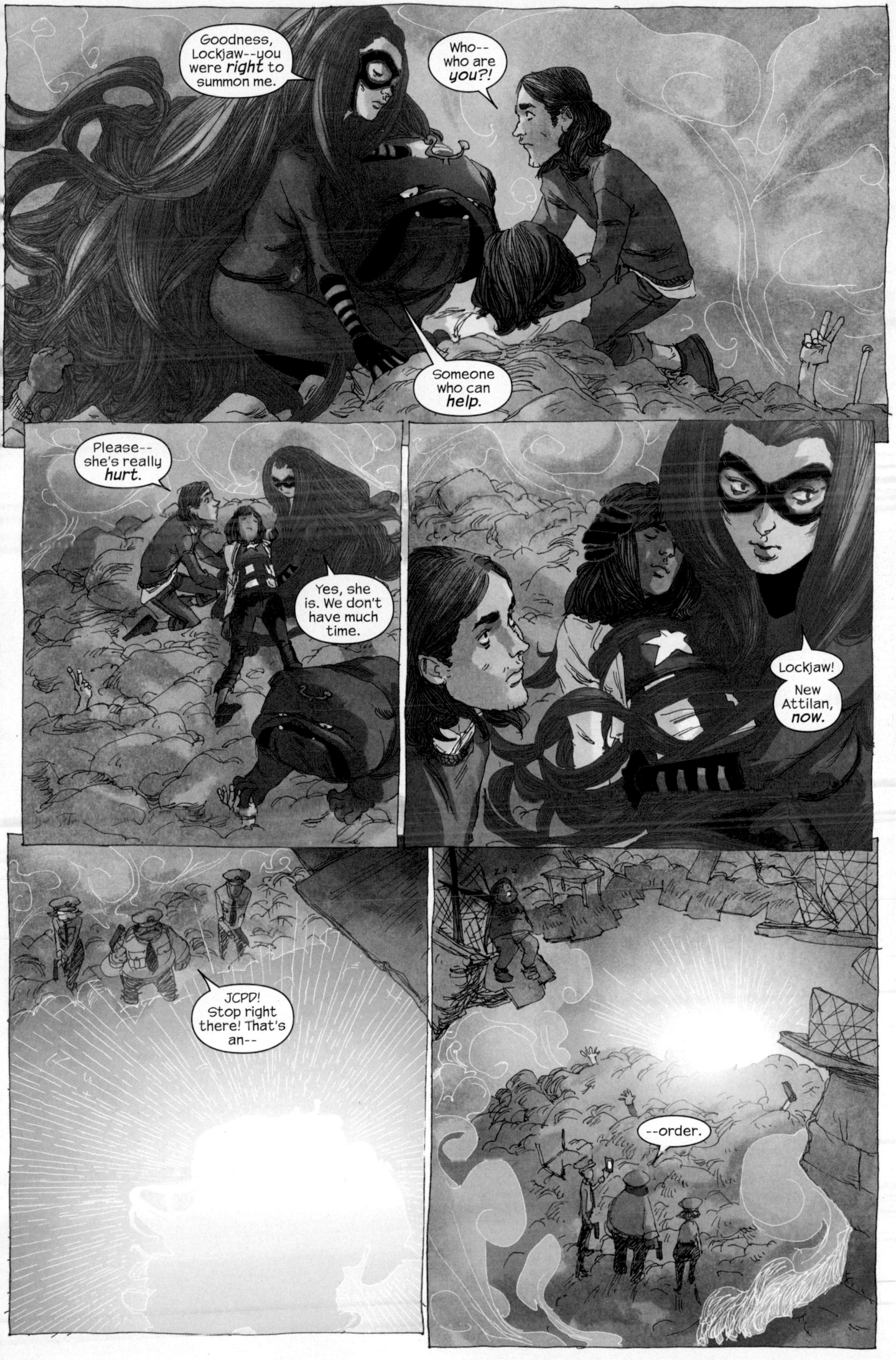
Goodness, Lockjaw--you were *right* to summon me.
Who-- who are *you*?!
Someone who can *help*.
Please-- she's really *hurt*.
Yes, she is. We don't have much time.
Lockjaw! New Attilan, *now*.
JCPD! Stop right there! That's an--
--order.

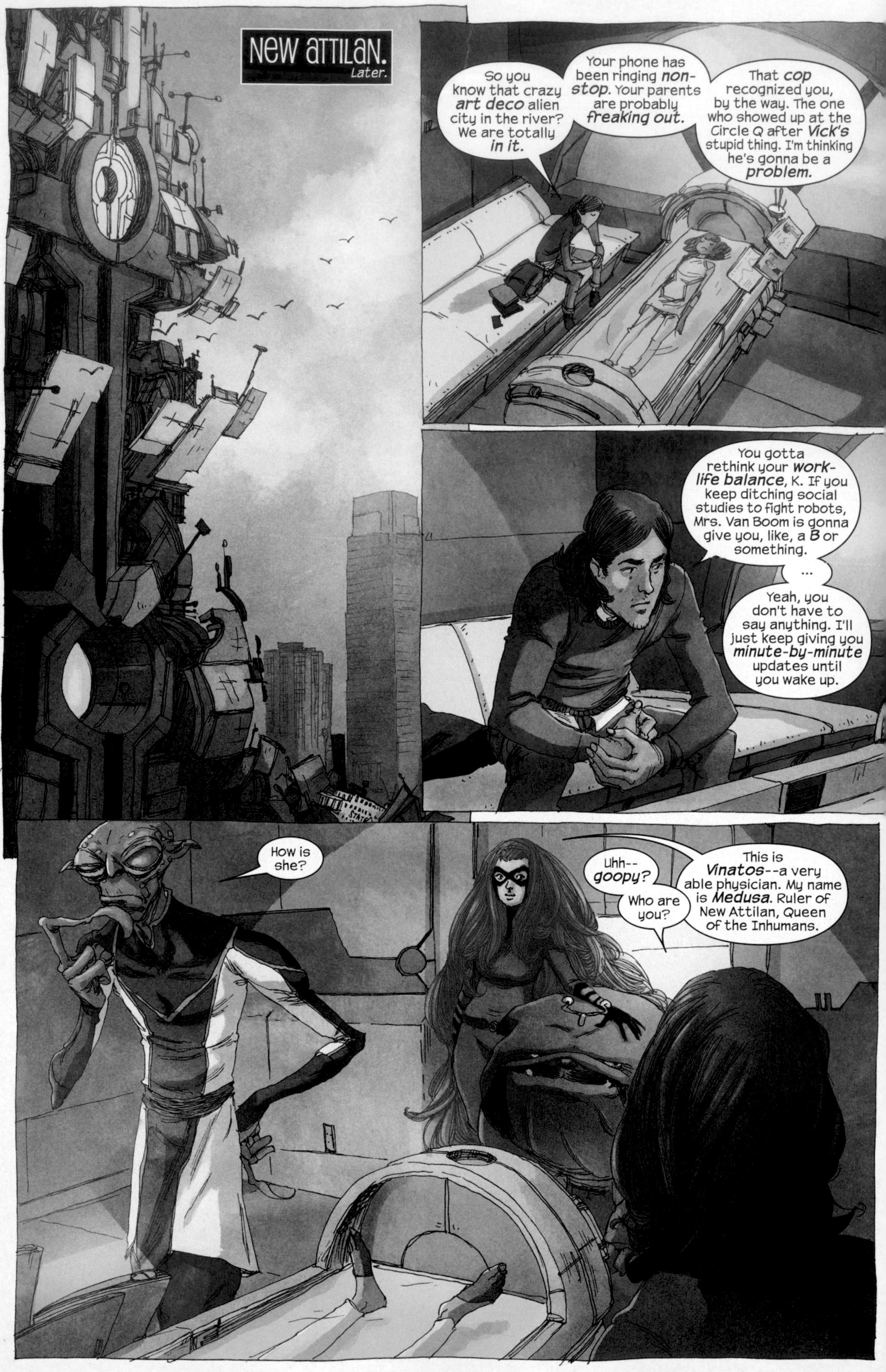
NEW ATTILAN.
Later.
So you know that crazy art deco alien city in the river? We are totally in it.
Your phone has been ringing non-stop. Your parents are probably freaking out.
That cop recognized you, by the way. The one who showed up at the Circle Q after Vick's stupid thing. I'm thinking he's gonna be a problem.
You gotta rethink your work-life balance, K. If you keep ditching social studies to fight robots, Mrs. Van Boom is gonna give you, like, a B or something.
...
Yeah, you don't have to say anything. I'll just keep giving you minute-by-minute updates until you wake up.
How is she?
Uhh-- goopy?
Who are you?
This is Vinatos--a very able physician. My name is Medusa. Ruler of New Attilan, Queen of the Inhumans.

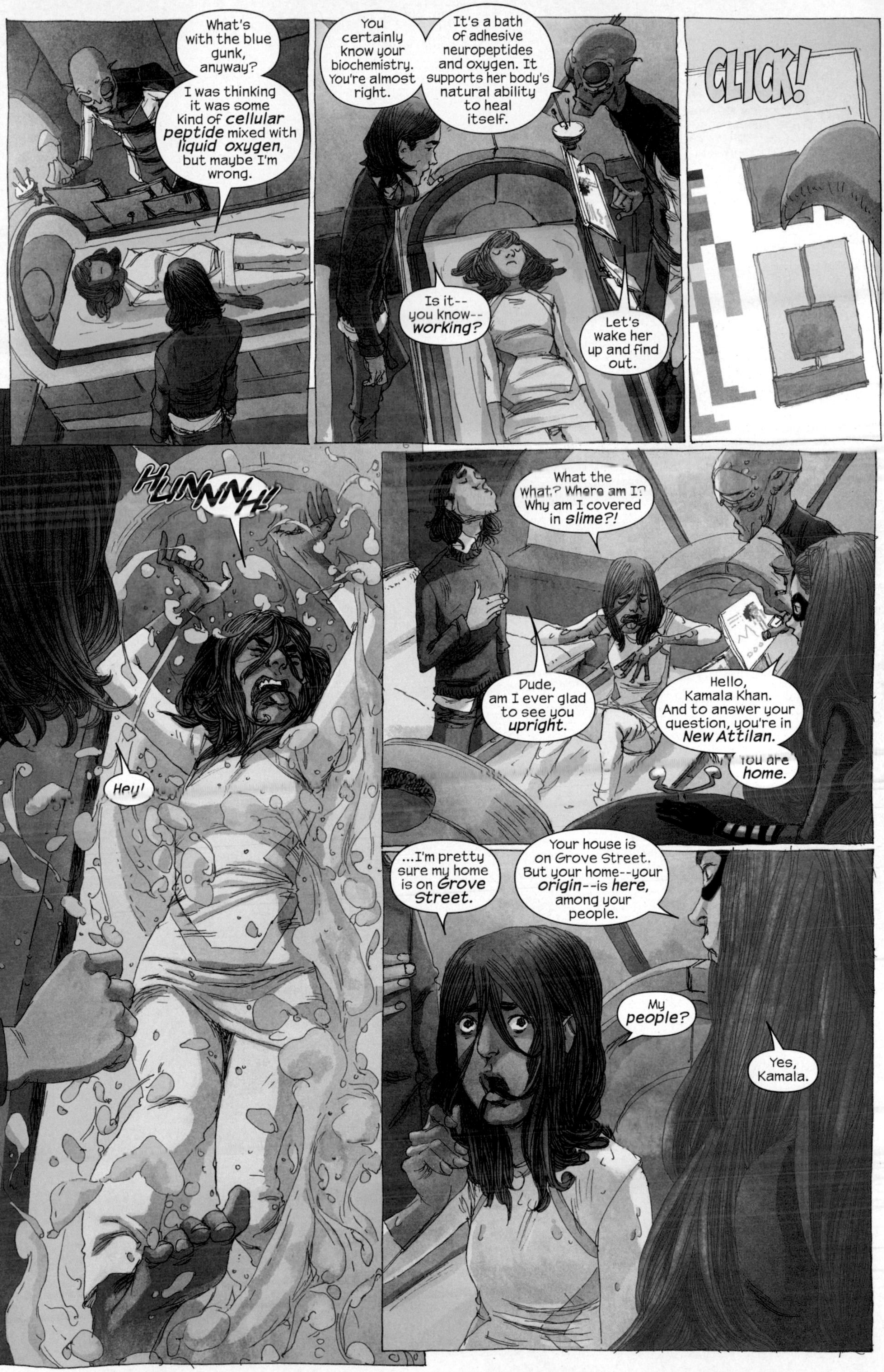
What's with the blue gunk, anyway?
I was thinking it was some kind of *cellular peptide* mixed with *liquid oxygen*, but maybe I'm wrong.
You certainly know your biochemistry. You're almost right.
It's a bath of adhesive neuropeptides and oxygen. It supports her body's natural ability to heal itself.
Is it-- you know-- *working?*
Let's wake her up and find out.
CLICK!
HLUNNNH!
Hey!
What the what? Where am I? Why am I covered in *slime?!*
Dude, am I ever glad to see you *upright*.
Hello, Kamala Khan. And to answer your question, you're in *New Attilan*.
You are *home*.
...I'm pretty sure my home is on *Grove Street*.
Your house is on Grove Street. But your home--your *origin*--is *here*, among your people.
My *people?*
Yes, Kamala.

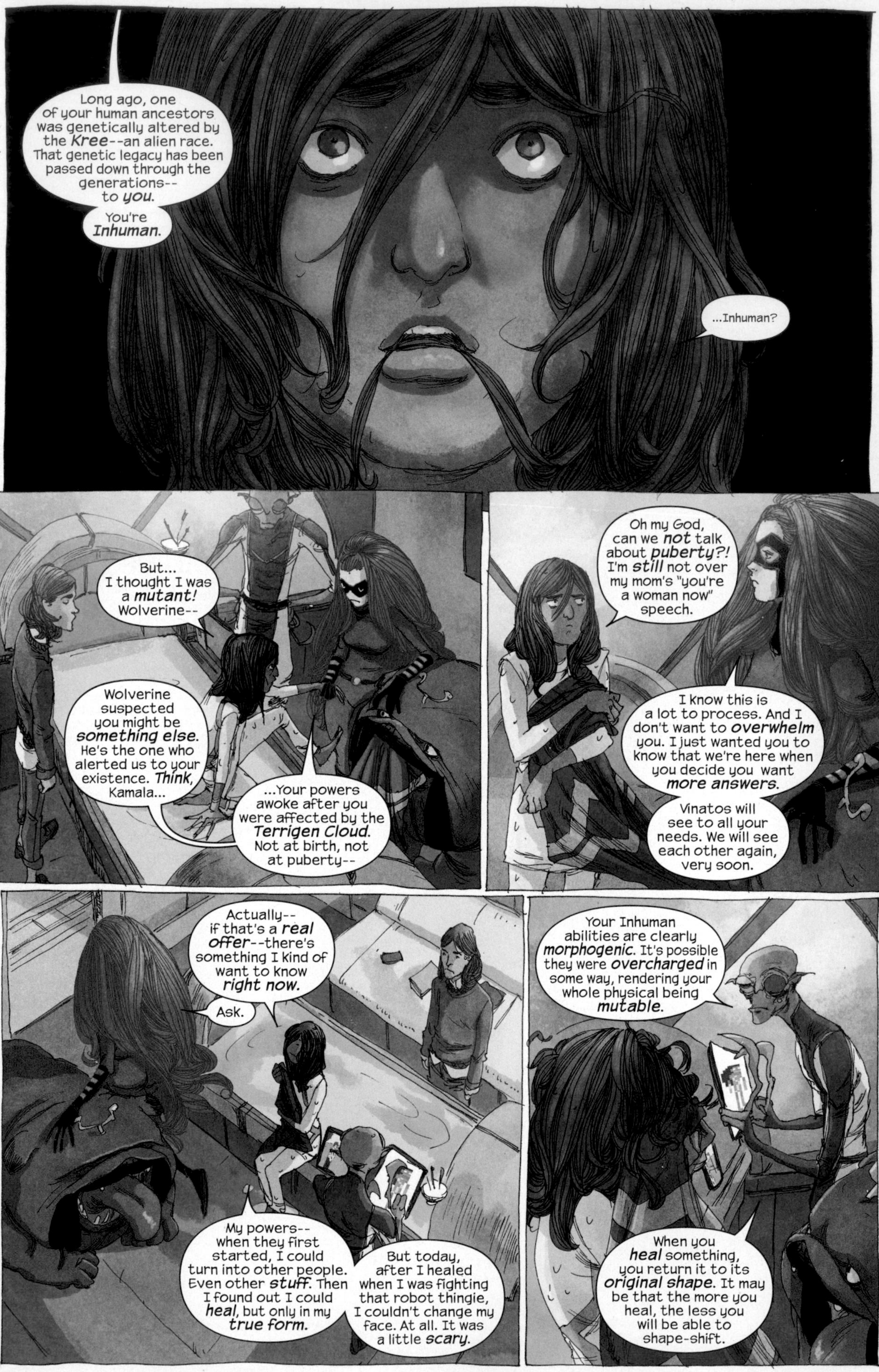

Long ago, one of your human ancestors was genetically altered by the Kree--an alien race. That genetic legacy has been passed down through the generations-- to you.
You're Inhuman.
...Inhuman?
But... I thought I was a mutant! Wolverine--
Wolverine suspected you might be something else. He's the one who alerted us to your existence. Think, Kamala...
...Your powers awoke after you were affected by the Terrigen Cloud. Not at birth, not at puberty--
Oh my God, can we not talk about puberty?! I'm still not over my mom's "you're a woman now" speech.
I know this is a lot to process. And I don't want to overwhelm you. I just wanted you to know that we're here when you decide you want more answers.
Vinatos will see to all your needs. We will see each other again, very soon.
Actually-- if that's a real offer--there's something I kind of want to know right now.
Ask.
My powers-- when they first started, I could turn into other people. Even other stuff. Then I found out I could heal, but only in my true form.
But today, after I healed when I was fighting that robot thingie, I couldn't change my face. At all. It was a little scary.
Your Inhuman abilities are clearly morphogenic. It's possible they were overcharged in some way, rendering your whole physical being mutable.
When you heal something, you return it to its original shape. It may be that the more you heal, the less you will be able to shape-shift.

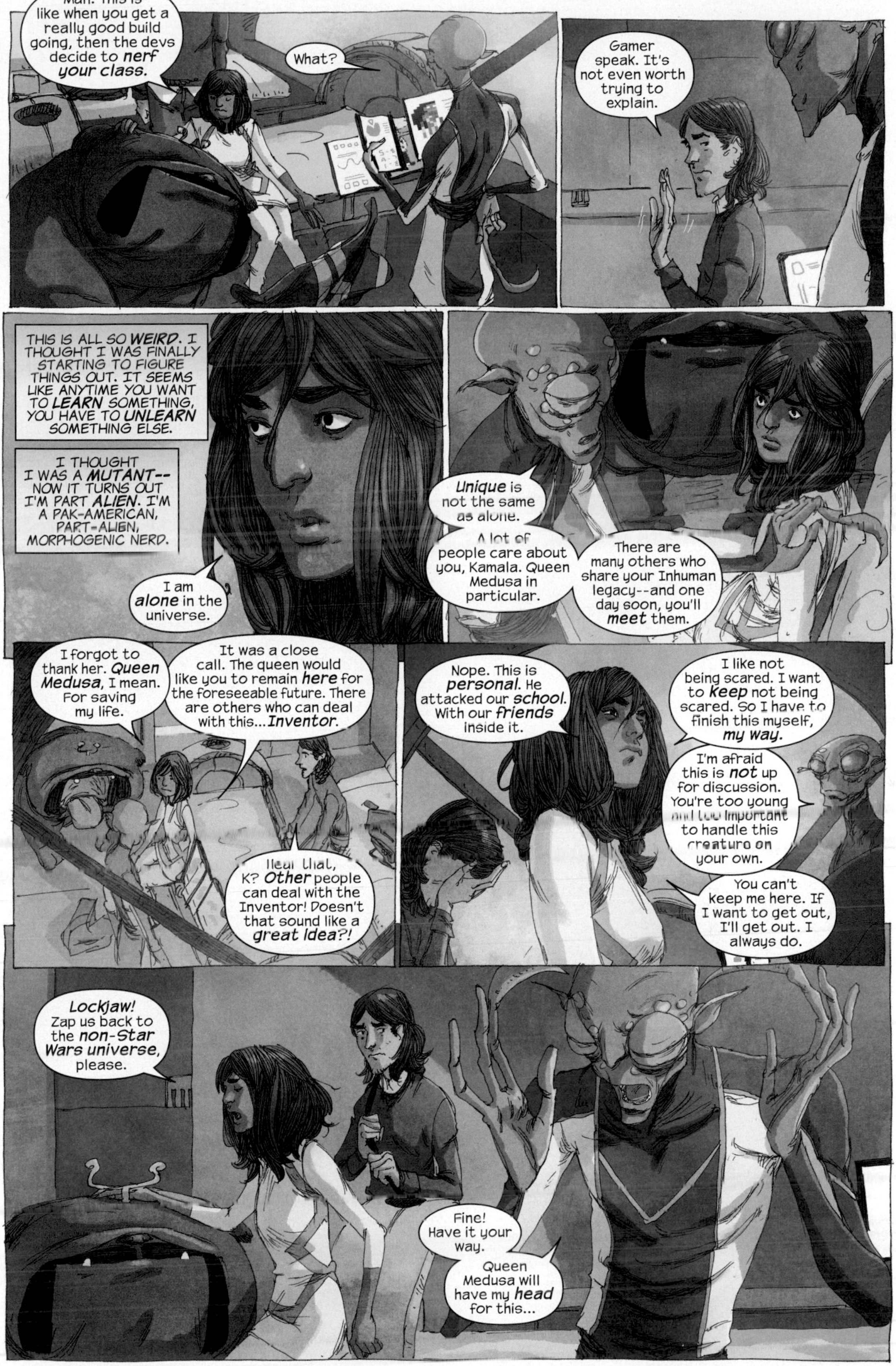
Man. This is like when you get a really good build going, then the devs decide to nerf your class.
What?
Gamer speak. It's not even worth trying to explain.
THIS IS ALL SO WEIRD. I THOUGHT I WAS FINALLY STARTING TO FIGURE THINGS OUT. IT SEEMS LIKE ANYTIME YOU WANT TO LEARN SOMETHING, YOU HAVE TO UNLEARN SOMETHING ELSE.
I THOUGHT I WAS A MUTANT-- NOW IT TURNS OUT I'M PART ALIEN. I'M A PAK-AMERICAN, PART-ALIEN, MORPHOGENIC NERD.
I am alone in the universe.
Unique is not the same as alone.
A lot of people care about you, Kamala. Queen Medusa in particular.
There are many others who share your Inhuman legacy--and one day soon, you'll meet them.
I forgot to thank her. Queen Medusa, I mean. For saving my life.
It was a close call. The queen would like you to remain here for the foreseeable future. There are others who can deal with this...Inventor.
Hear that, K? Other people can deal with the Inventor! Doesn't that sound like a great Idea?!
Nope. This is personal. He attacked our school. With our friends inside it.
I like not being scared. I want to keep not being scared. So I have to finish this myself, my way.
I'm afraid this is not up for discussion. You're too young and too important to handle this creature on your own.
You can't keep me here. If I want to get out, I'll get out. I always do.
Lockjaw! Zap us back to the non-Star Wars universe, please.
Fine! Have it your way.
Queen Medusa will have my head for this...

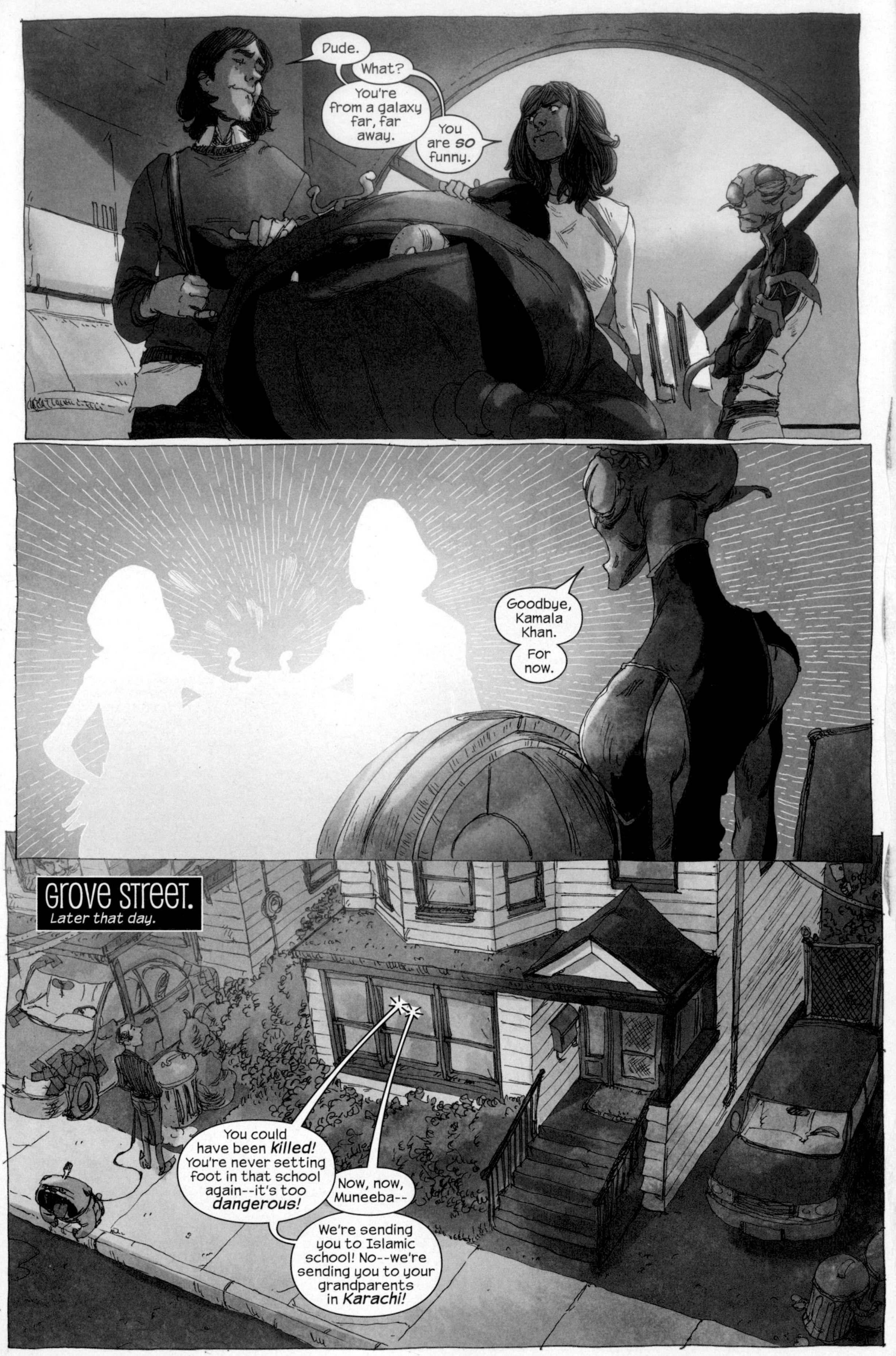
Dude.
What?
You're from a galaxy far, far away.
You are *SO* funny.
Goodbye, Kamala Khan.
For now.
GROVE STREET.
Later that day.
You could have been *killed!* You're never setting foot in that school again--it's too *dangerous!*
Now, now, Muneeba--
We're sending you to Islamic school! No--we're sending you to your grandparents in *Karachi!*

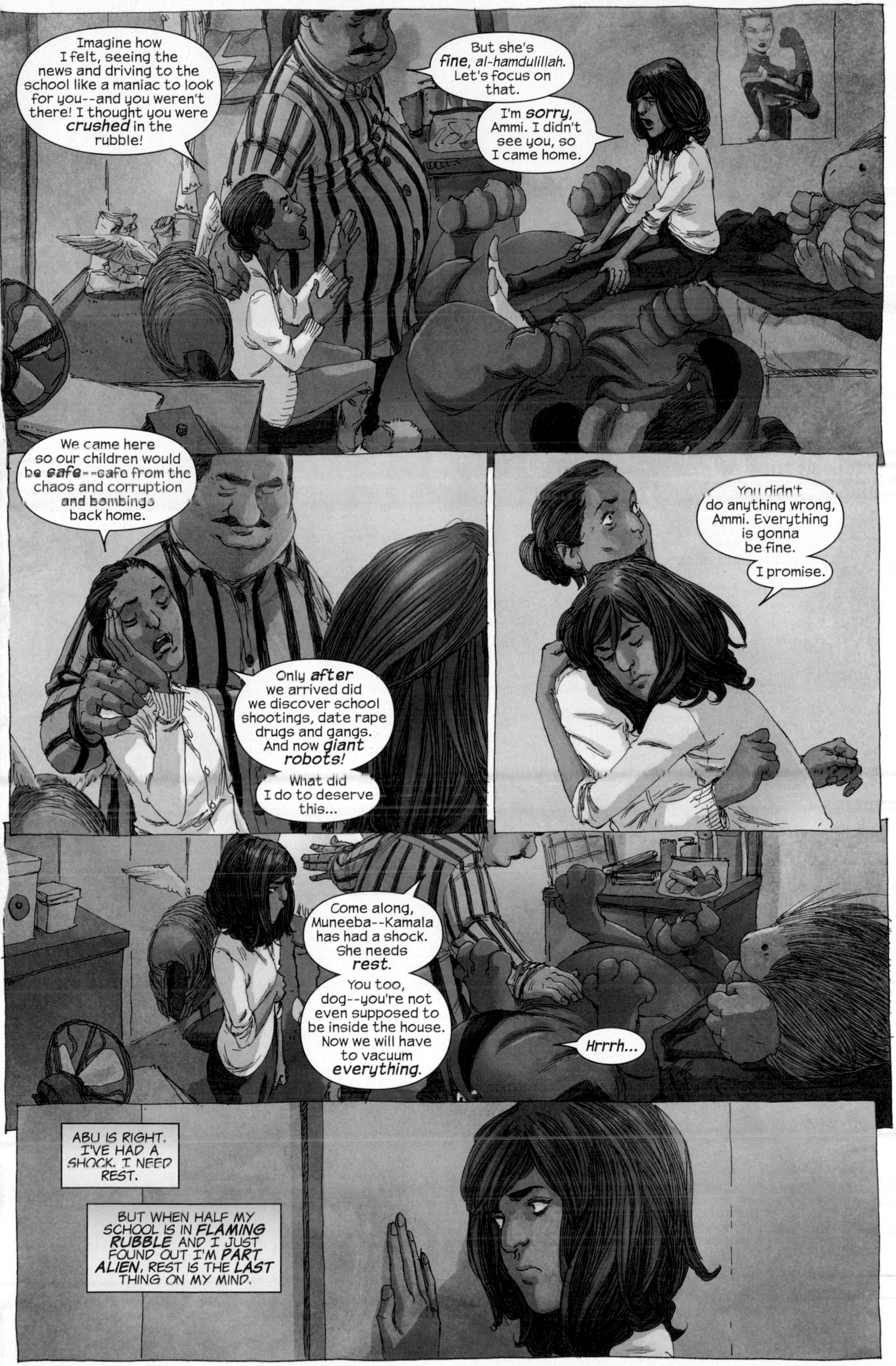
Imagine how I felt, seeing the news and driving to the school like a maniac to look for you--and you weren't there! I thought you were crushed in the rubble!
But she's fine, al-hamdulillah. Let's focus on that.
I'm sorry, Ammi. I didn't see you, so I came home.
We came here so our children would be safe--safe from the chaos and corruption and bombings back home.
Only after we arrived did we discover school shootings, date rape drugs and gangs. And now giant robots!
What did I do to deserve this...
You didn't do anything wrong, Ammi. Everything is gonna be fine.
I promise.
Come along, Muneeba--Kamala has had a shock. She needs rest.
You too, dog--you're not even supposed to be inside the house. Now we will have to vacuum everything.
Hrrrh...
ABU IS RIGHT. I'VE HAD A SHOCK. I NEED REST.
BUT WHEN HALF MY SCHOOL IS IN FLAMING RUBBLE AND I JUST FOUND OUT I'M PART ALIEN, REST IS THE LAST THING ON MY MIND.

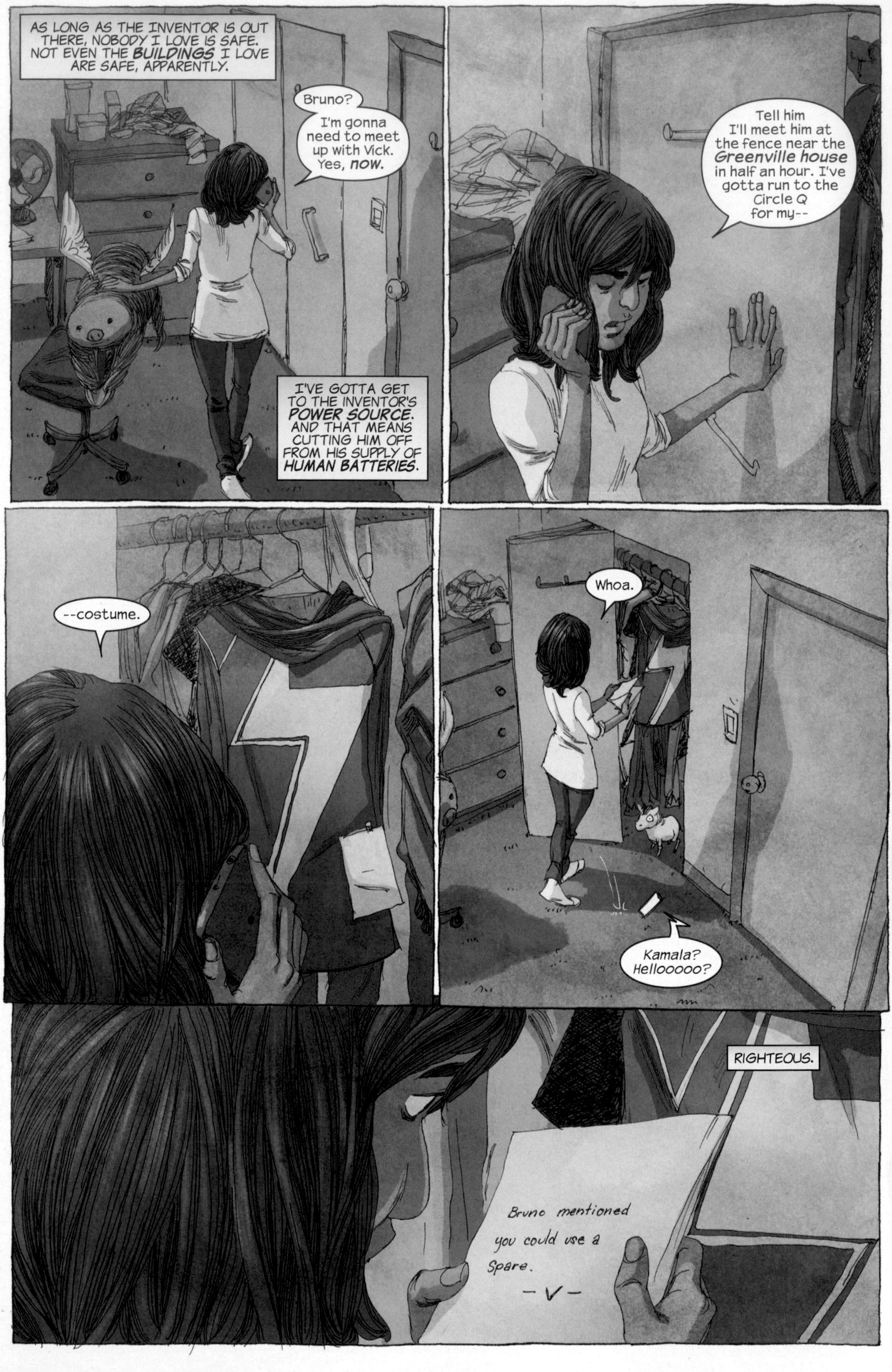
AS LONG AS THE INVENTOR IS OUT THERE, NOBODY I LOVE IS SAFE. NOT EVEN THE BUILDINGS I LOVE ARE SAFE, APPARENTLY.
Bruno?
I'm gonna need to meet up with Vick. Yes, now.
I'VE GOTTA GET TO THE INVENTOR'S POWER SOURCE. AND THAT MEANS CUTTING HIM OFF FROM HIS SUPPLY OF HUMAN BATTERIES.
Tell him I'll meet him at the fence near the Greenville house in half an hour. I've gotta run to the Circle Q for my--
--costume.
Whoa.
Kamala? Hellooooo?
RIGHTEOUS.
Bruno mentioned you could use a spare.
-V-

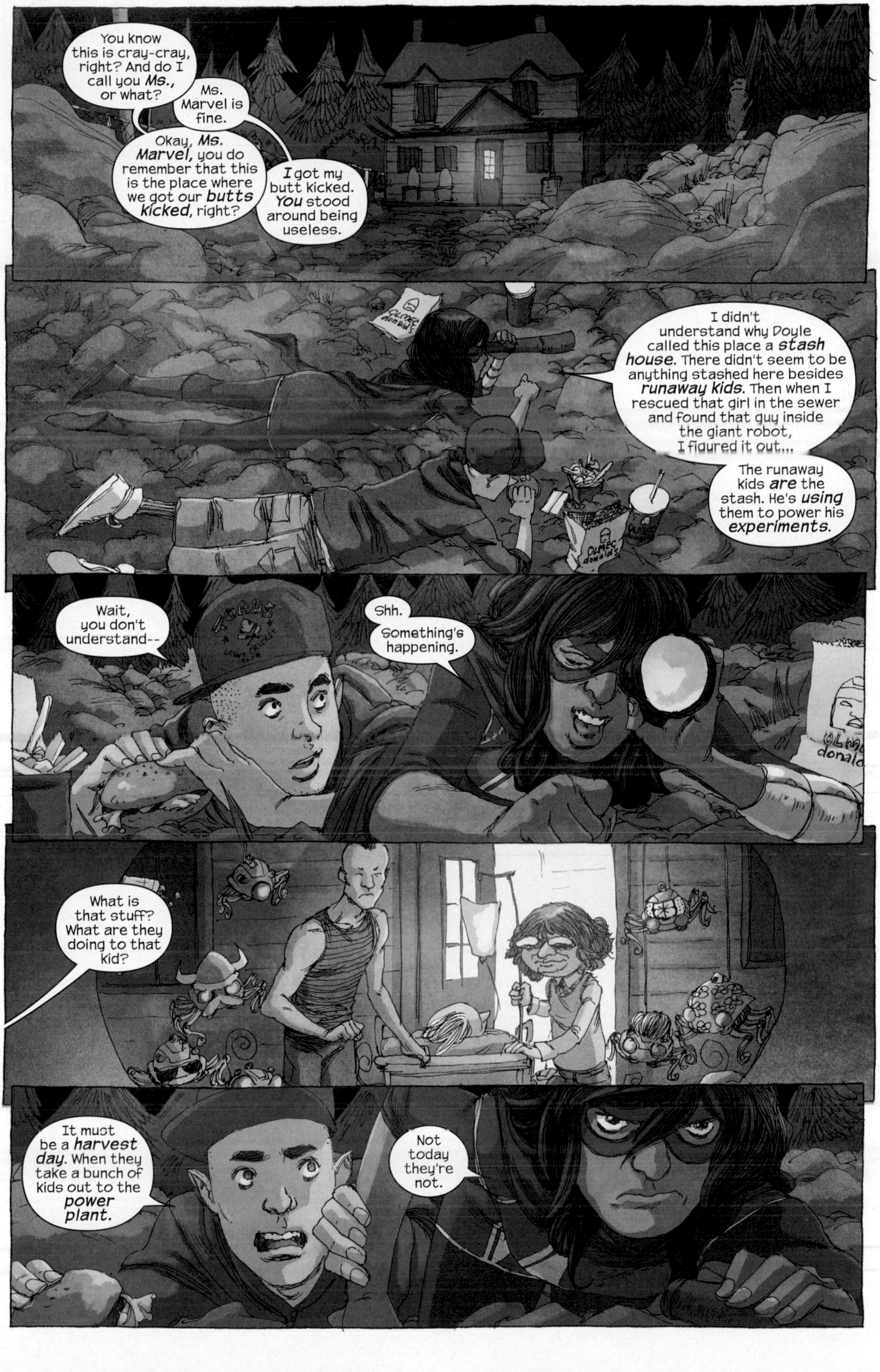
You know this is cray-cray, right? And do I call you Ms., or what?
Ms. Marvel is fine.
Okay, Ms. Marvel, you do remember that this is the place where we got our butts kicked, right?
I got my butt kicked. You stood around being useless.
I didn't understand why Doyle called this place a stash house. There didn't seem to be anything stashed here besides runaway kids. Then when I rescued that girl in the sewer and found that guy inside the giant robot, I figured it out...
The runaway kids are the stash. He's using them to power his experiments.
Wait, you don't understand--
Shh.
Something's happening.
What is that stuff? What are they doing to that kid?
It must be a harvest day. When they take a bunch of kids out to the power plant.
Not today they're not.

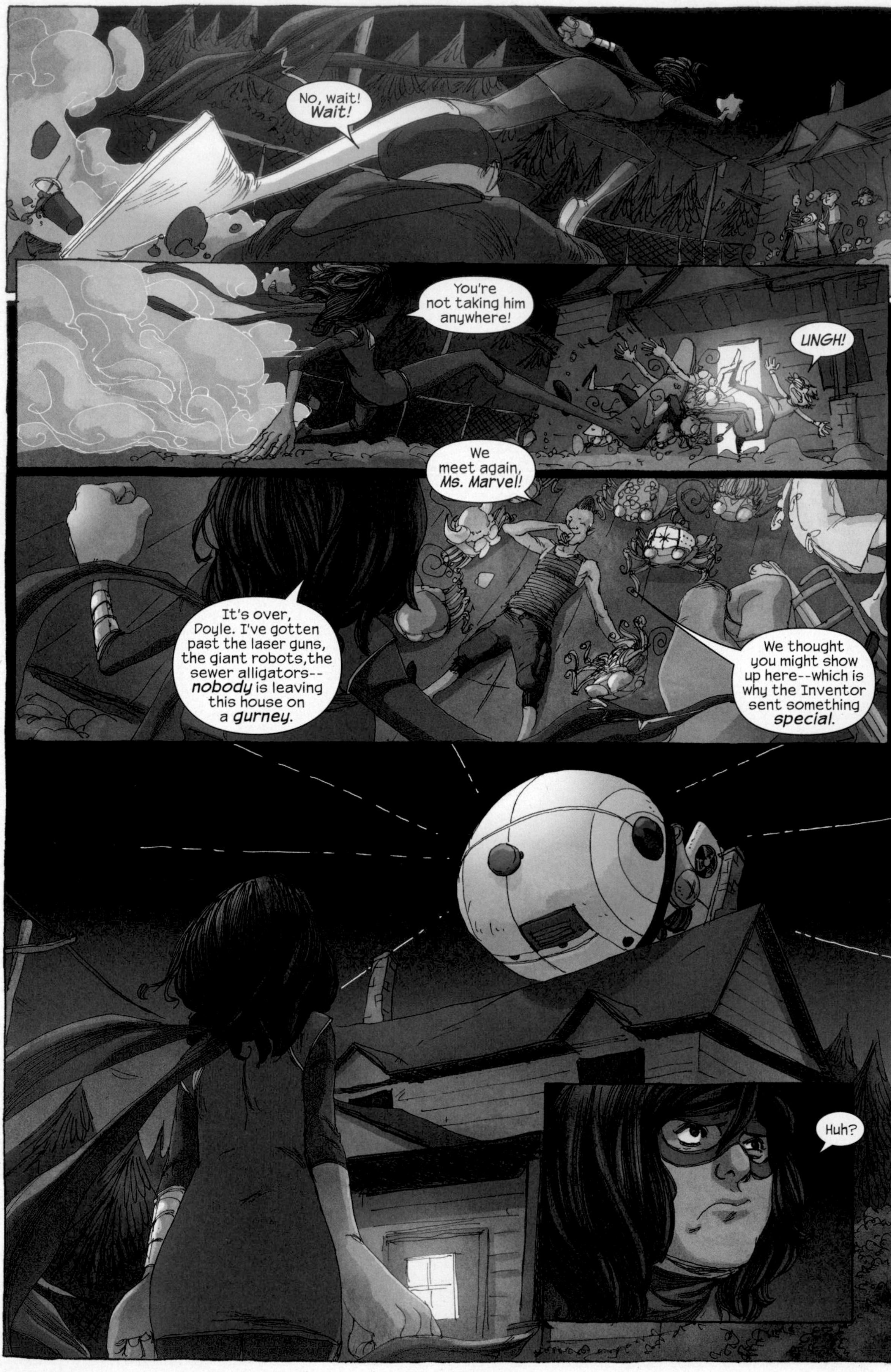
No, wait! Wait!
You're not taking him anywhere!
UNGH!
We meet again, Ms. Marvel!
It's over, Doyle. I've gotten past the laser guns, the giant robots, the sewer alligators-- nobody is leaving this house on a gurney.
We thought you might show up here--which is why the Inventor sent something special.
Huh?

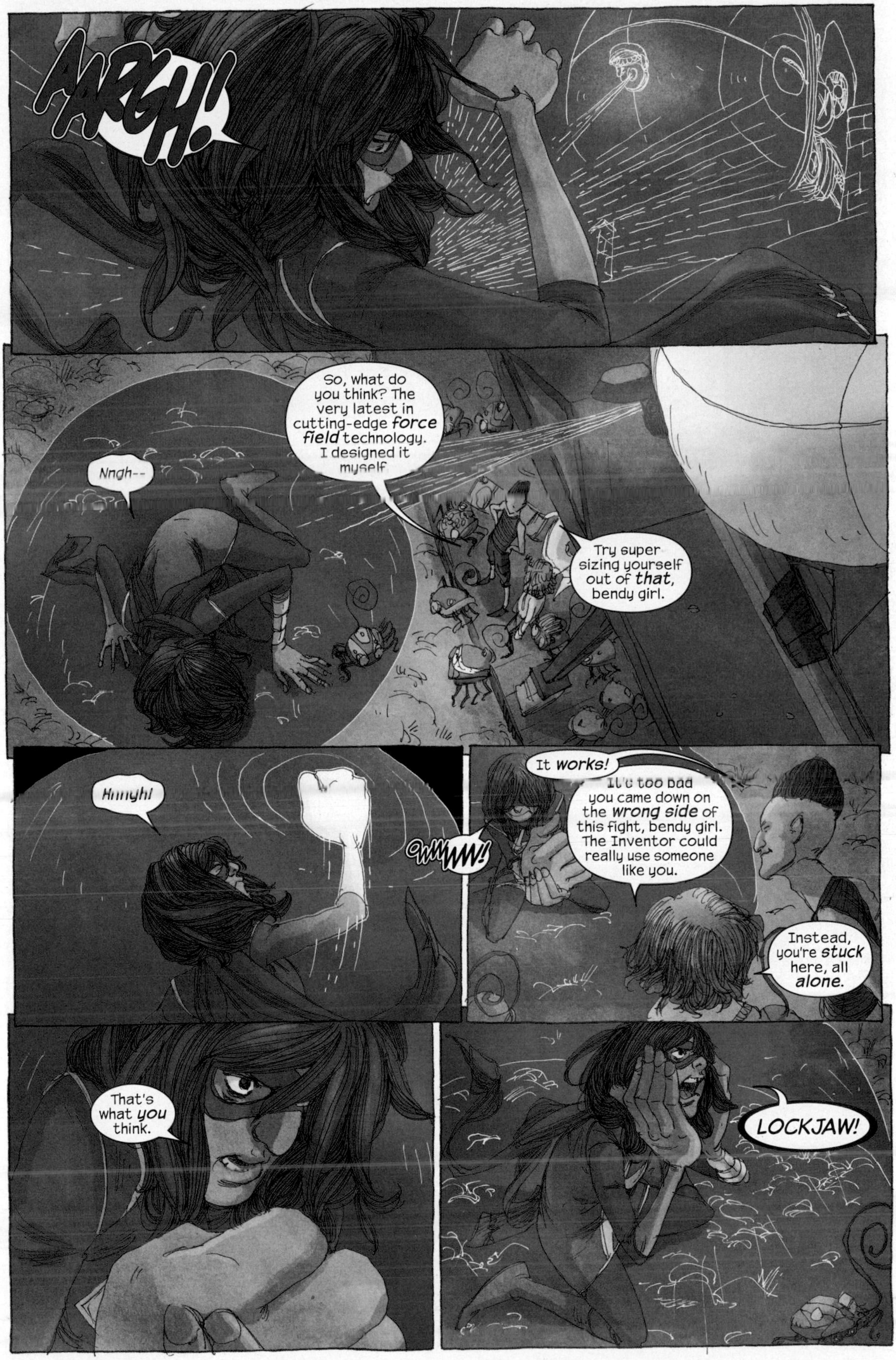
AARGH!
So, what do you think? The very latest in cutting-edge force field technology. I designed it myself.
Nngh--
Try super sizing yourself out of that, bendy girl.
Hnngh!
WMWW!
It works!
It's too bad you came down on the wrong side of this fight, bendy girl. The Inventor could really use someone like you.
Instead, you're stuck here, all alone.
That's what you think.
LOCKJAW!

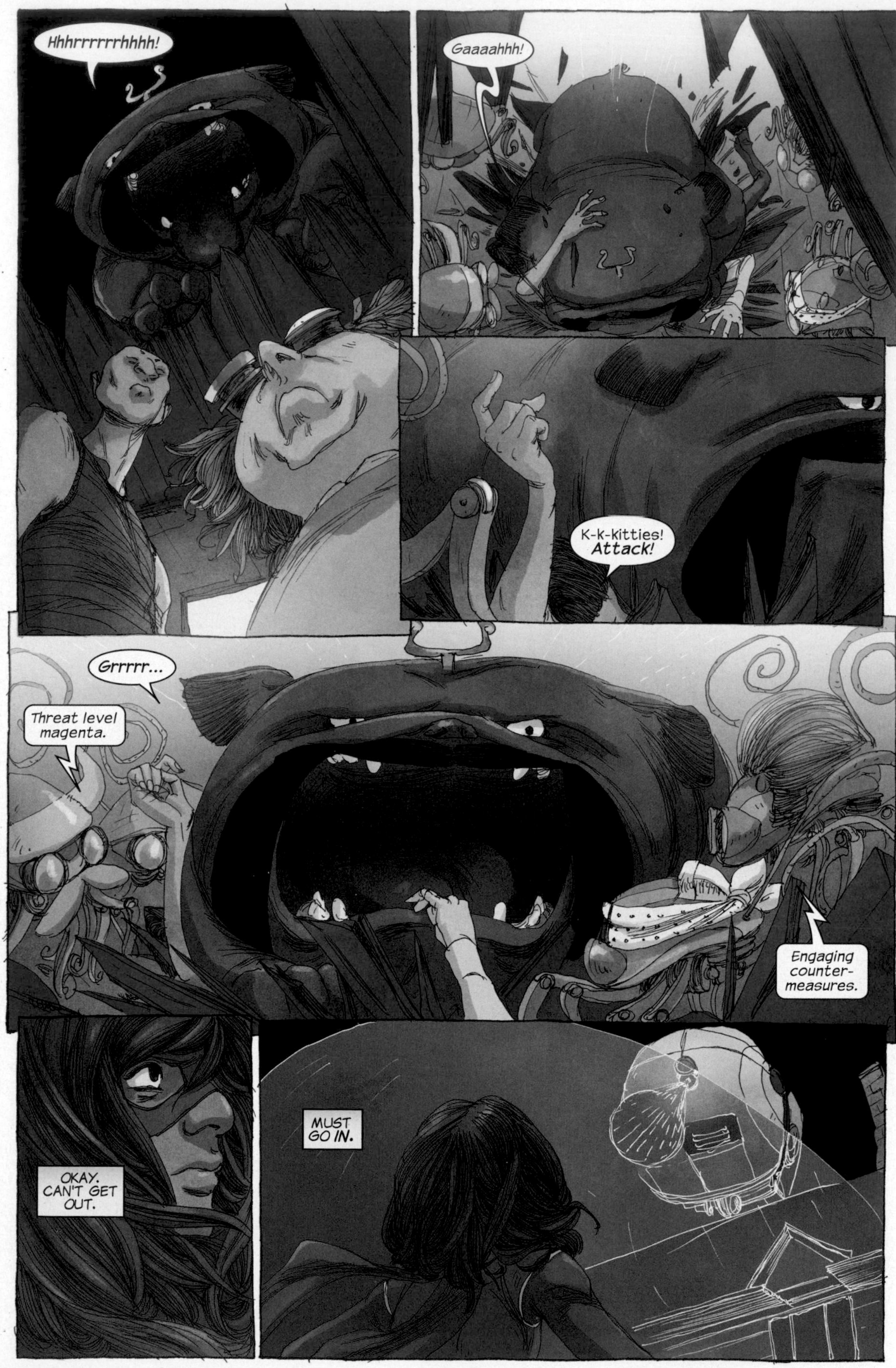
Hhhrrrrrrhhhh!
Gaaaahhh!
K-k-kitties! Attack!
Grrrrr...
Threat level magenta.
Engaging counter-measures.
OKAY. CAN'T GET OUT.
MUST GO IN.

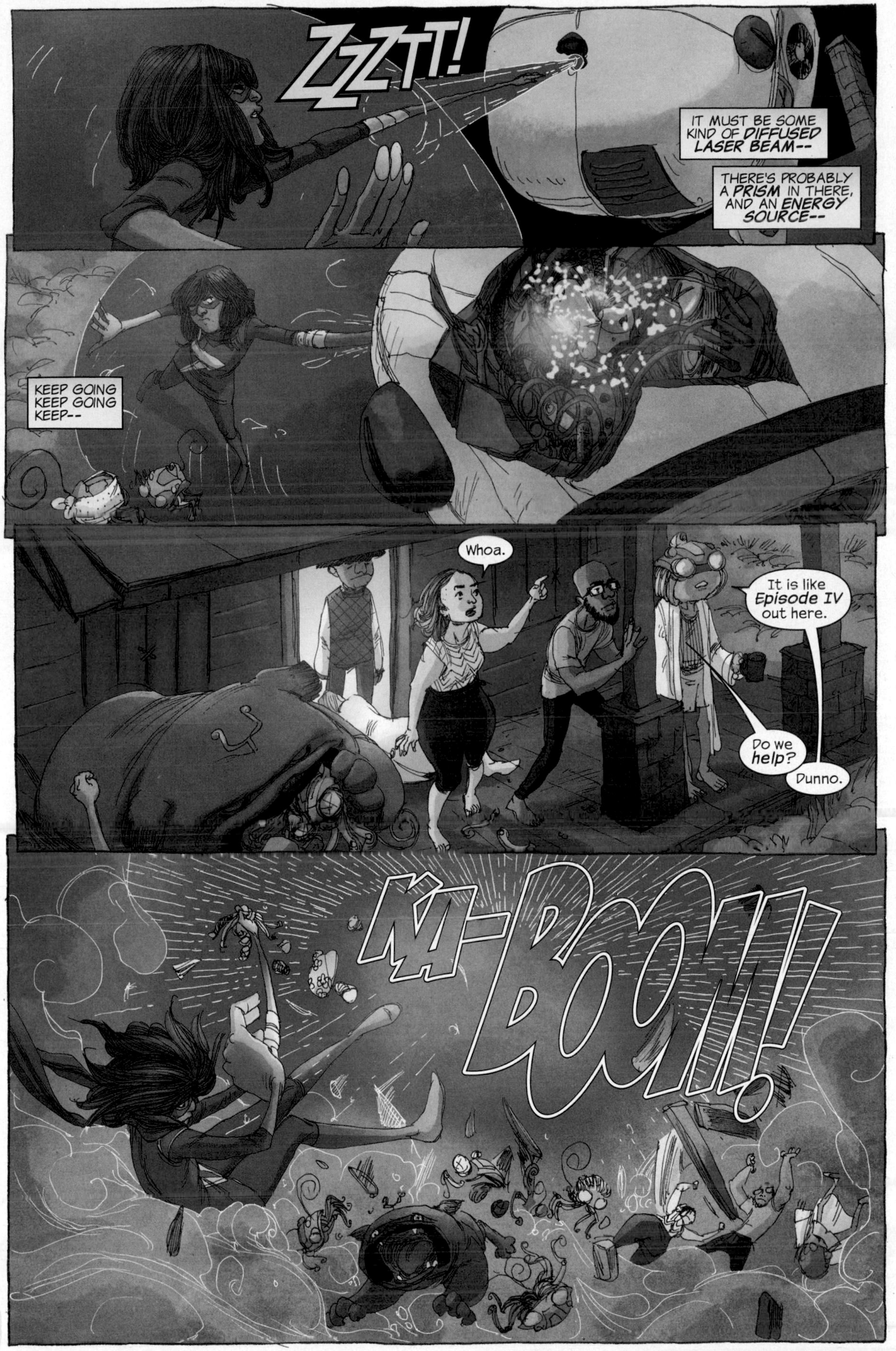
ZZZTT!
IT MUST BE SOME KIND OF DIFFUSED LASER BEAM--
THERE'S PROBABLY A PRISM IN THERE, AND AN ENERGY SOURCE--
KEEP GOING KEEP GOING KEEP--
Whoa.
It is like Episode IV out here.
Do we help?
Dunno.
KA-BOOM!

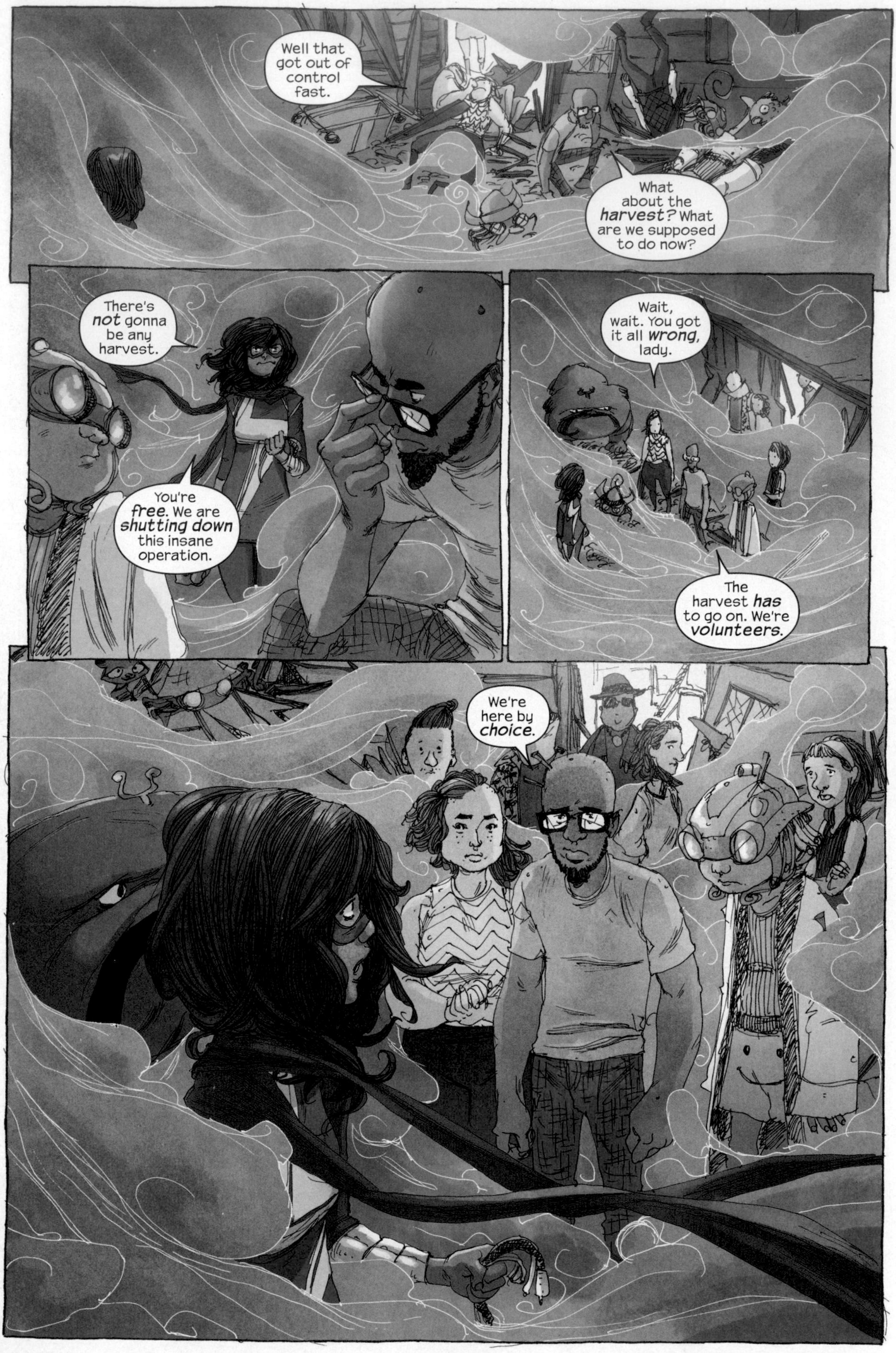
Well that got out of control fast.
What about the harvest? What are we supposed to do now?
There's not gonna be any harvest.
You're free. We are shutting down this insane operation.
Wait, wait. You got it all wrong, lady.
The harvest has to go on. We're volunteers.
We're here by choice.

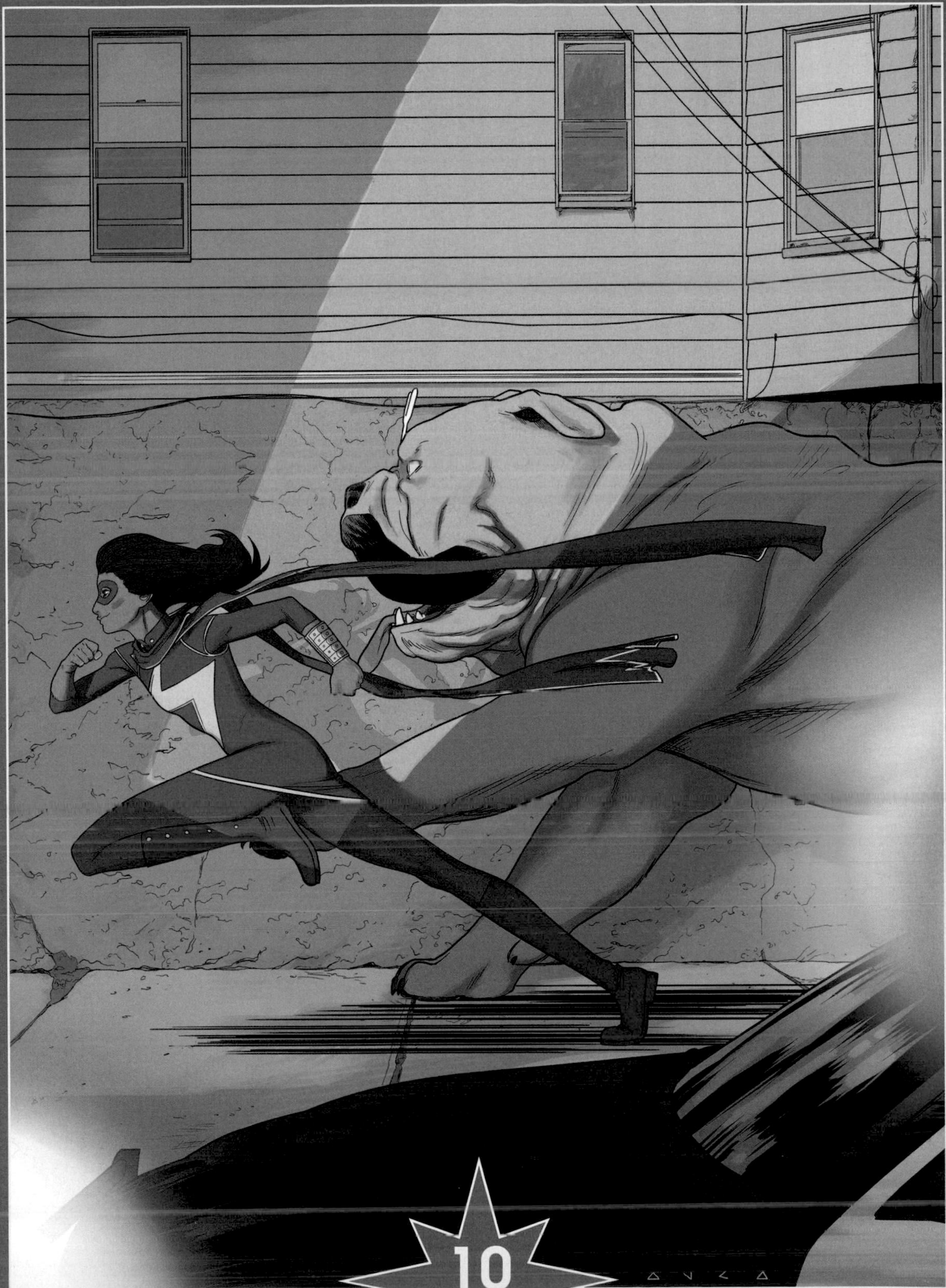
10

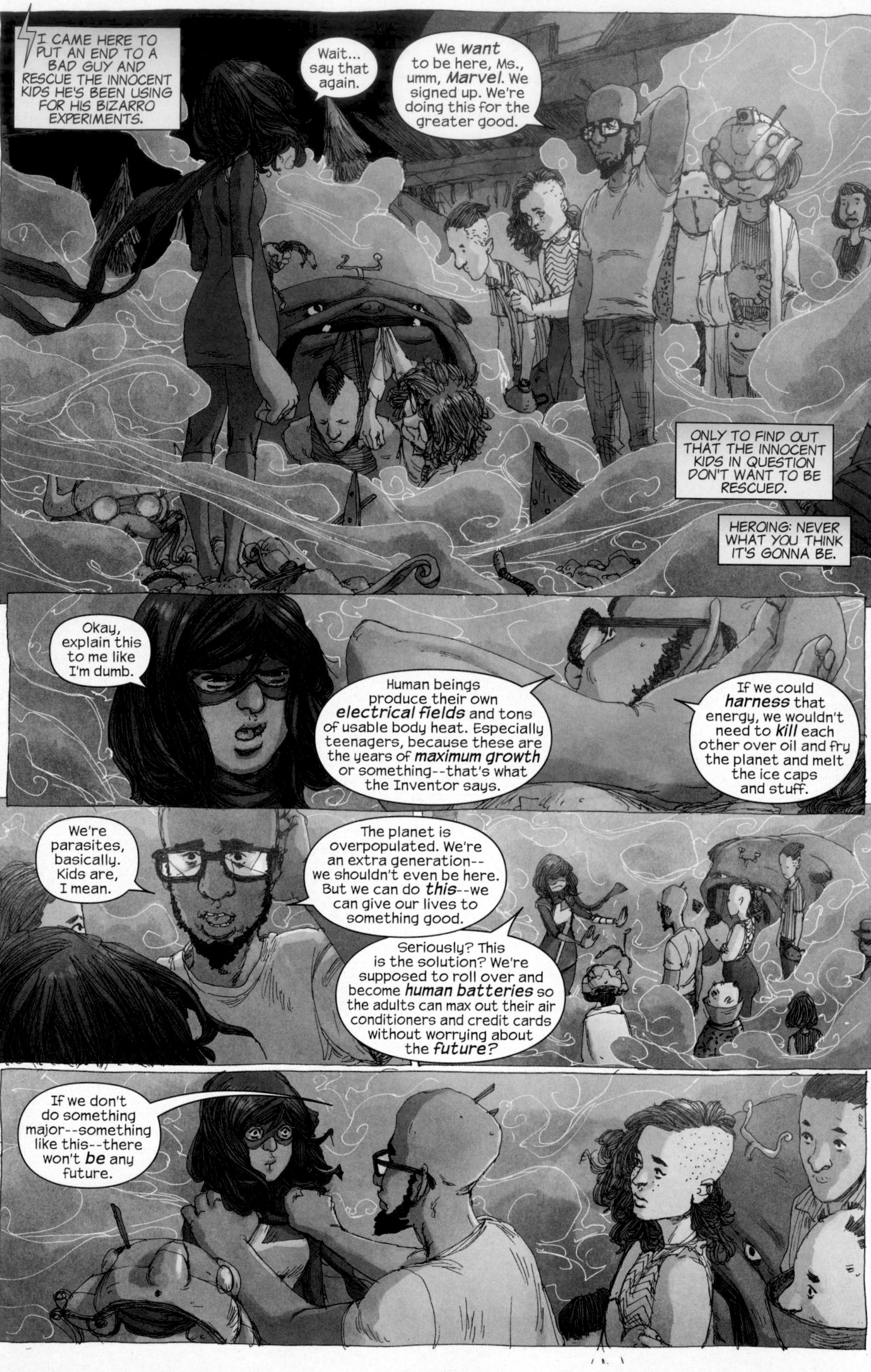
I CAME HERE TO PUT AN END TO A BAD GUY AND RESCUE THE INNOCENT KIDS HE'S BEEN USING FOR HIS BIZARRO EXPERIMENTS.
Wait... say that again.
We *want* to be here, Ms., umm, *Marvel*. We signed up. We're doing this for the greater good.
ONLY TO FIND OUT THAT THE INNOCENT KIDS IN QUESTION DON'T WANT TO BE RESCUED.
HEROING: NEVER WHAT YOU THINK IT'S GONNA BE.
Okay, explain this to me like I'm dumb.
Human beings produce their own *electrical fields* and tons of usable body heat. Especially teenagers, because these are the years of *maximum growth* or something--that's what the Inventor says.
If we could *harness* that energy, we wouldn't need to *kill* each other over oil and fry the planet and melt the ice caps and stuff.
We're parasites, basically. Kids are, I mean.
The planet is overpopulated. We're an extra generation--we shouldn't even be here. But we can do *this*--we can give our lives to something good.
Seriously? This is the solution? We're supposed to roll over and become *human batteries* so the adults can max out their air conditioners and credit cards without worrying about the *future?*
If we don't do something major--something like this--there won't *be* any future.

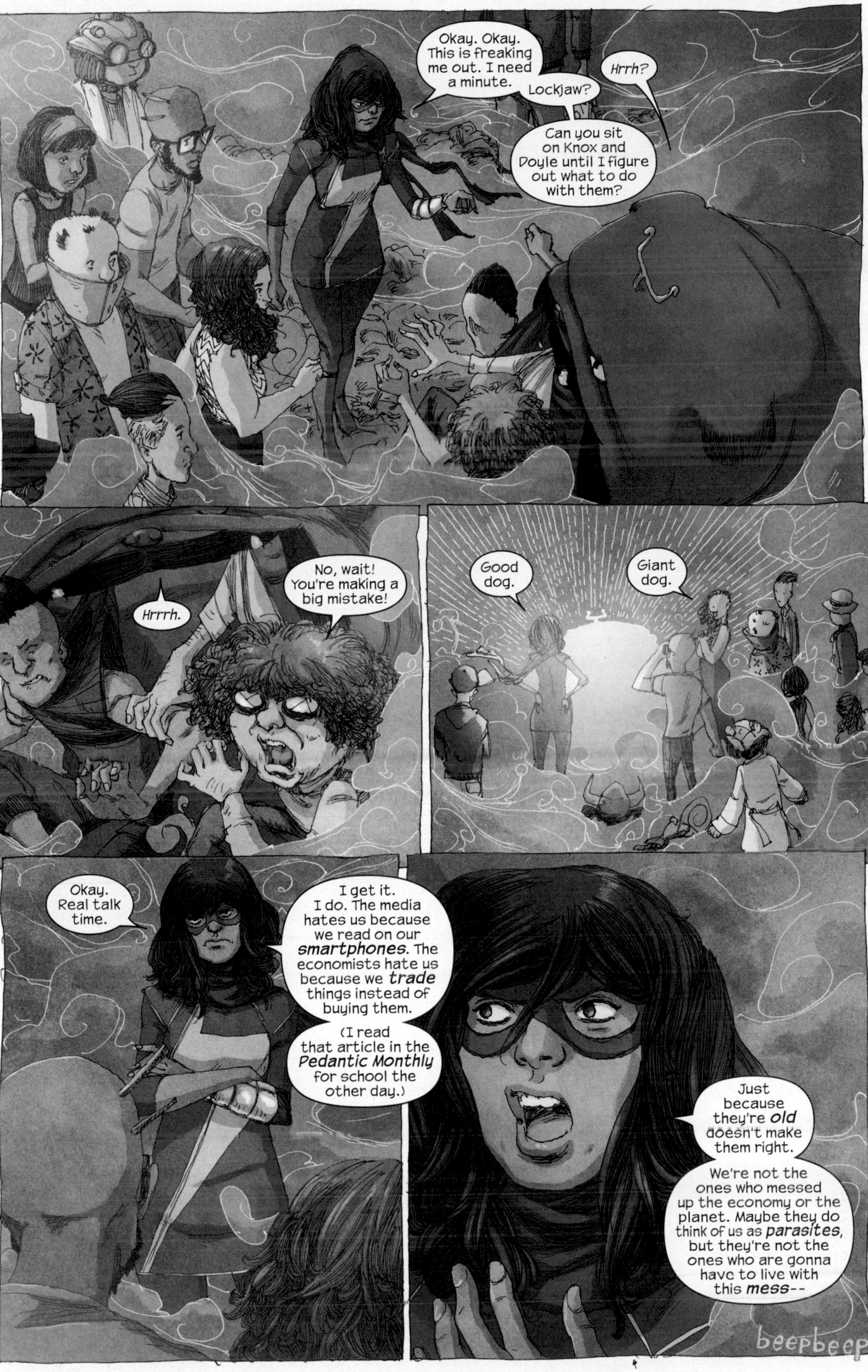

Okay. Okay. This is freaking me out. I need a minute.
Lockjaw?
Hrrh?
Can you sit on Knox and Doyle until I figure out what to do with them?
Hrrrh.
No, wait! You're making a big mistake!
Good dog.
Giant dog.
Okay. Real talk time.
I get it. I do. The media hates us because we read on our smartphones. The economists hate us because we trade things instead of buying them.
(I read that article in the Pedantic Monthly for school the other day.)
Just because they're old doesn't make them right.
We're not the ones who messed up the economy or the planet. Maybe they do think of us as parasites, but they're not the ones who are gonna have to live with this mess--
beepbeep

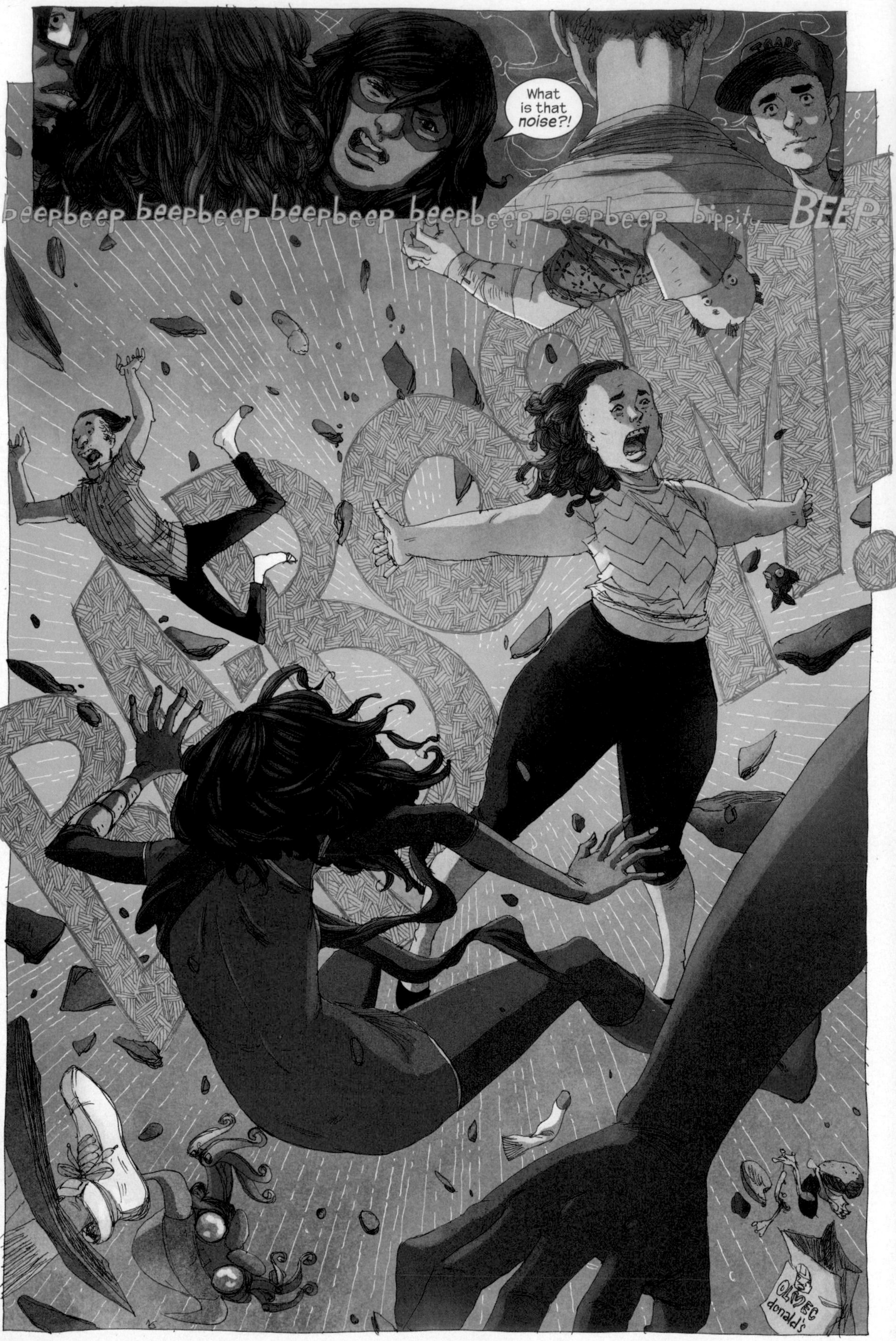

What is that noise?!
beepbeep beepbeep beepbeep beepbeep beepbeep bippity BEEP!

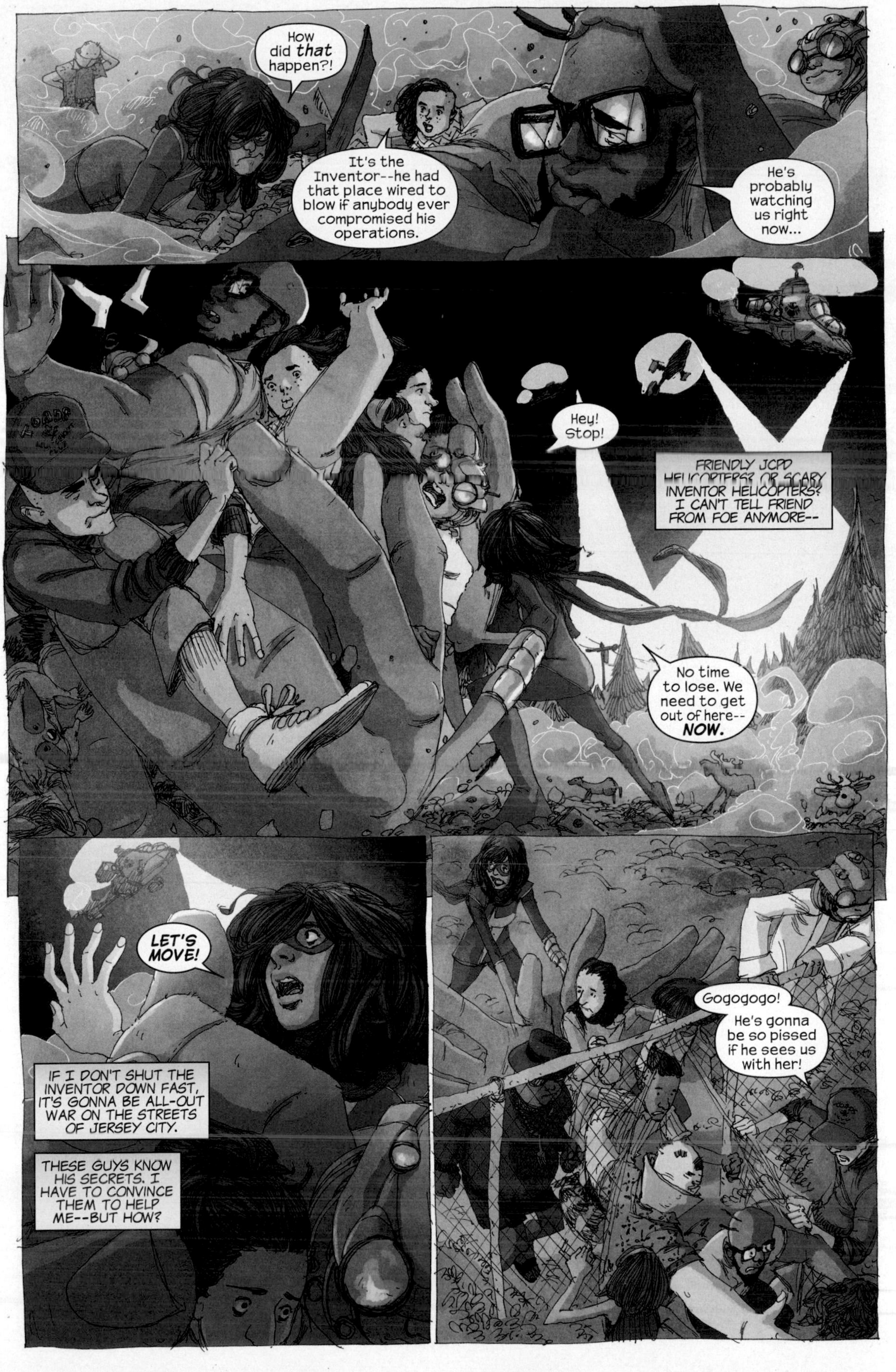
How did *that* happen?!
It's the Inventor--he had that place wired to blow if anybody ever compromised his operations.
He's probably watching us right now...
Hey! Stop!
FRIENDLY JCPD HELICOPTERS? OR SCARY INVENTOR HELICOPTERS? I CAN'T TELL FRIEND FROM FOE ANYMORE--
No time to lose. We need to get out of here-- **NOW.**
LET'S MOVE!
IF I DON'T SHUT THE INVENTOR DOWN FAST, IT'S GONNA BE ALL-OUT WAR ON THE STREETS OF JERSEY CITY.
THESE GUYS KNOW HIS SECRETS. I HAVE TO CONVINCE THEM TO HELP ME--BUT HOW?
Gogogogo!
He's gonna be so pissed if he sees us with her!

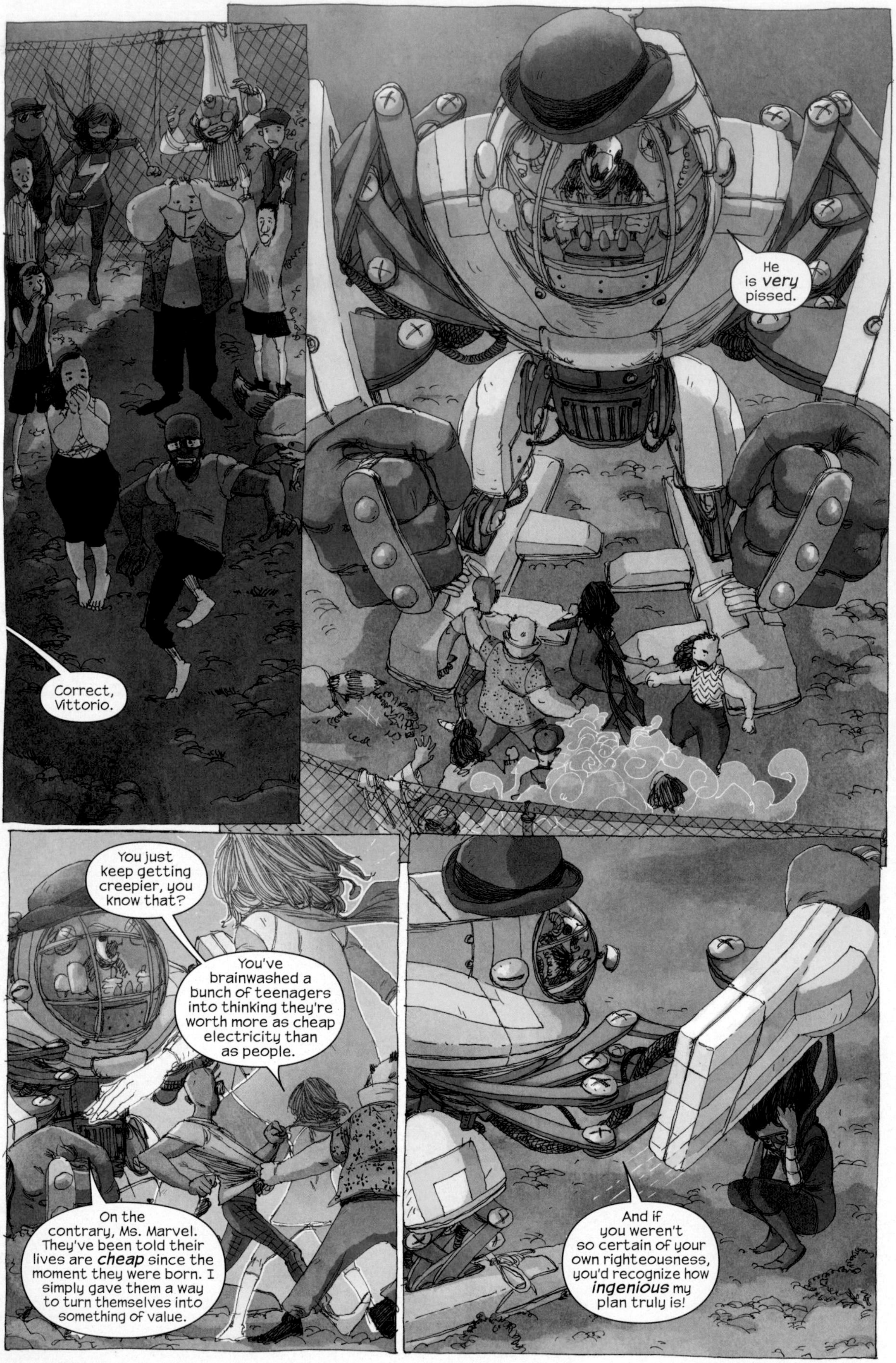
He is *very* pissed.
Correct, Vittorio.
You just keep getting creepier, you know that?
You've brainwashed a bunch of teenagers into thinking they're worth more as cheap electricity than as people.
On the contrary, Ms. Marvel. They've been told their lives are *cheap* since the moment they were born. I simply gave them a way to turn themselves into something of value.
And if you weren't so certain of your own righteousness, you'd recognize how *ingenious* my plan truly is!

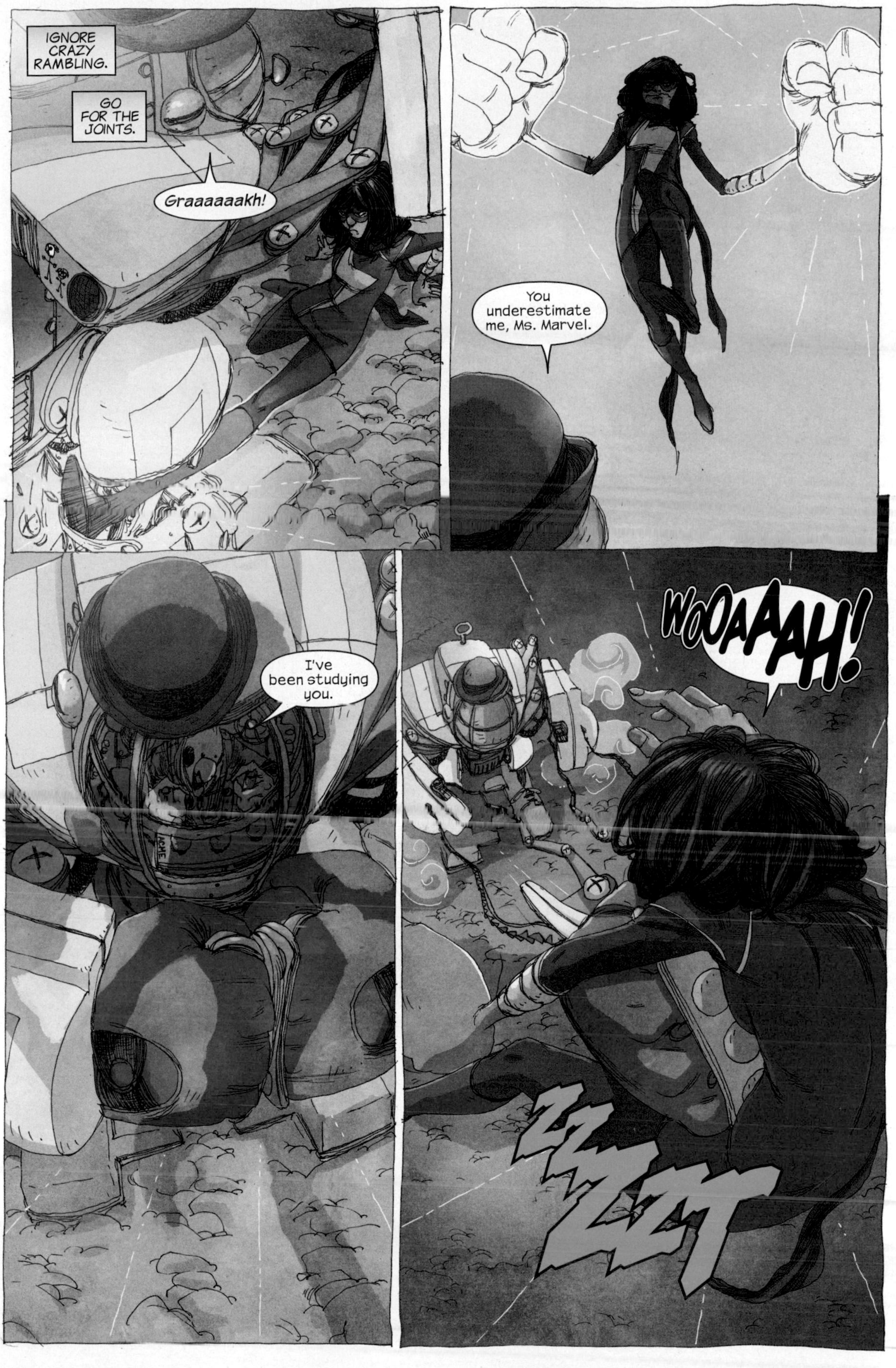
IGNORE CRAZY RAMBLING.
GO FOR THE JOINTS.
Graaaaaakh!
You underestimate me, Ms. Marvel.
I've been studying you.
WOOAAAAH!
ZZZZT

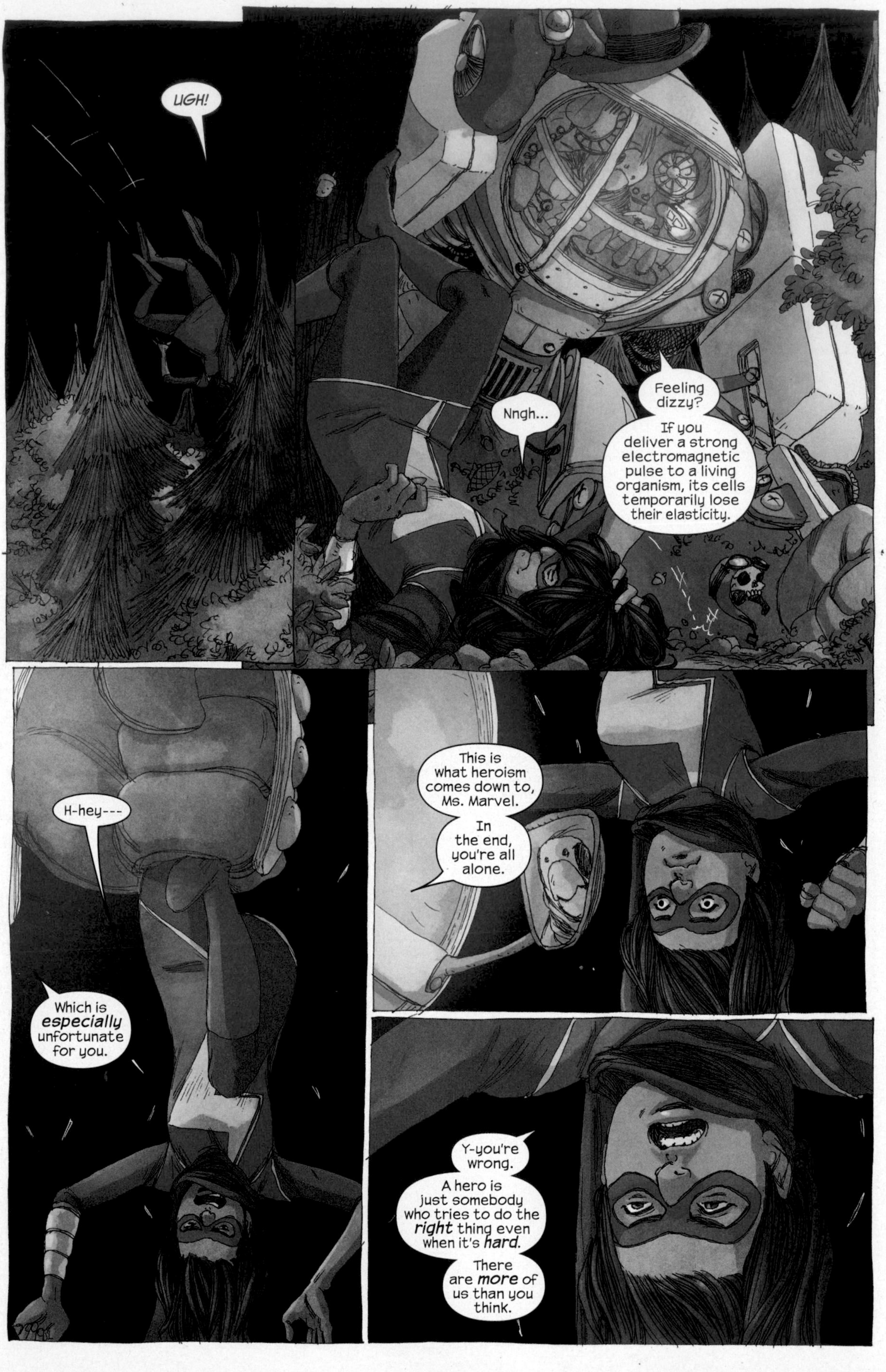
UGH!
Nngh...
Feeling dizzy?
If you deliver a strong electromagnetic pulse to a living organism, its cells temporarily lose their elasticity.
H-hey---
Which is *especially* unfortunate for you.
This is what heroism comes down to, Ms. Marvel.
In the end, you're all alone.
Y-you're wrong.
A hero is just somebody who tries to do the *right* thing even when it's *hard*.
There are *more* of us than you think.

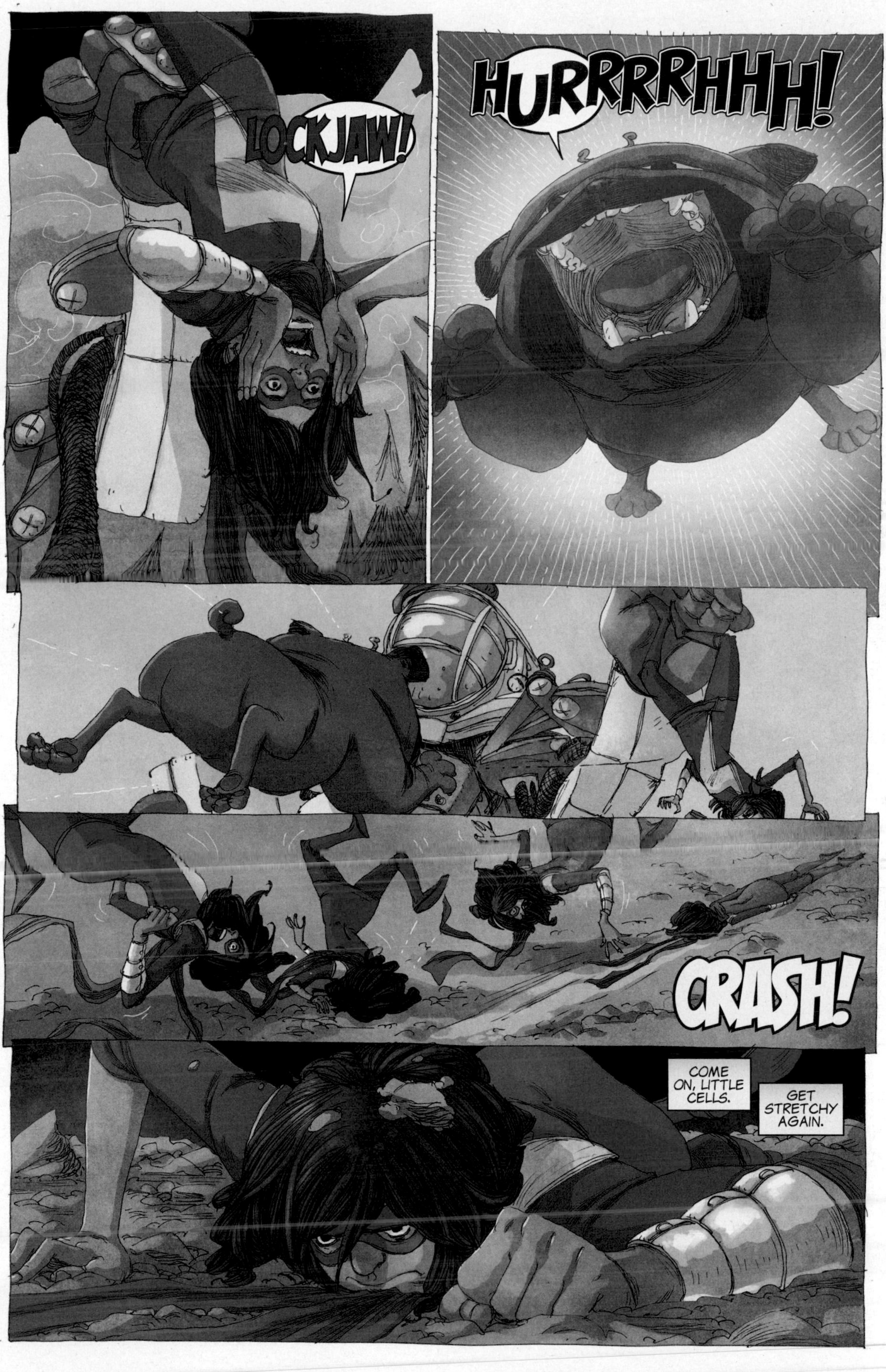
LOCKJAW!
HURRRRRHHH!
CRASH!
COME ON, LITTLE CELLS.
GET STRETCHY AGAIN.

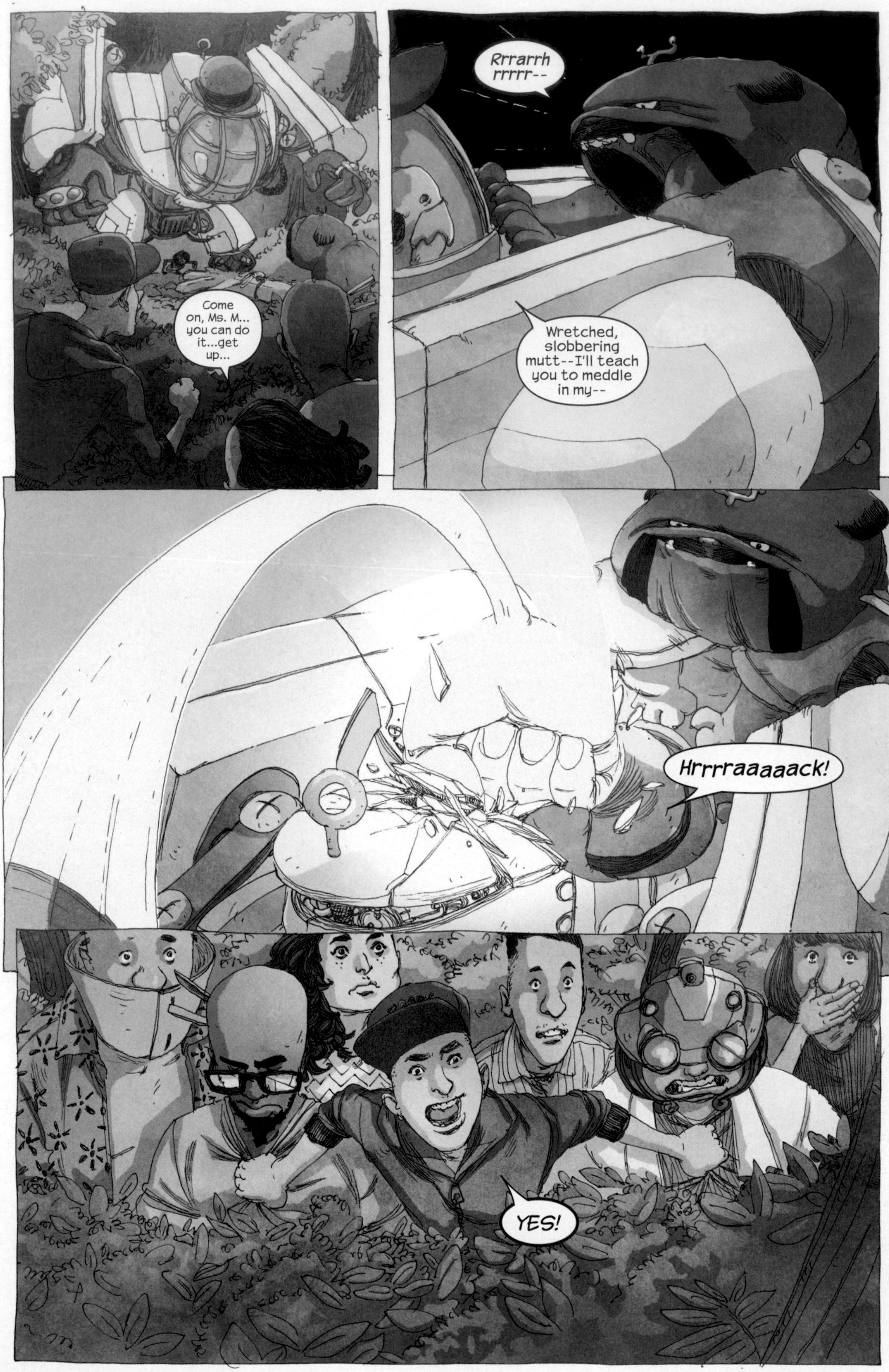
Come on, Ms. M... you can do it...get up...
Rrrarrh rrrrr--
Wretched, slobbering mutt--I'll teach you to meddle in my--
Hrrrraaaaack!
YES!

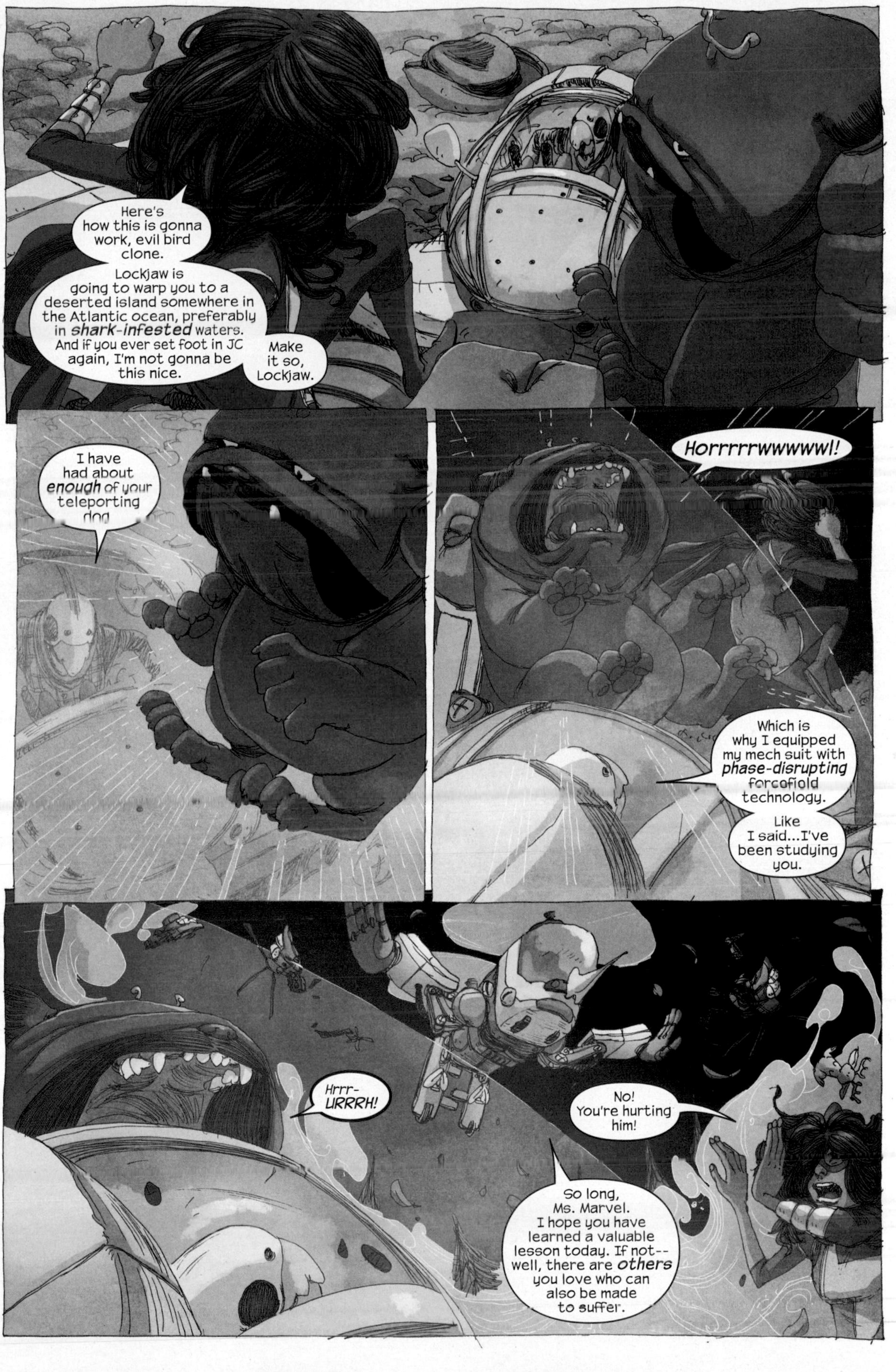
Here's how this is gonna work, evil bird clone.
Lockjaw is going to warp you to a deserted island somewhere in the Atlantic ocean, preferably in *shark-infested* waters. And if you ever set foot in JC again, I'm not gonna be this nice.
Make it so, Lockjaw.
I have had about *enough* of your teleporting dog
Horrrrrwwwwwl!
Which is why I equipped my mech suit with *phase-disrupting* forcefield technology.
Like I said...I've been studying you.
Hrrr-URRRH!
No! You're hurting him!
So long, Ms. Marvel. I hope you have learned a valuable lesson today. If not-- well, there are *others* you love who can also be made to suffer.

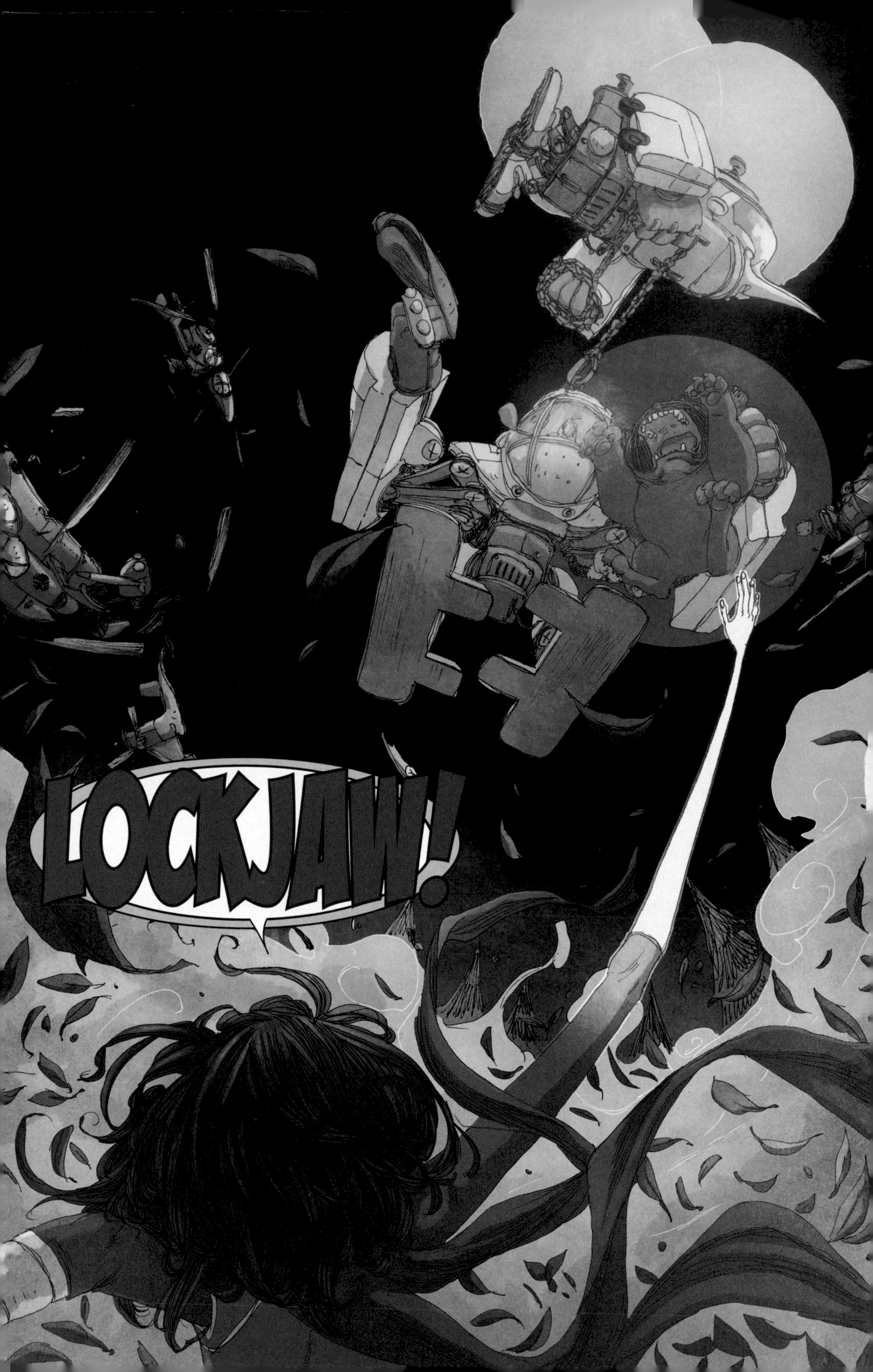
LOCKJAW!

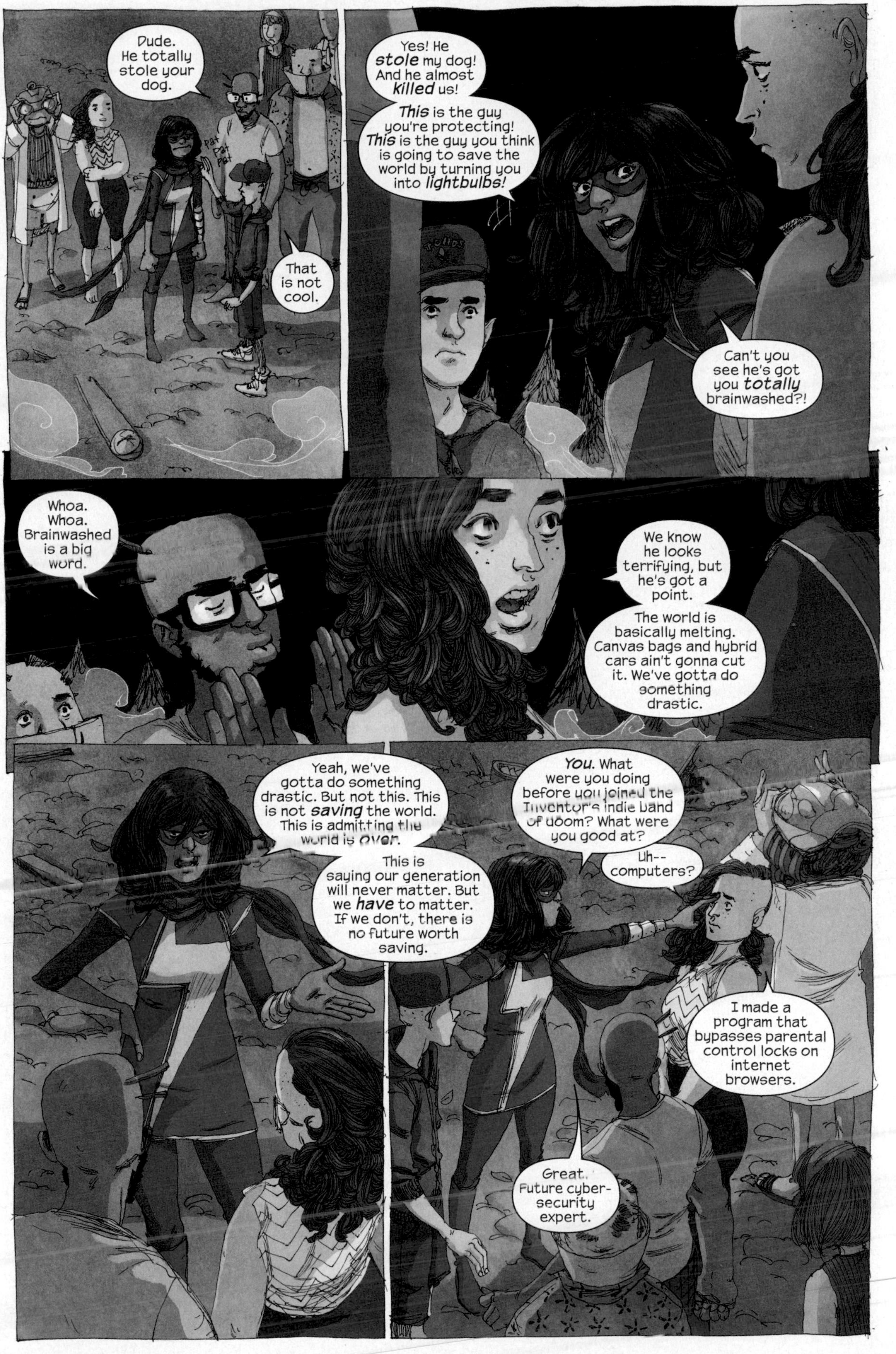
Dude. He totally stole your dog.
Pat Pat Pat
That is not cool.
Yes! He stole my dog! And he almost killed us!
This is the guy you're protecting! This is the guy you think is going to save the world by turning you into lightbulbs!
Can't you see he's got you totally brainwashed?!
Whoa. Whoa. Brainwashed is a big word.
We know he looks terrifying, but he's got a point.
The world is basically melting. Canvas bags and hybrid cars ain't gonna cut it. We've gotta do something drastic.
Yeah, we've gotta do something drastic. But not this. This is not saving the world. This is admitting the world is over.
This is saying our generation will never matter. But we have to matter. If we don't, there is no future worth saving.
You. What were you doing before you joined the Inventor's indie band of doom? What were you good at?
Uh-- computers?
I made a program that bypasses parental control locks on internet browsers.
Great. Future cyber-security expert.

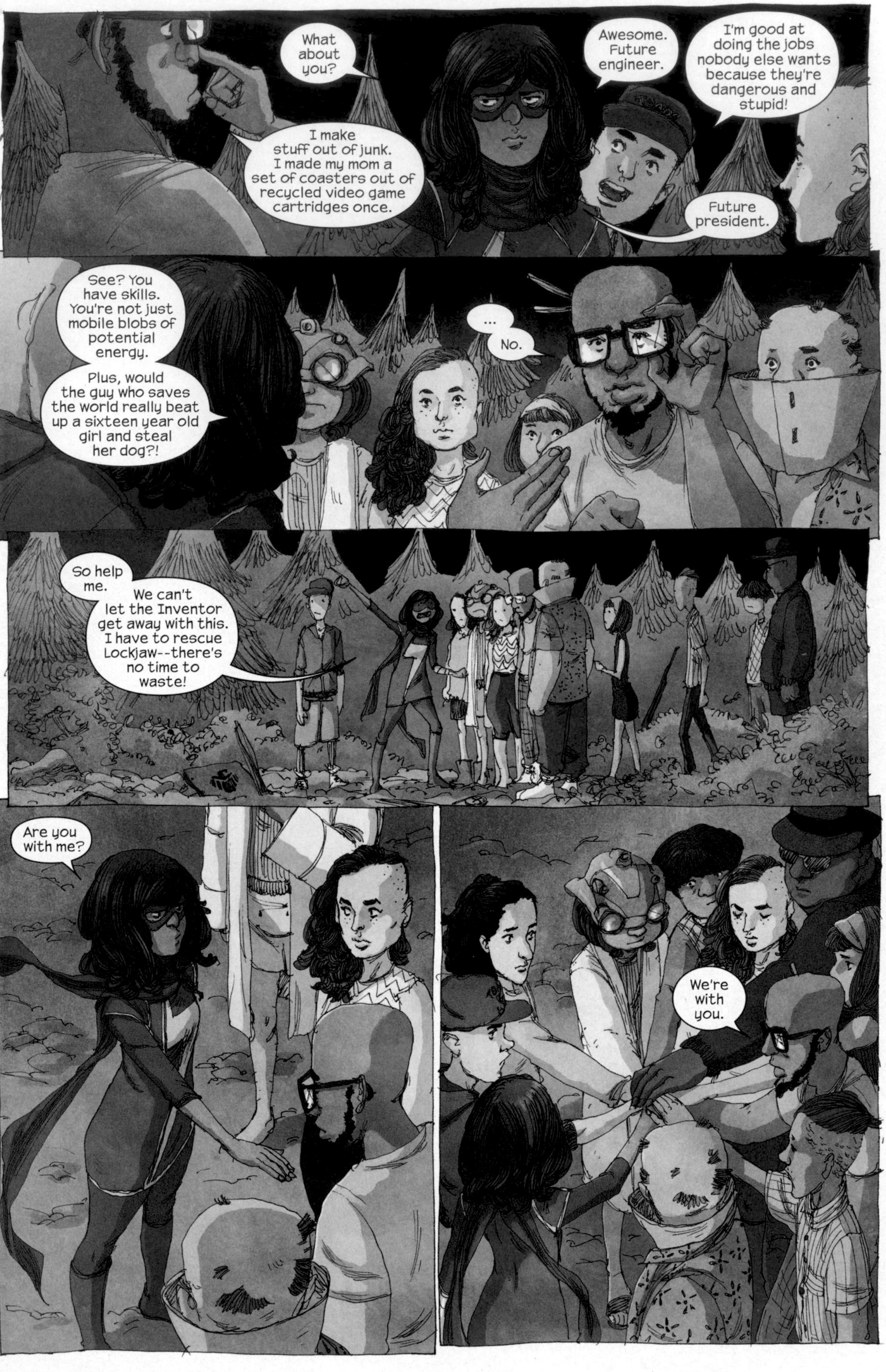

What about you?
I make stuff out of junk. I made my mom a set of coasters out of recycled video game cartridges once.
Awesome. Future engineer.
I'm good at doing the jobs nobody else wants because they're dangerous and stupid!
Future president.
See? You have skills. You're not just mobile blobs of potential energy.
Plus, would the guy who saves the world really beat up a sixteen year old girl and steal her dog?!
...
No.
So help me.
We can't let the Inventor get away with this. I have to rescue Lockjaw--there's no time to waste!
Are you with me?
We're with you.

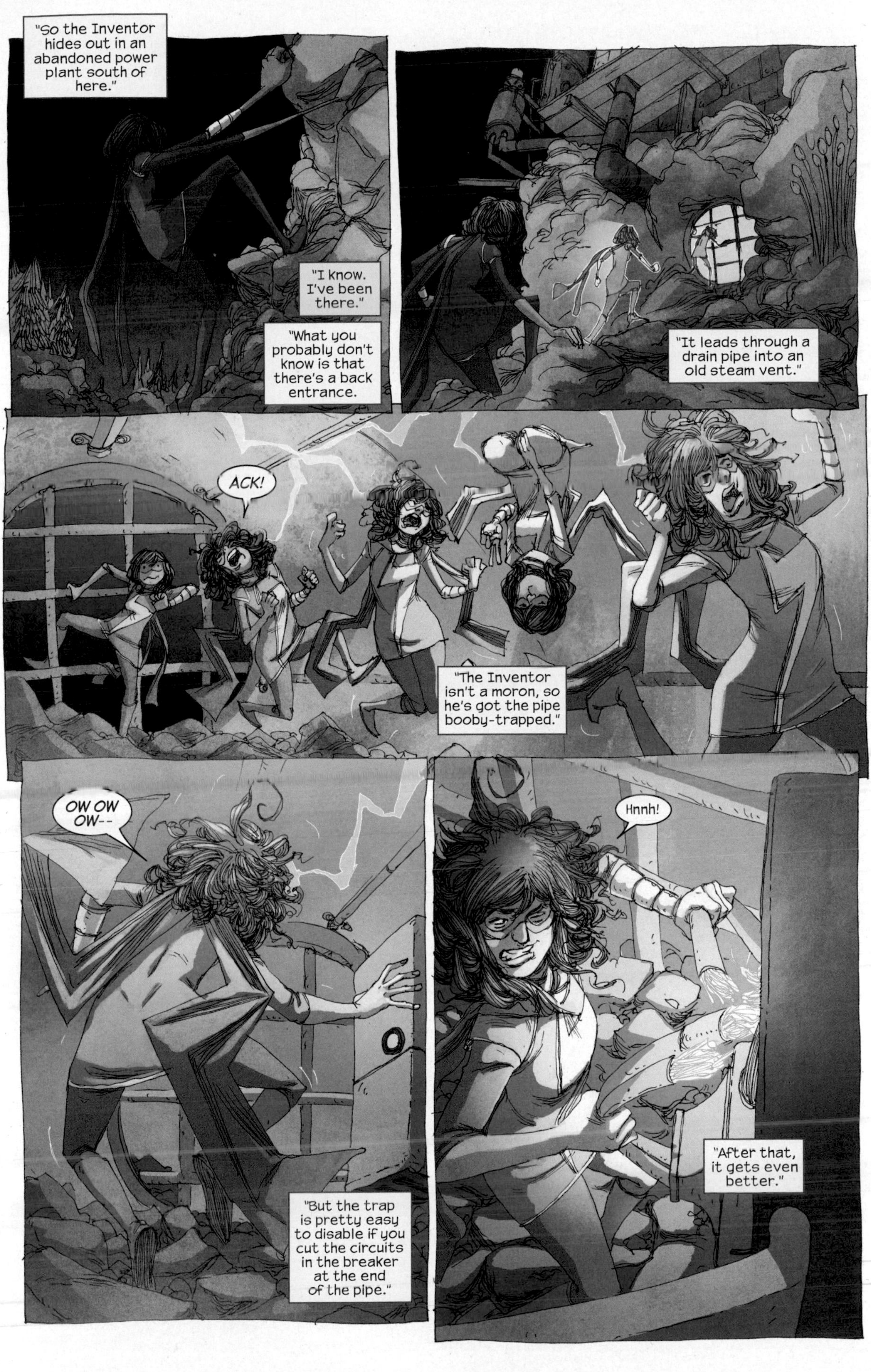
"So the Inventor hides out in an abandoned power plant south of here."
"I know. I've been there."
"What you probably don't know is that there's a back entrance.
"It leads through a drain pipe into an old steam vent."
ACK!
"The Inventor isn't a moron, so he's got the pipe booby-trapped."
OW OW OW--
"But the trap is pretty easy to disable if you cut the circuits in the breaker at the end of the pipe."
Hnnh!
"After that, it gets even better."

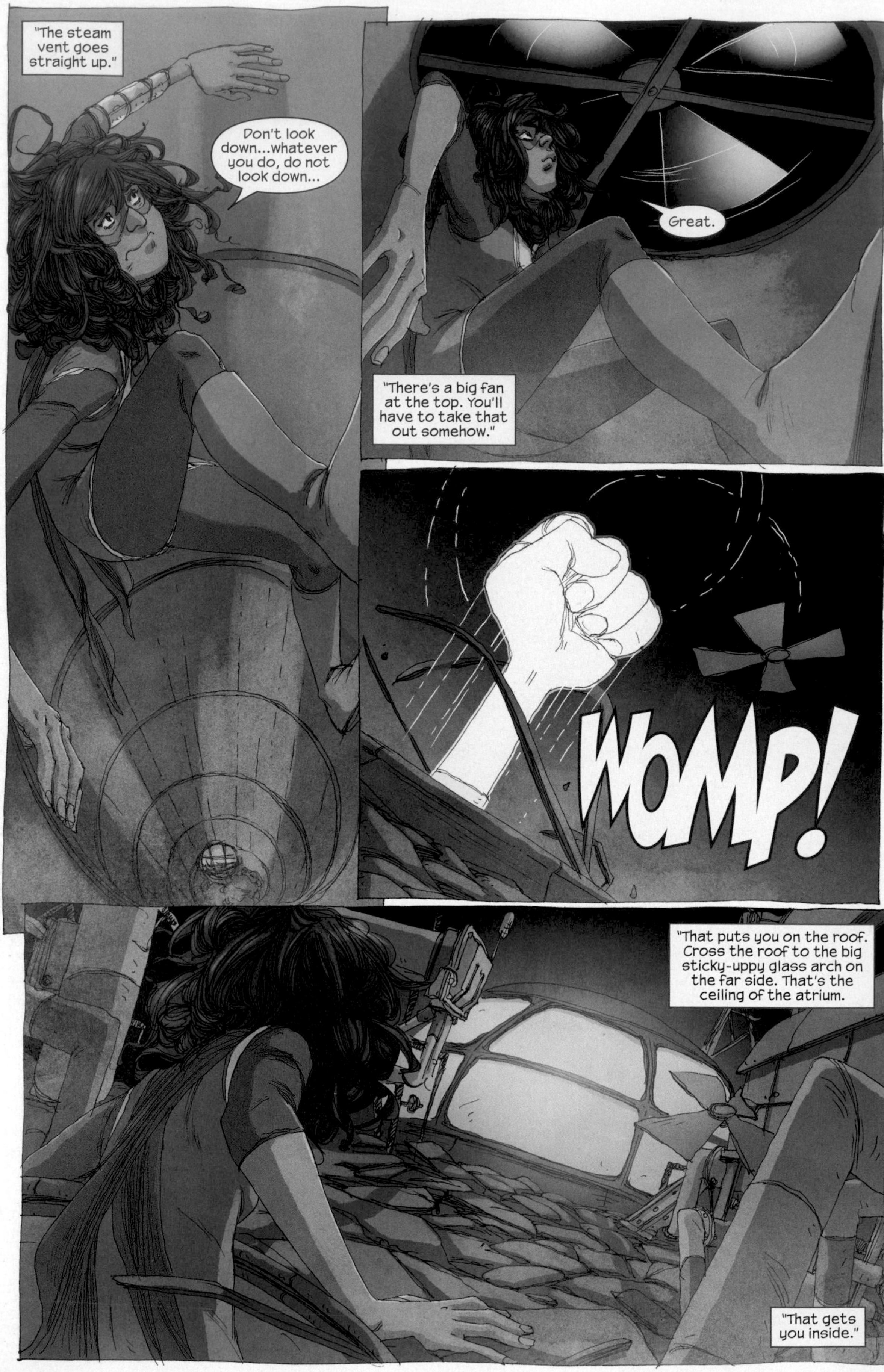
"The steam vent goes straight up."
Don't look down...whatever you do, do not look down...
Great.
"There's a big fan at the top. You'll have to take that out somehow."
WOMP!
"That puts you on the roof. Cross the roof to the big sticky-uppy glass arch on the far side. That's the ceiling of the atrium.
"That gets you inside."

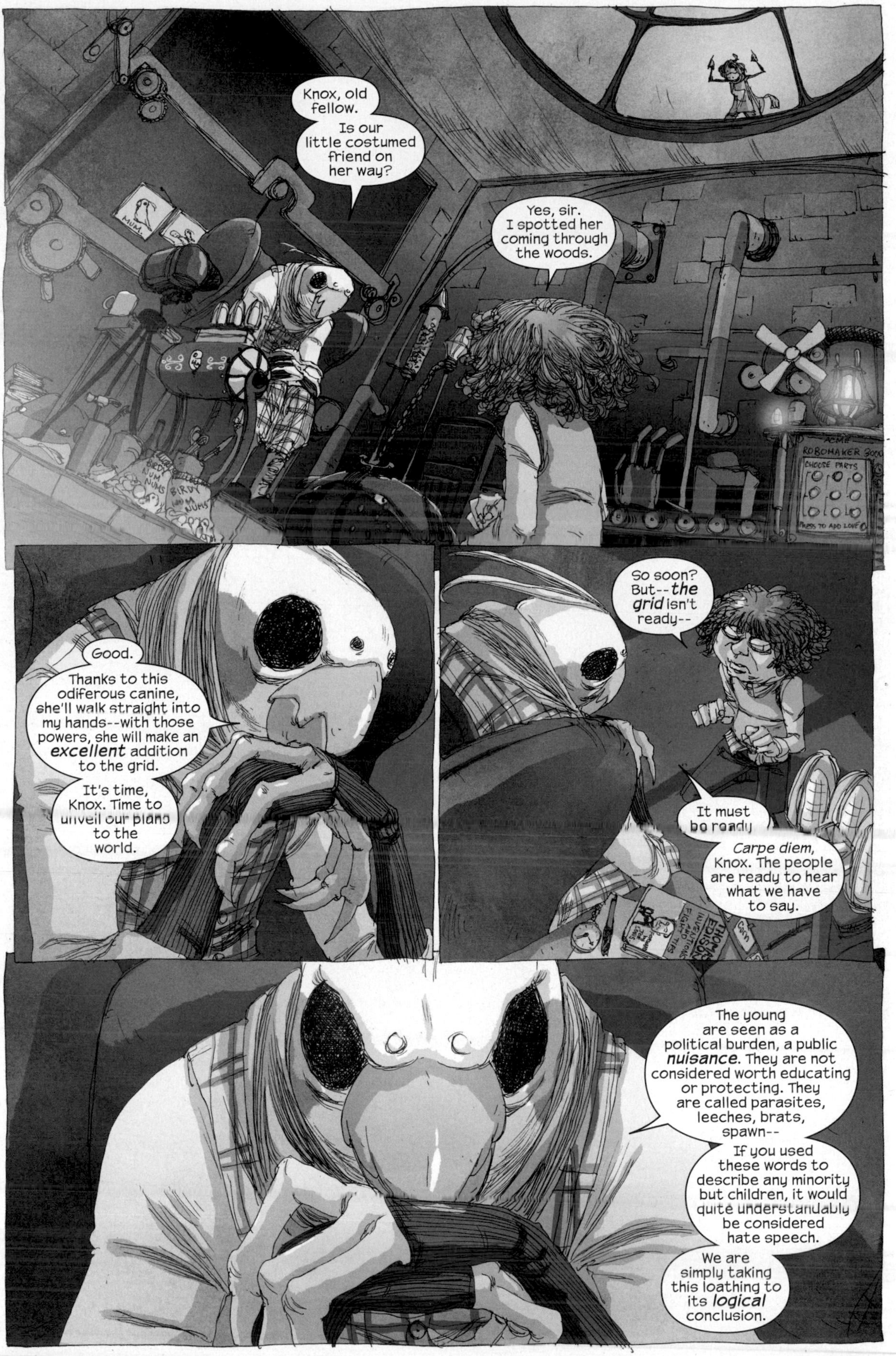

Knox, old fellow.
Is our little costumed friend on her way?
Yes, sir. I spotted her coming through the woods.
MUM.
BIRDY NUM NUMS
ROBOMAKER
CHOOSE PARTS
Good.
Thanks to this odiferous canine, she'll walk straight into my hands--with those powers, she will make an ***excellent*** addition to the grid.
It's time, Knox. Time to unveil our plans to the world.
So soon? But--***the grid*** isn't ready--
It must be ready
Carpe diem, Knox. The people are ready to hear what we have to say.
The young are seen as a political burden, a public ***nuisance***. They are not considered worth educating or protecting. They are called parasites, leeches, brats, spawn--
If you used these words to describe any minority but children, it would quite understandably be considered hate speech.
We are simply taking this loathing to its ***logical*** conclusion.

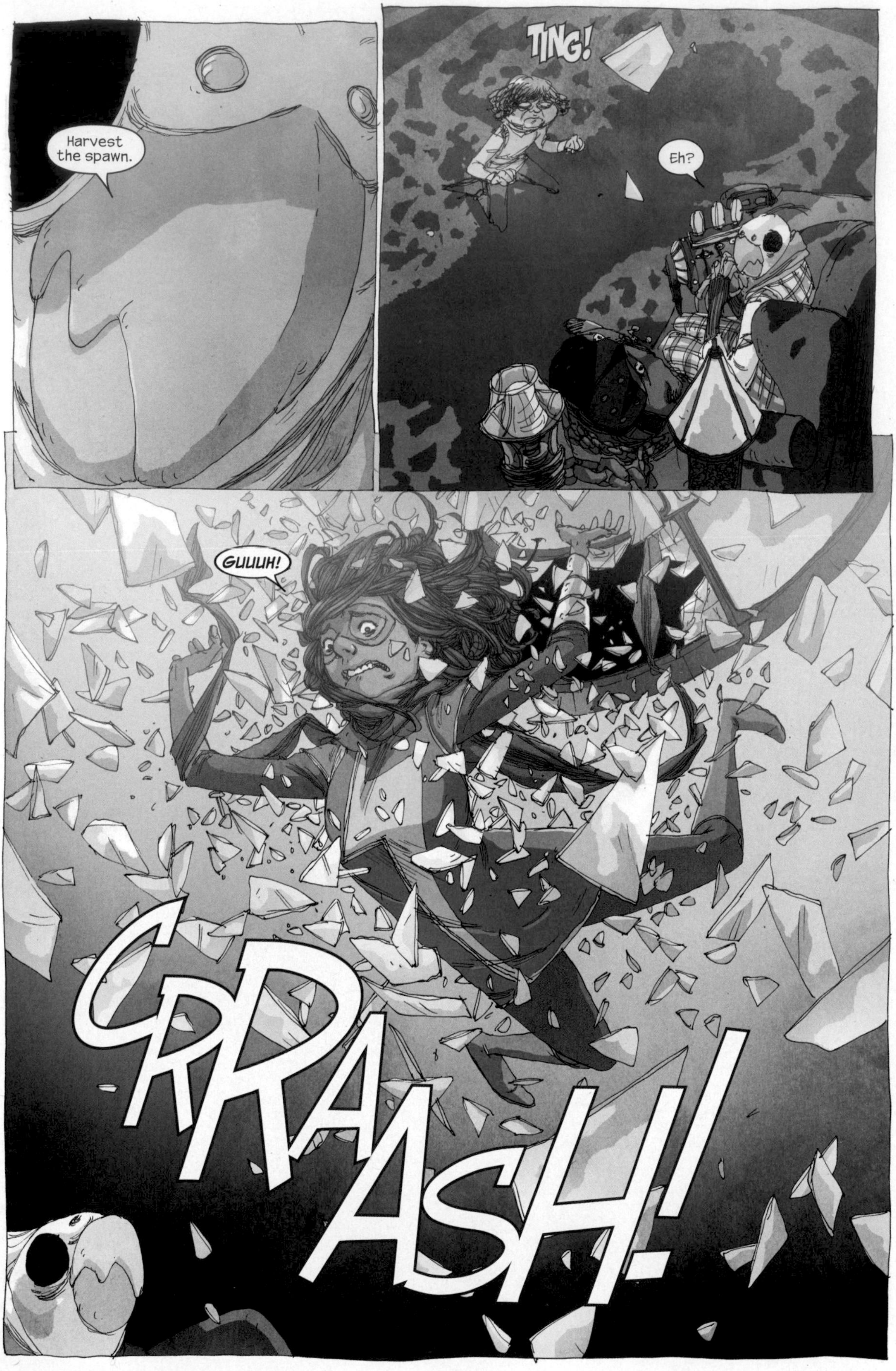
Harvest the spawn.
TING!
Eh?
GUUUH!
CRRAASH!

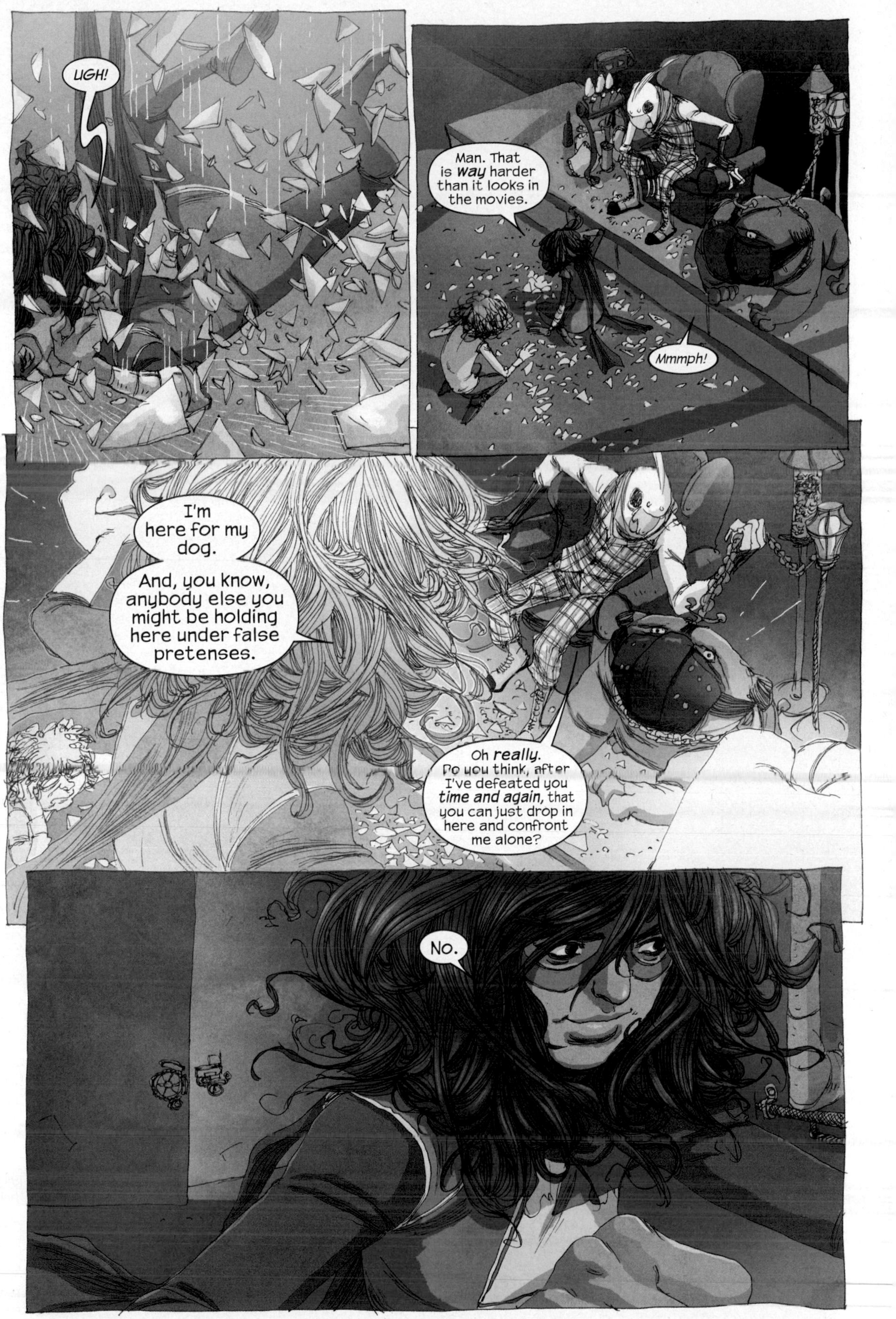
UGH!
Man. That is way harder than it looks in the movies.
Mmmph!
I'm here for my dog.
And, you know, anybody else you might be holding here under false pretenses.
Oh really. Do you think, after I've defeated you time and again, that you can just drop in here and confront me alone?
No.

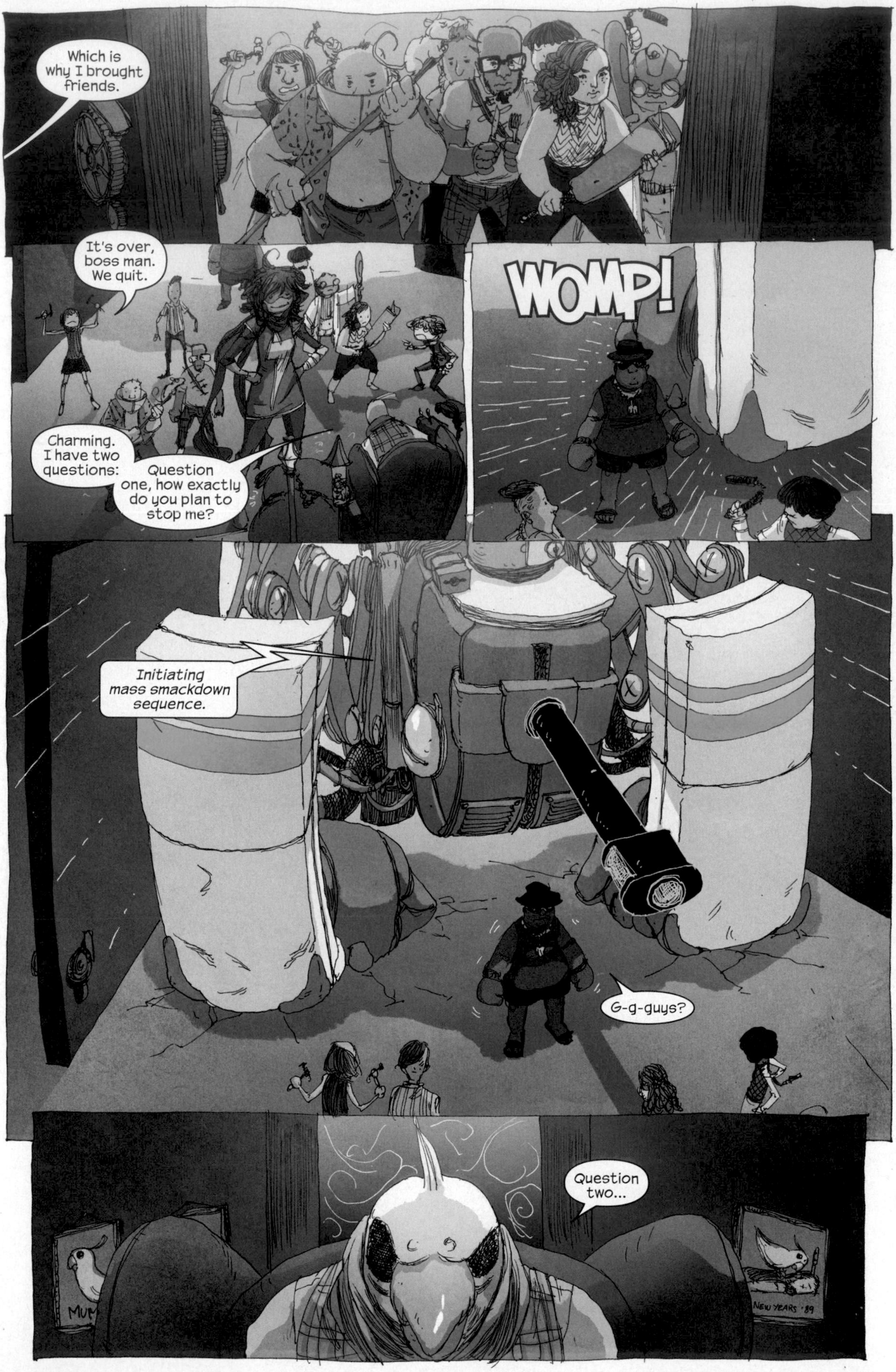

Which is why I brought friends.
It's over, boss man. We quit.
WOMP!
Charming. I have two questions:
Question one, how exactly do you plan to stop me?
Initiating mass smackdown sequence.
G-g-guys?
Question two...
MUM
NEW YEARS '89

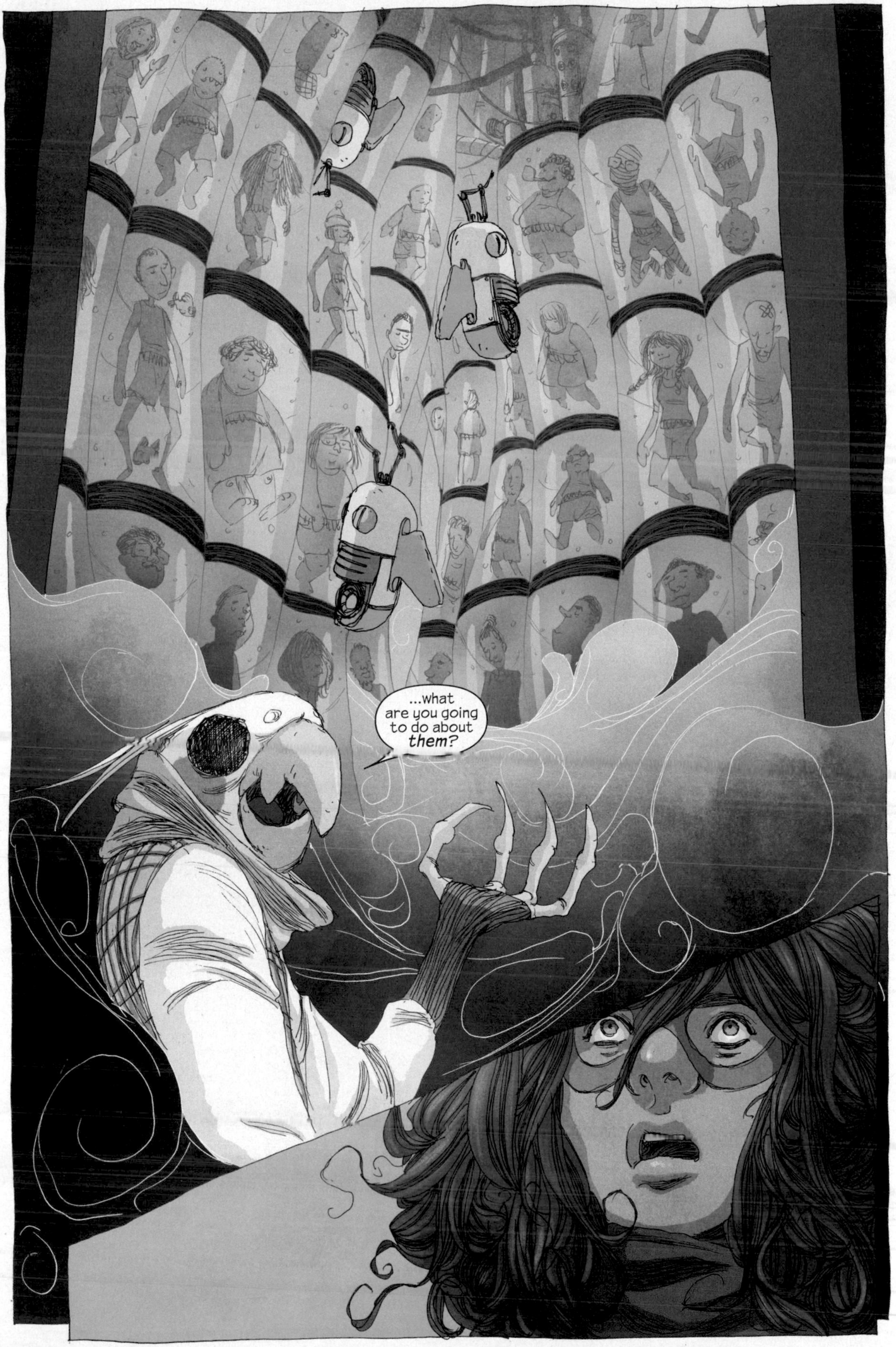
...what are you going to do about *them*?

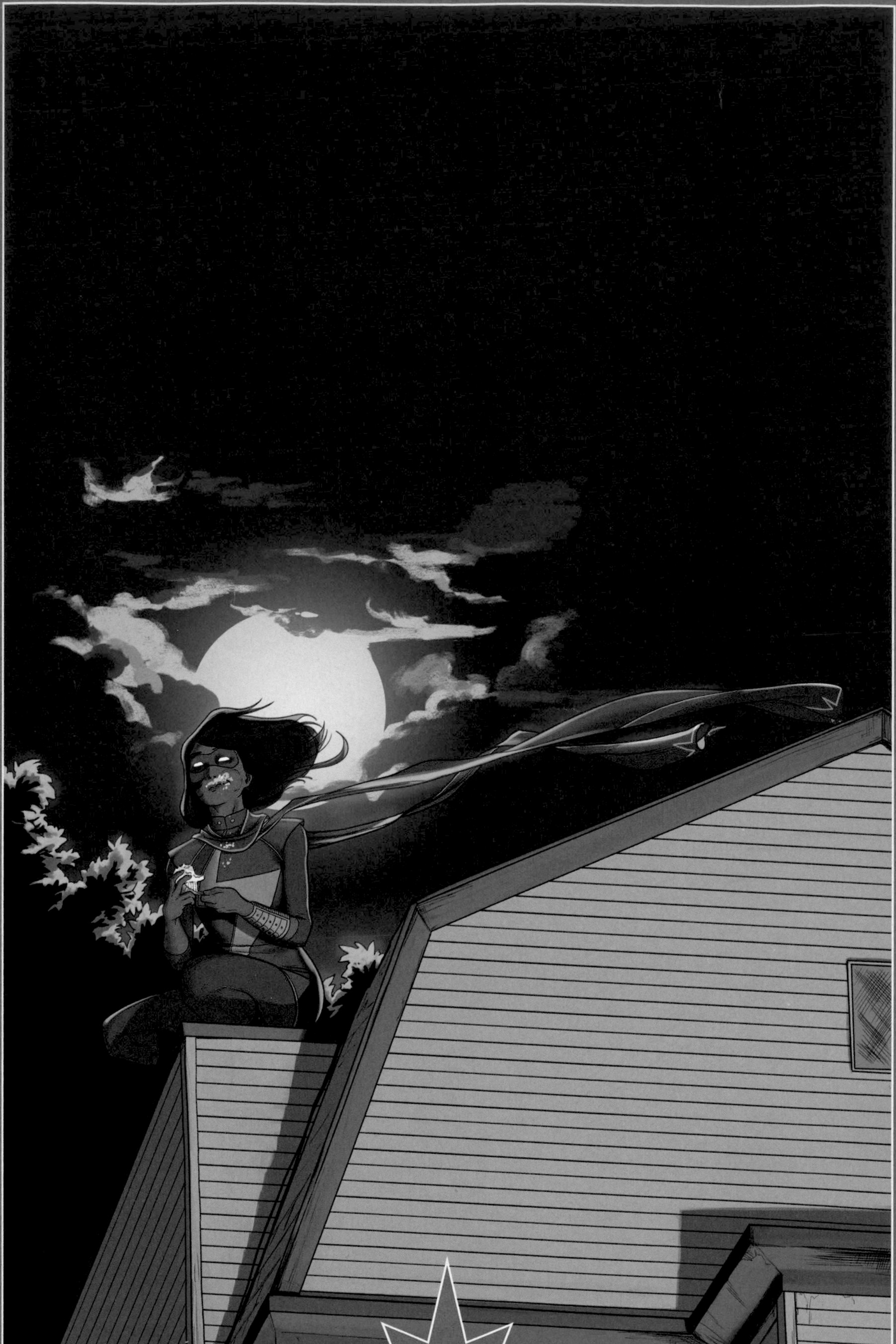
11

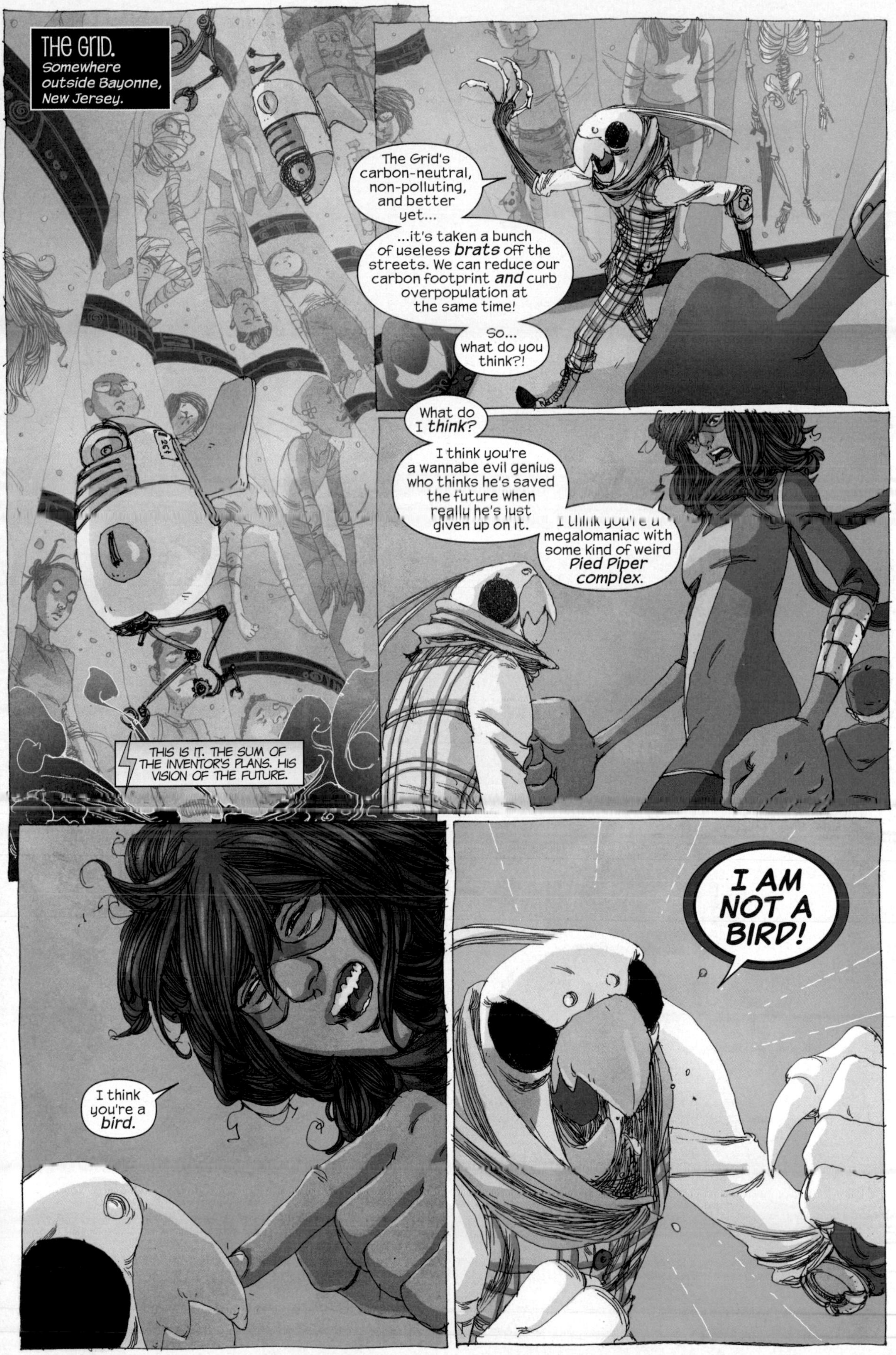
THE GRID.
Somewhere outside Bayonne, New Jersey.
The Grid's carbon-neutral, non-polluting, and better yet...
...it's taken a bunch of useless brats off the streets. We can reduce our carbon footprint and curb overpopulation at the same time!
So... what do you think?!
THIS IS IT. THE SUM OF THE INVENTOR'S PLANS. HIS VISION OF THE FUTURE.
What do I think?
I think you're a wannabe evil genius who thinks he's saved the future when really he's just given up on it.
I think you're a megalomaniac with some kind of weird Pied Piper complex.
I think you're a bird.
I AM NOT A BIRD!

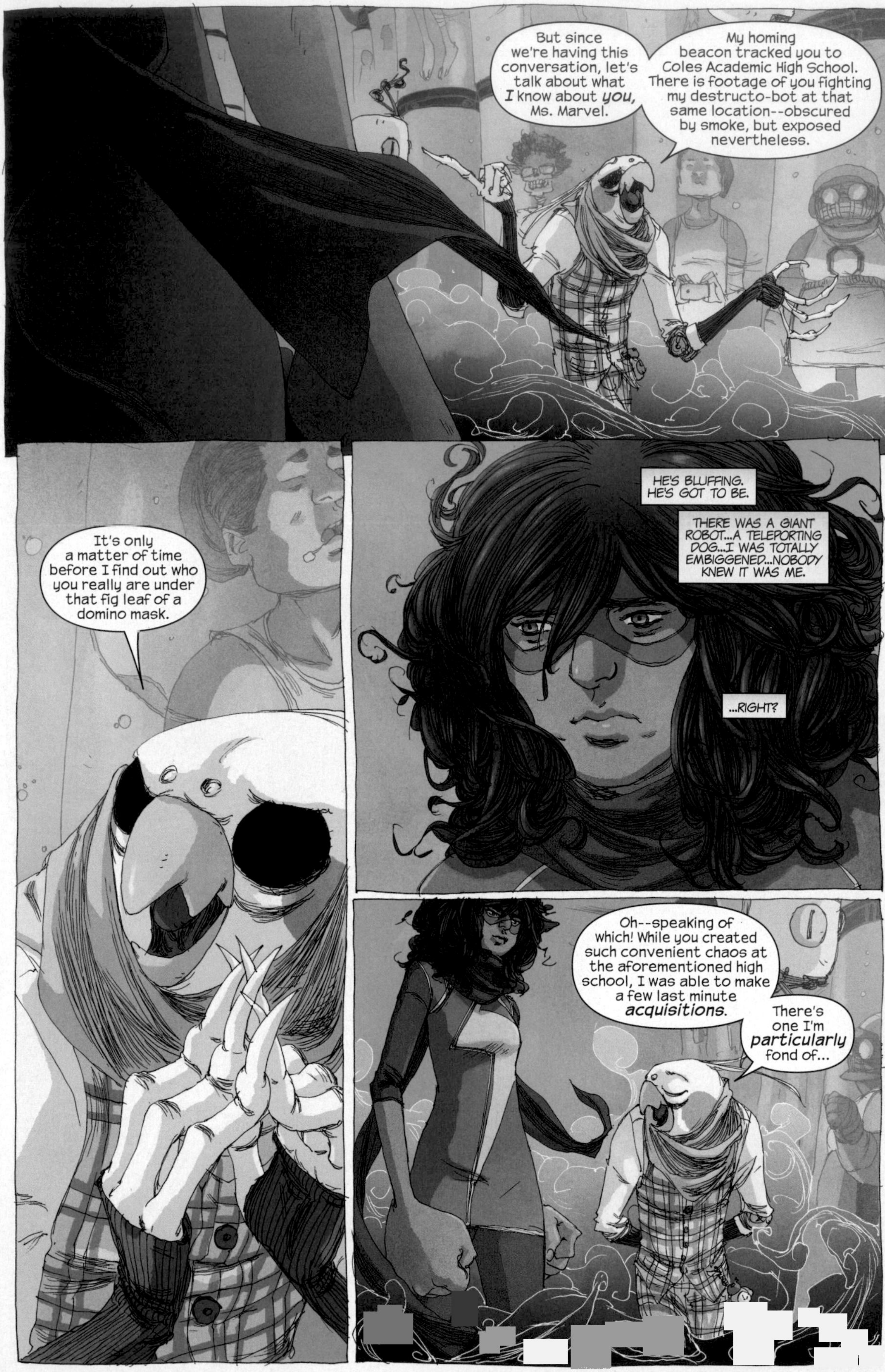
But since we're having this conversation, let's talk about what I know about *you,* Ms. Marvel.
My homing beacon tracked you to Coles Academic High School. There is footage of you fighting my destructo-bot at that same location--obscured by smoke, but exposed nevertheless.
It's only a matter of time before I find out who you really are under that fig leaf of a domino mask.
HE'S BLUFFING. HE'S GOT TO BE.
THERE WAS A GIANT ROBOT...A TELEPORTING DOG...I WAS TOTALLY EMBIGGENED...NOBODY KNEW IT WAS ME.
...RIGHT?
Oh--speaking of which! While you created such convenient chaos at the aforementioned high school, I was able to make a few last minute **acquisitions**.
There's one I'm *particularly* fond of...

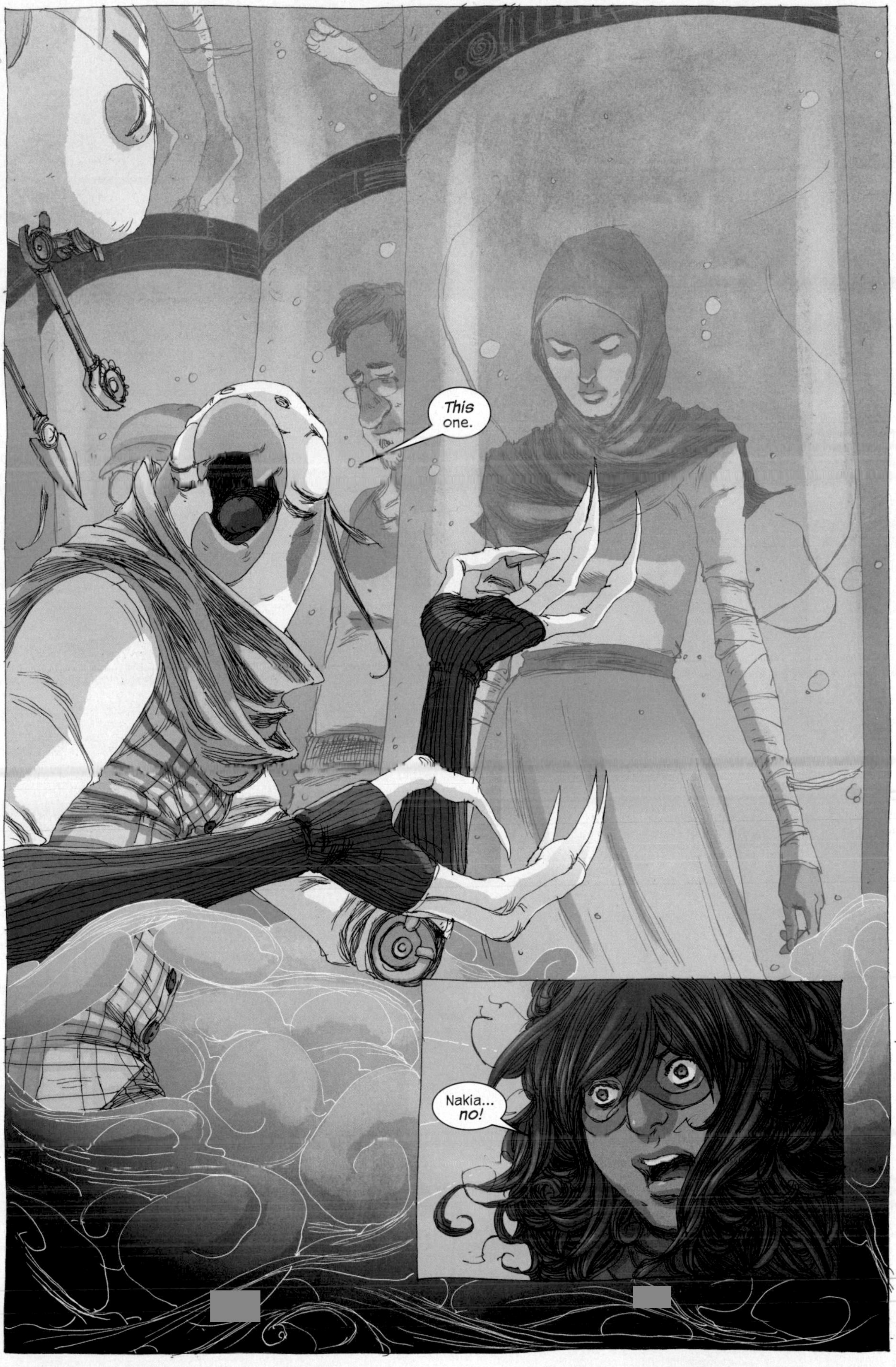
This one.
Nakia... no!

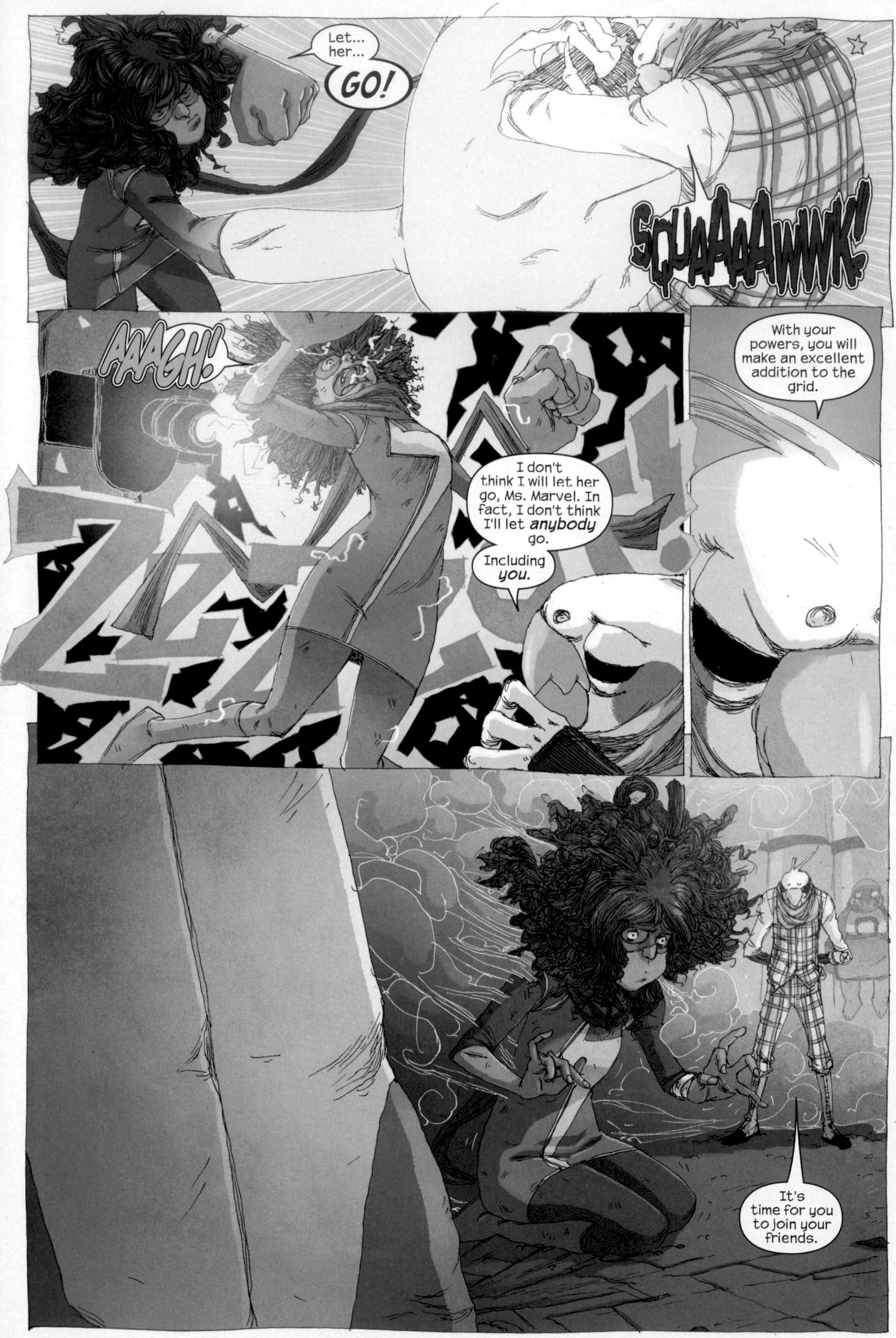
Let... her... GO!
SQUAAAAWWK!
AAAGH!
With your powers, you will make an excellent addition to the grid.
I don't think I will let her go, Ms. Marvel. In fact, I don't think I'll let *anybody* go.
Including *you.*
It's time for you to join your friends.

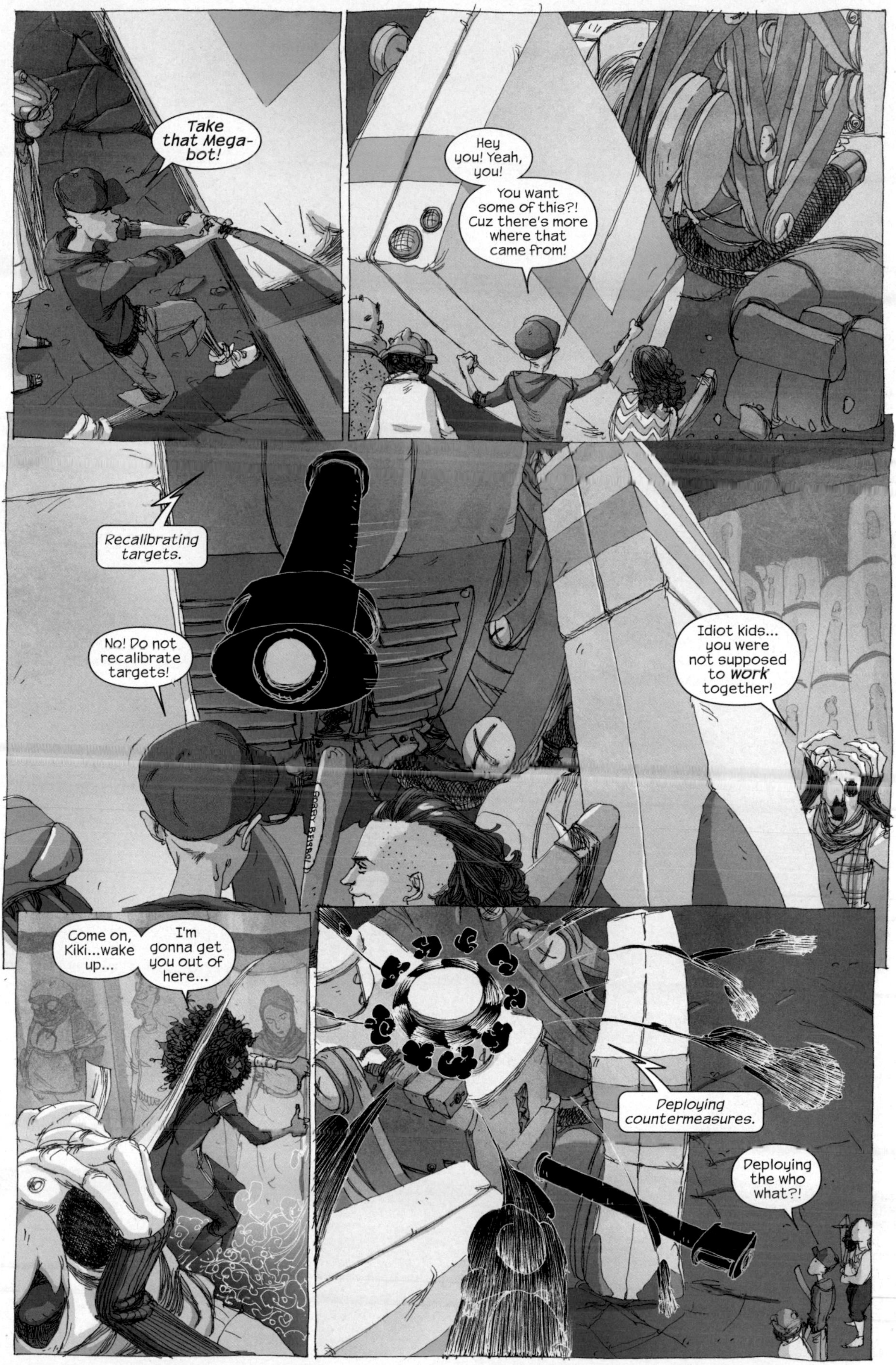
Take that Mega-bot!
Hey you! Yeah, you!
You want some of this?! Cuz there's more where that came from!
Recalibrating targets.
No! Do not recalibrate targets!
Idiot kids... you were not supposed to *work* together!
Come on, Kiki...wake up...
I'm gonna get you out of here...
Deploying countermeasures.
Deploying the who what?!

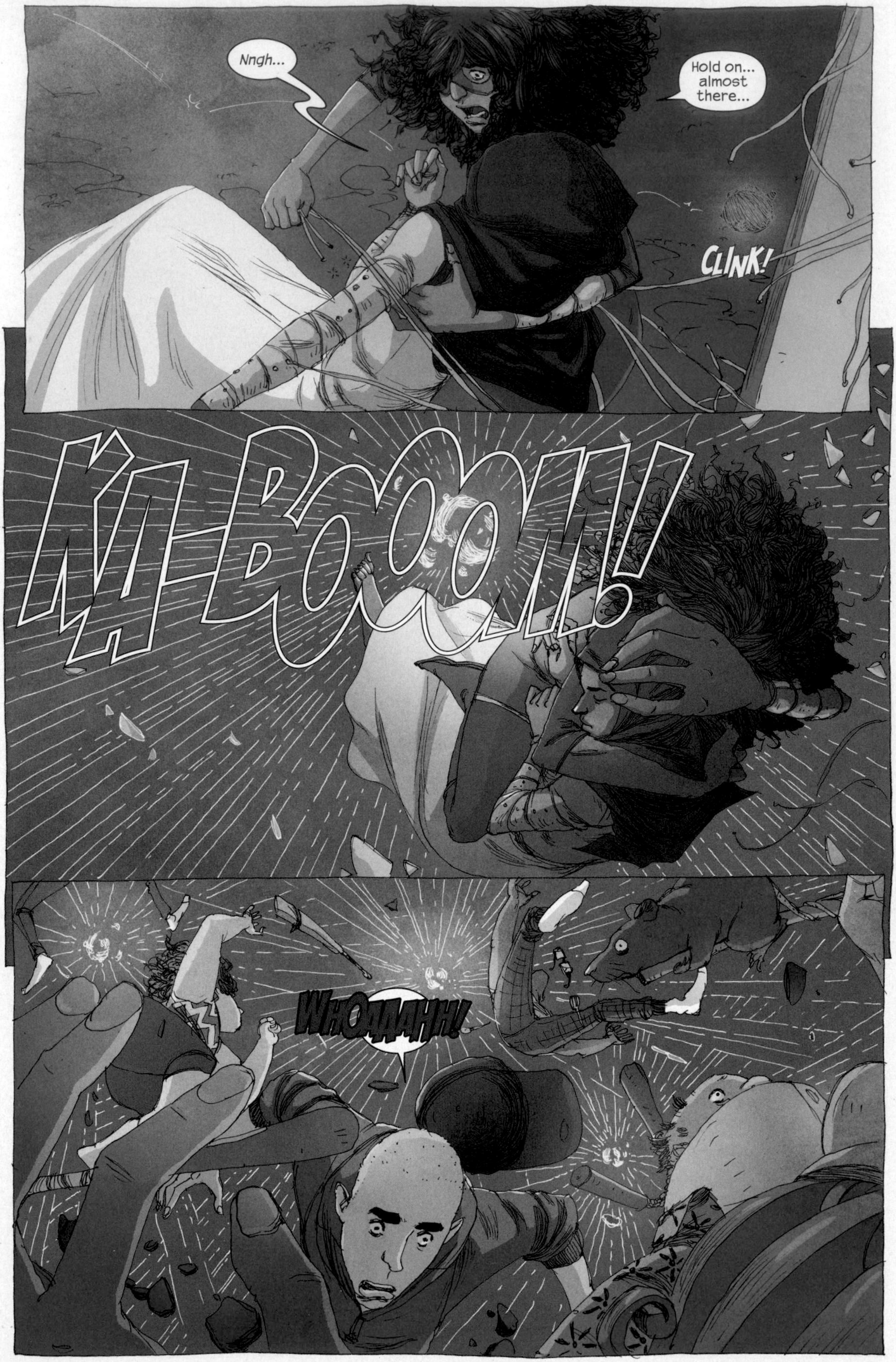
Nngh...
Hold on... almost there...
CLINK!
KA-BOOOM!
WHOAAAHH!

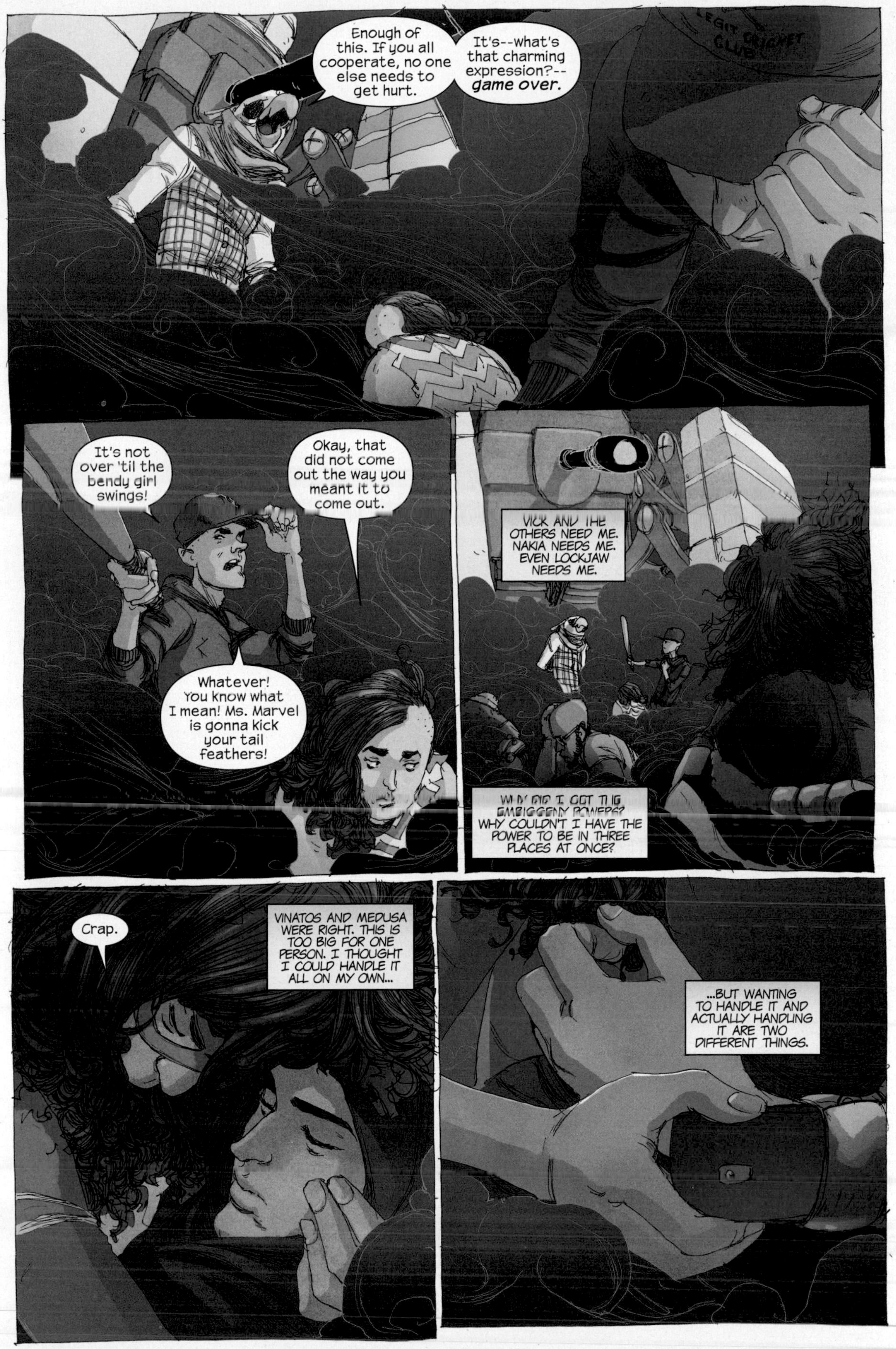
Enough of this. If you all cooperate, no one else needs to get hurt.
It's--what's that charming expression?-- *game over.*
LEGIT CRICKET CLUB
It's not over 'til the bendy girl swings!
Okay, that did not come out the way you meant it to come out.
Whatever! You know what I mean! Ms. Marvel is gonna kick your tail feathers!
VICK AND THE OTHERS NEED ME. NAKIA NEEDS ME. EVEN LOCKJAW NEEDS ME.
WHY COULDN'T I HAVE THE POWER TO BE IN THREE PLACES AT ONCE?
Crap.
VINATOS AND MEDUSA WERE RIGHT. THIS IS TOO BIG FOR ONE PERSON. I THOUGHT I COULD HANDLE IT ALL ON MY OWN...
...BUT WANTING TO HANDLE IT AND ACTUALLY HANDLING IT ARE TWO DIFFERENT THINGS.

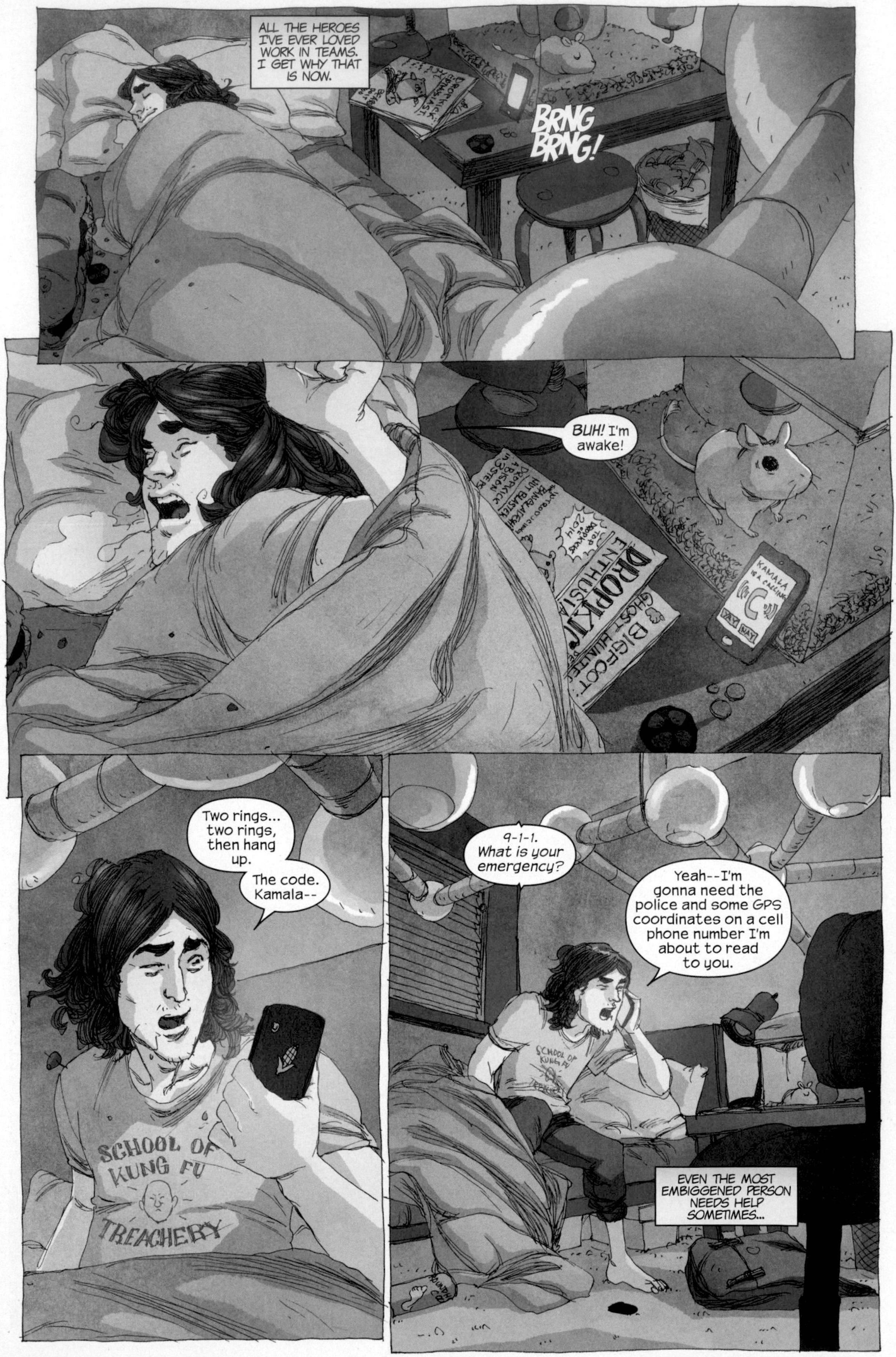

ALL THE HEROES I'VE EVER LOVED WORK IN TEAMS. I GET WHY THAT IS NOW.
BRNG BRNG!
BUH! I'm awake!
KAMALA IS A CALLING
Two rings... two rings, then hang up.
The code. Kamala--
SCHOOL OF KUNG FU
TREACHERY
9-1-1. What is your emergency?
Yeah--I'm gonna need the police and some GPS coordinates on a cell phone number I'm about to read to you.
EVEN THE MOST EMBIGGENED PERSON NEEDS HELP SOMETIMES...

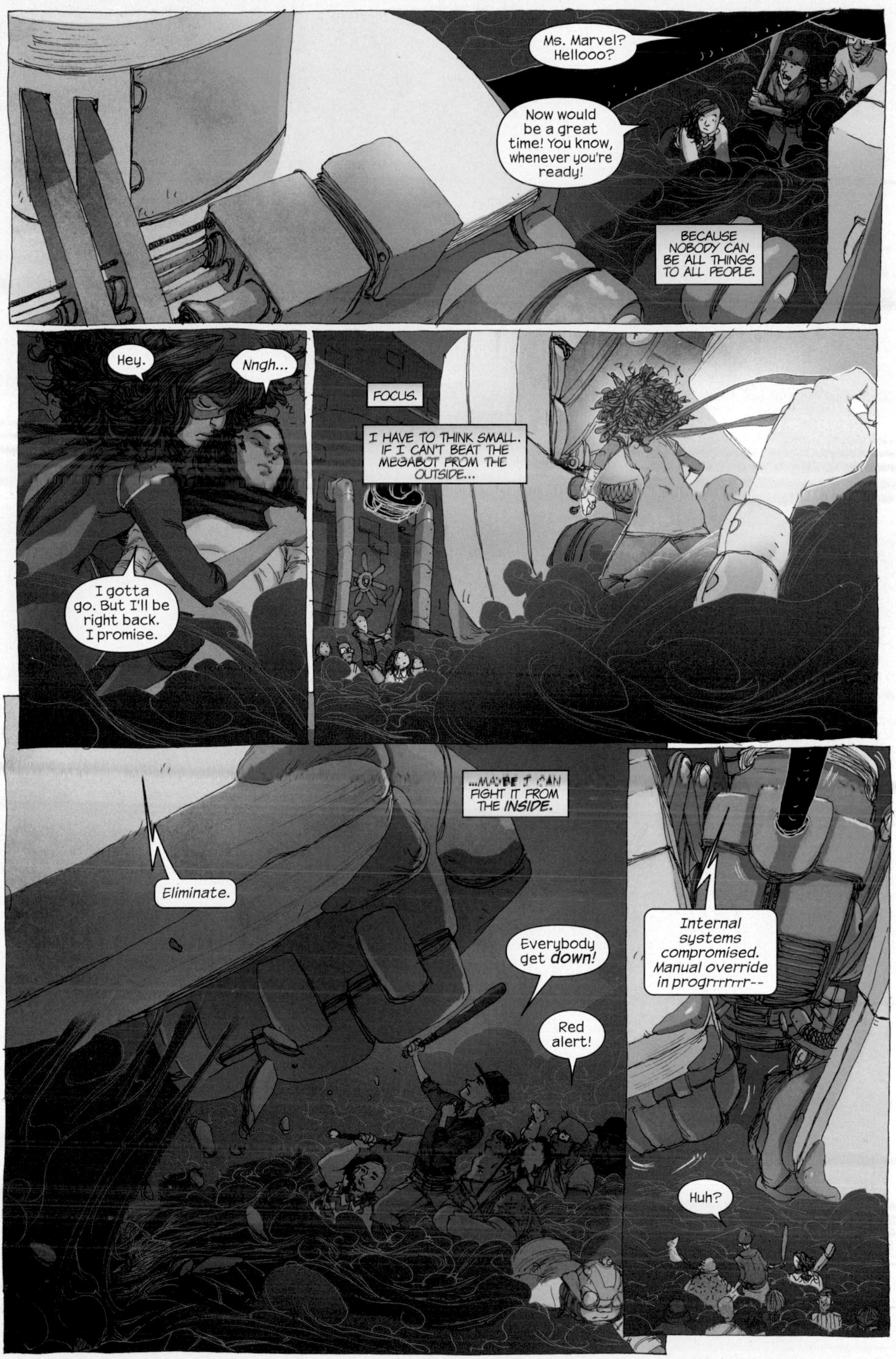
Ms. Marvel? Hellooo?
Now would be a great time! You know, whenever you're ready!
BECAUSE NOBODY CAN BE ALL THINGS TO ALL PEOPLE.
Hey.
Nngh...
I gotta go. But I'll be right back. I promise.
FOCUS.
I HAVE TO THINK SMALL. IF I CAN'T BEAT THE MEGABOT FROM THE OUTSIDE...
...MAYBE I CAN FIGHT IT FROM THE *INSIDE.*
Eliminate.
Everybody get *down!*
Red alert!
Internal systems compromised. Manual override in progrrrrrr--
Huh?

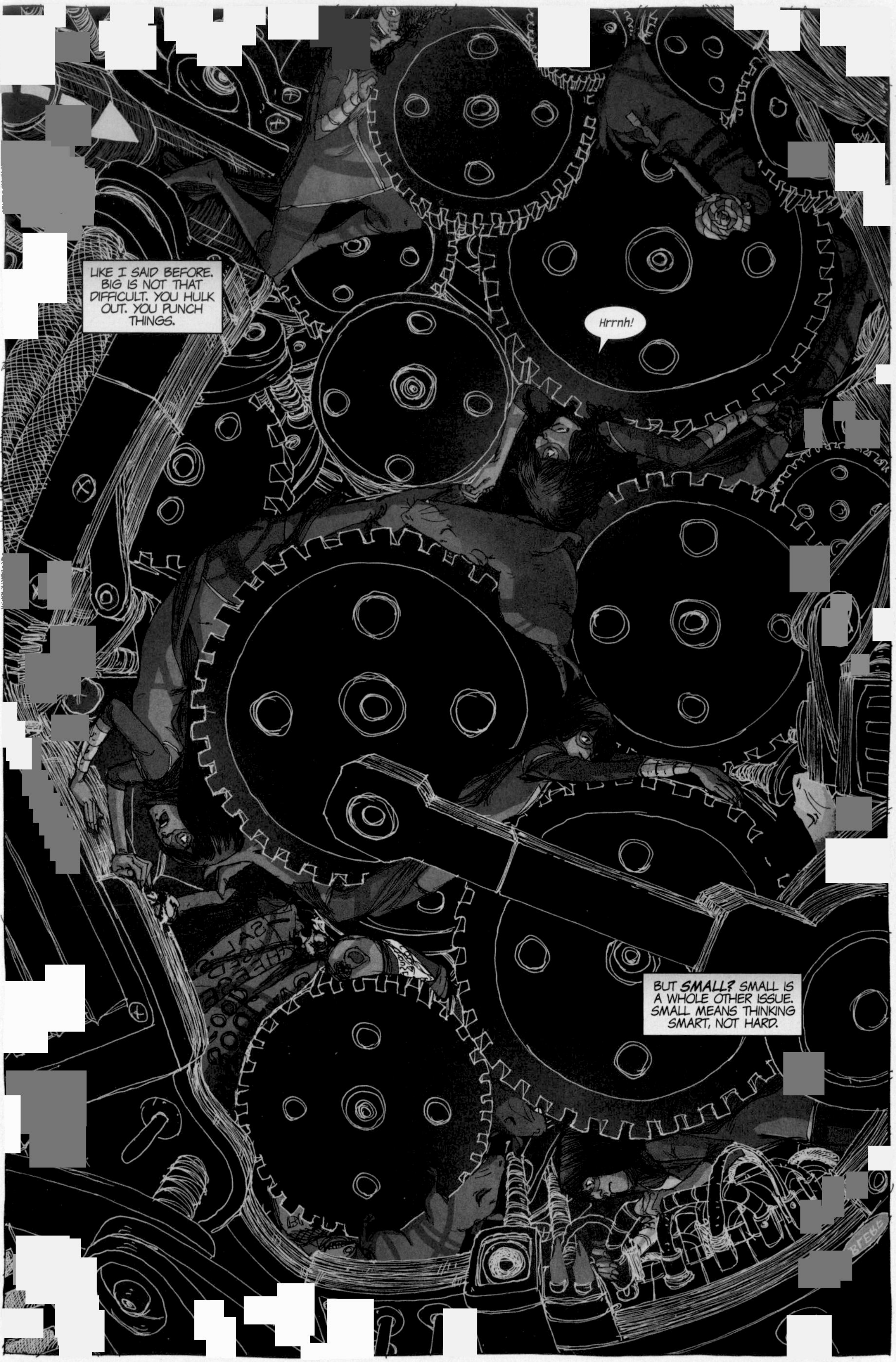
LIKE I SAID BEFORE. BIG IS NOT THAT DIFFICULT. YOU HULK OUT. YOU PUNCH THINGS.
Hrrnh!
BUT SMALL? SMALL IS A WHOLE OTHER ISSUE. SMALL MEANS THINKING SMART, NOT HARD.

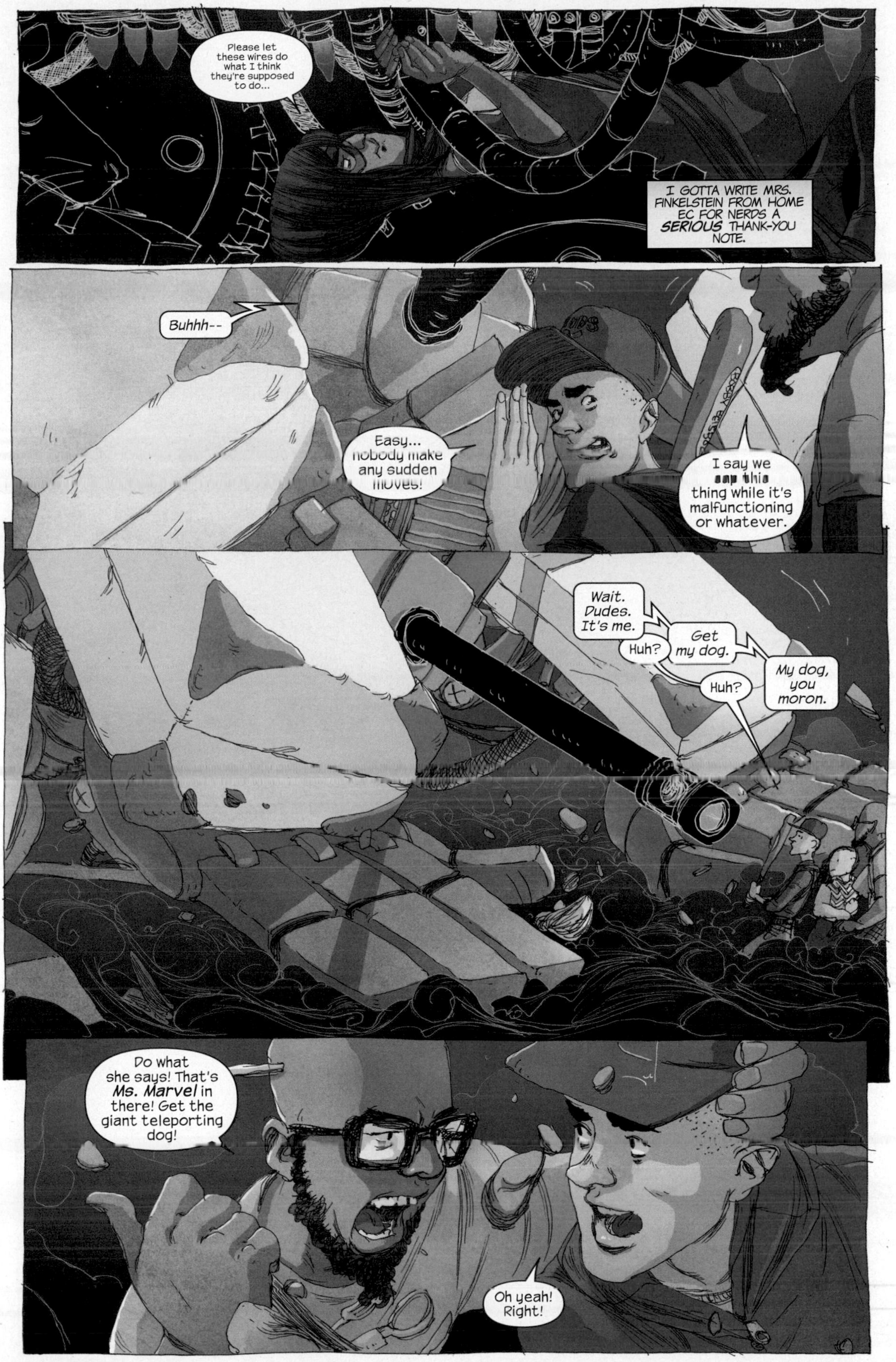
Please let these wires do what I think they're supposed to do...
I GOTTA WRITE MRS. FINKELSTEIN FROM HOME EC FOR NERDS A SERIOUS THANK-YOU NOTE.
Buhhh--
Easy... nobody make any sudden moves!
I say we thing while it's malfunctioning or whatever.
Wait. Dudes. It's me.
Huh?
Get my dog.
Huh?
My dog, you moron.
Do what she says! That's Ms. Marvel in there! Get the giant teleporting dog!
Oh yeah! Right!

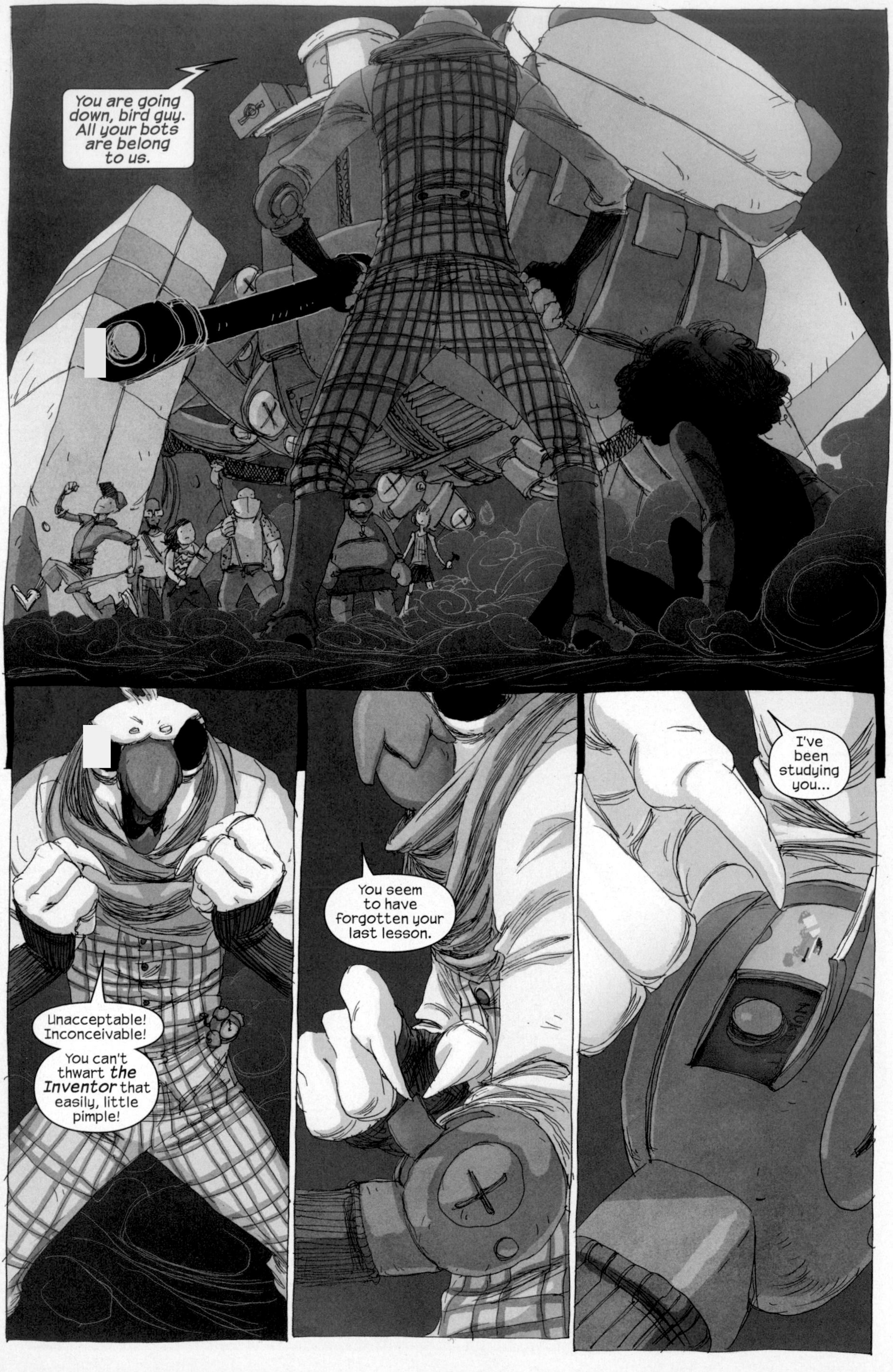
You are going down, bird guy. All your bots are belong to us.
Unacceptable! Inconceivable!
You can't thwart **the Inventor** that easily, little pimple!
You seem to have forgotten your last lesson.
I've been studying you...

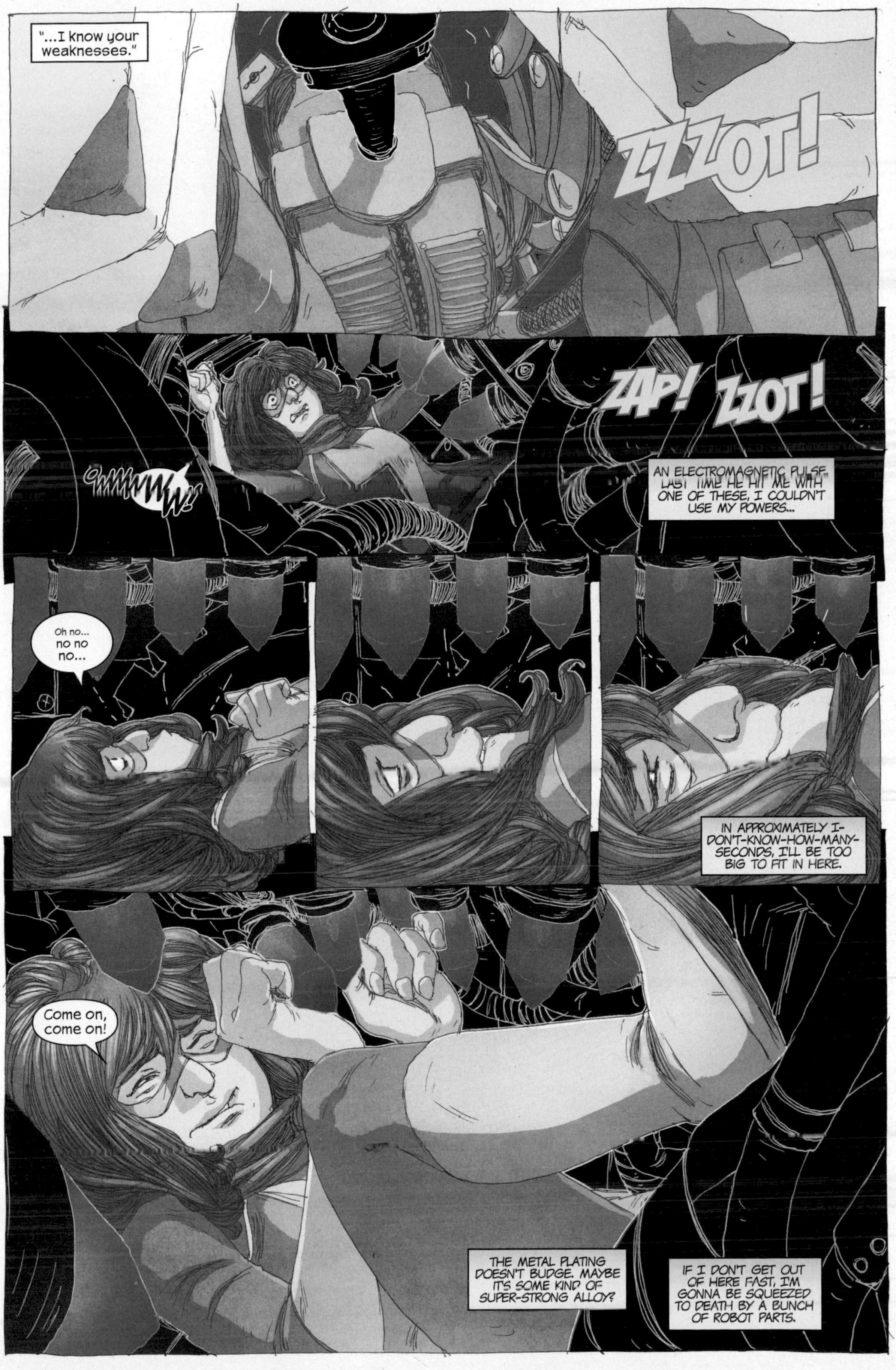
"...I know your weaknesses."
ZZZOT!
ZAP! ZZOT!
OWWWWW!
AN ELECTROMAGNETIC PULSE. LAST TIME HE HIT ME WITH ONE OF THESE, I COULDN'T USE MY POWERS...
Oh no... no no no...
IN APPROXIMATELY I-DON'T-KNOW-HOW-MANY-SECONDS, I'LL BE TOO BIG TO FIT IN HERE.
Come on, come on!
THE METAL PLATING DOESN'T BUDGE. MAYBE IT'S SOME KIND OF SUPER-STRONG ALLOY?
IF I DON'T GET OUT OF HERE FAST, I'M GONNA BE SQUEEZED TO DEATH BY A BUNCH OF ROBOT PARTS.

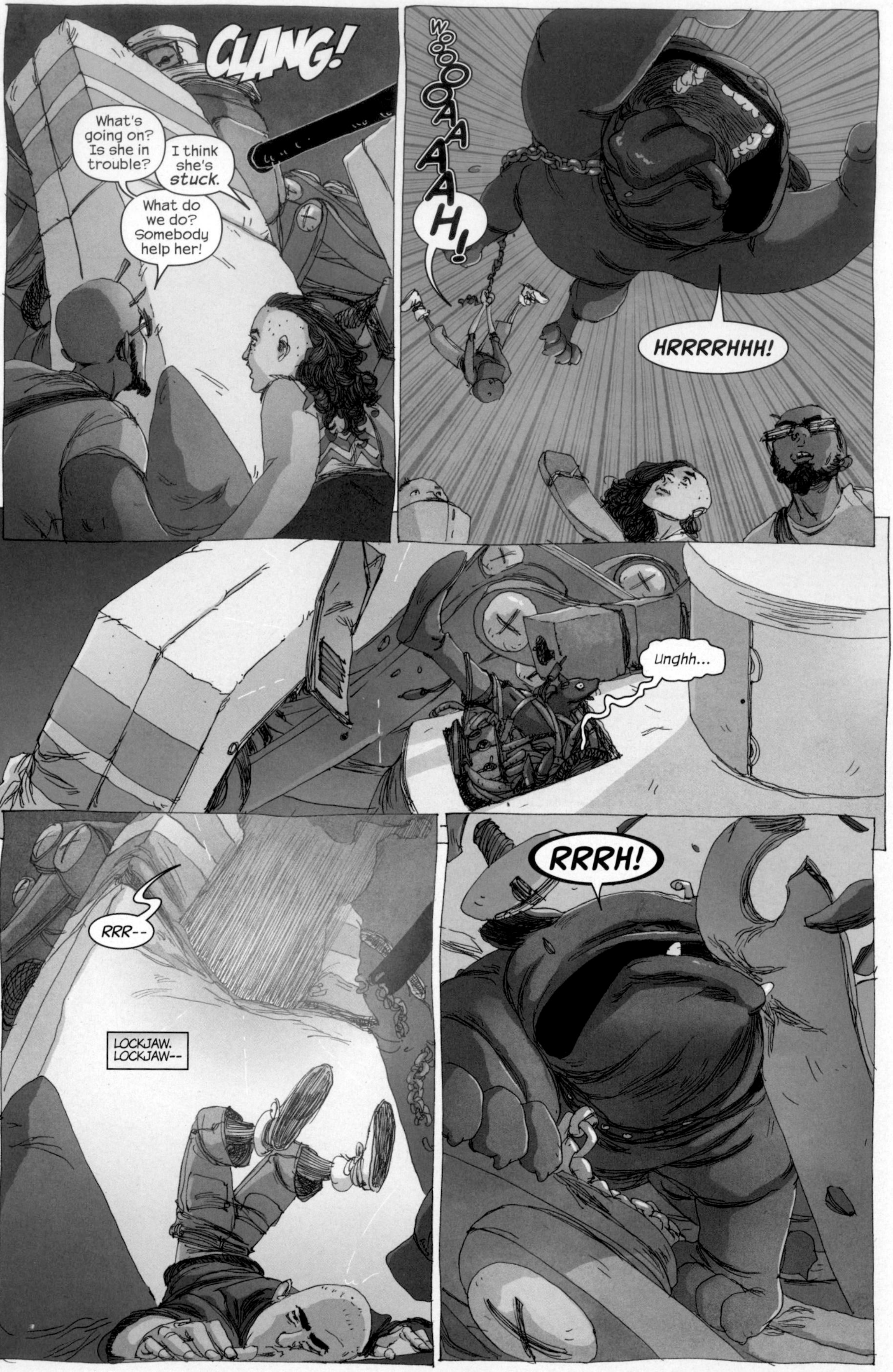
CLANG!
What's going on? Is she in trouble?
I think she's stuck.
What do we do? Somebody help her!
WOOOOAAAAAH!
HRRRRHHH!
Unghh...
RRR--
LOCKJAW. LOCKJAW--
RRRH!

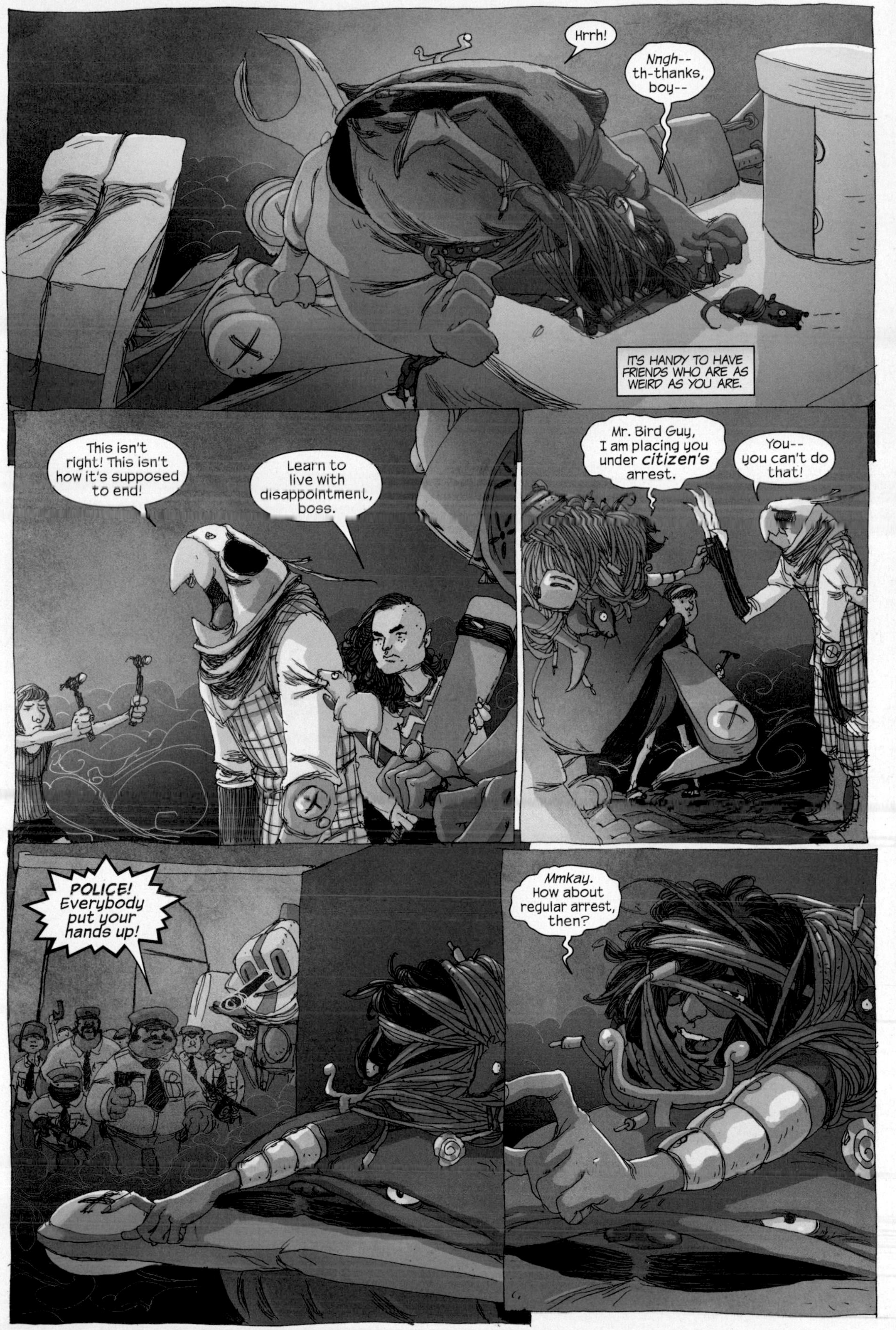

Hrrh!
Nngh-- th-thanks, boy--
IT'S HANDY TO HAVE FRIENDS WHO ARE AS WEIRD AS YOU ARE.
This isn't right! This isn't how it's supposed to end!
Learn to live with disappointment, boss.
Mr. Bird Guy, I am placing you under *citizen's* arrest.
You-- you can't do that!
POLICE! Everybody put your hands up!
Mmkay. How about regular arrest, then?

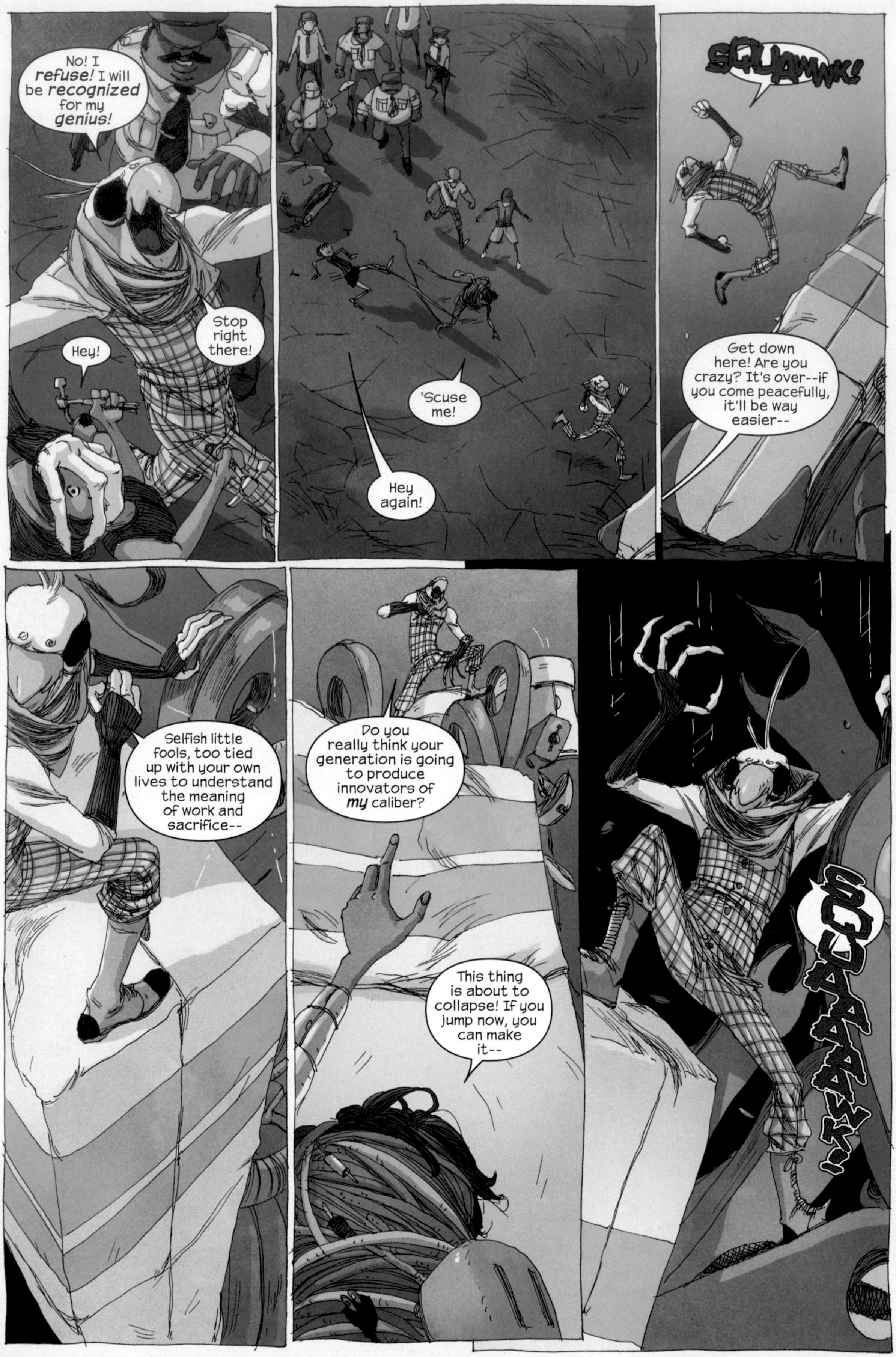
No! I refuse! I will be recognized for my genius!
Stop right there!
Hey!
'Scuse me!
Hey again!
SQUAWWK!
Get down here! Are you crazy? It's over--if you come peacefully, it'll be way easier--
Selfish little fools, too tied up with your own lives to understand the meaning of work and sacrifice--
Do you really think your generation is going to produce innovators of my caliber?
This thing is about to collapse! If you jump now, you can make it--

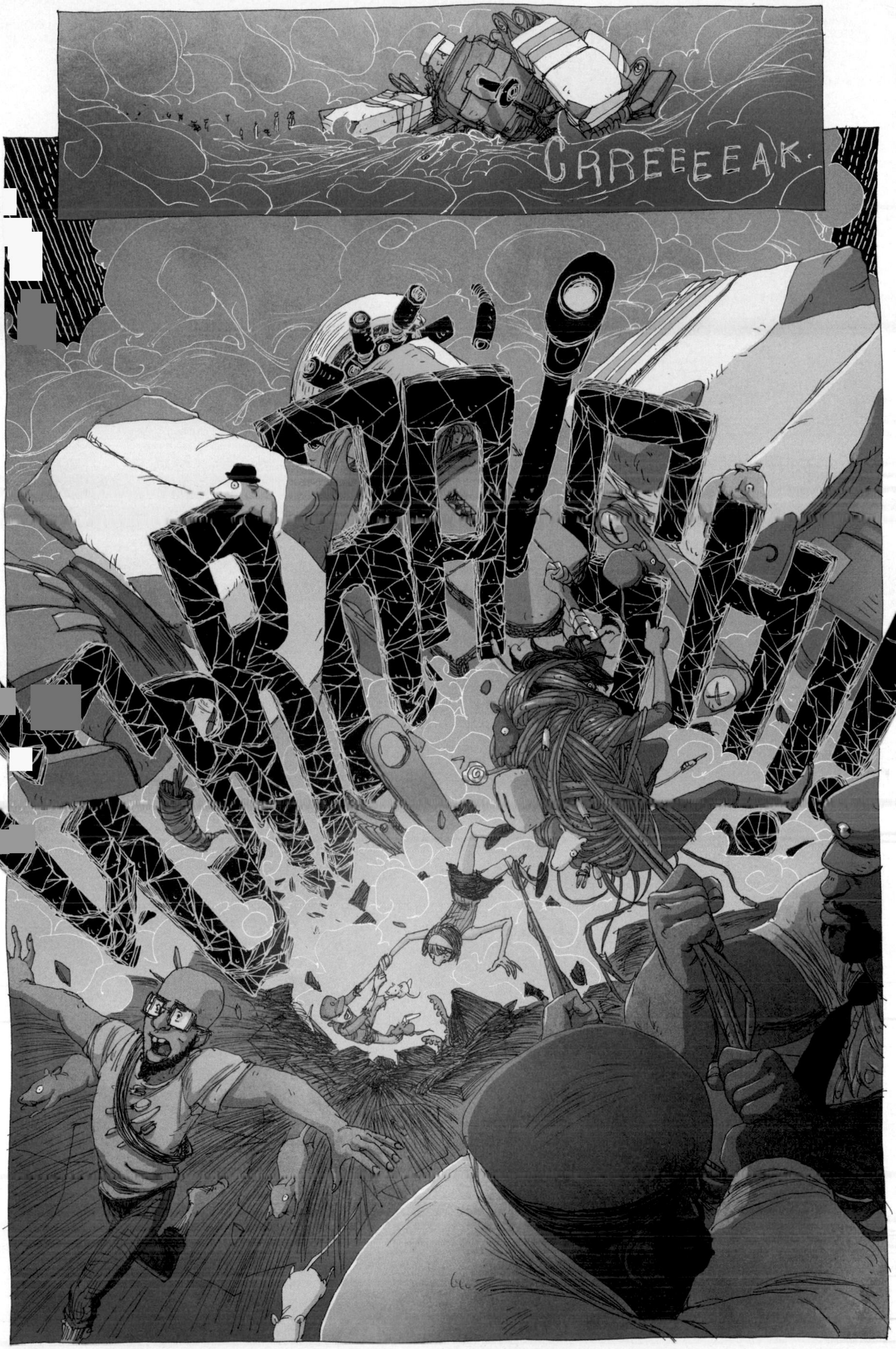
CRREEEEAK.

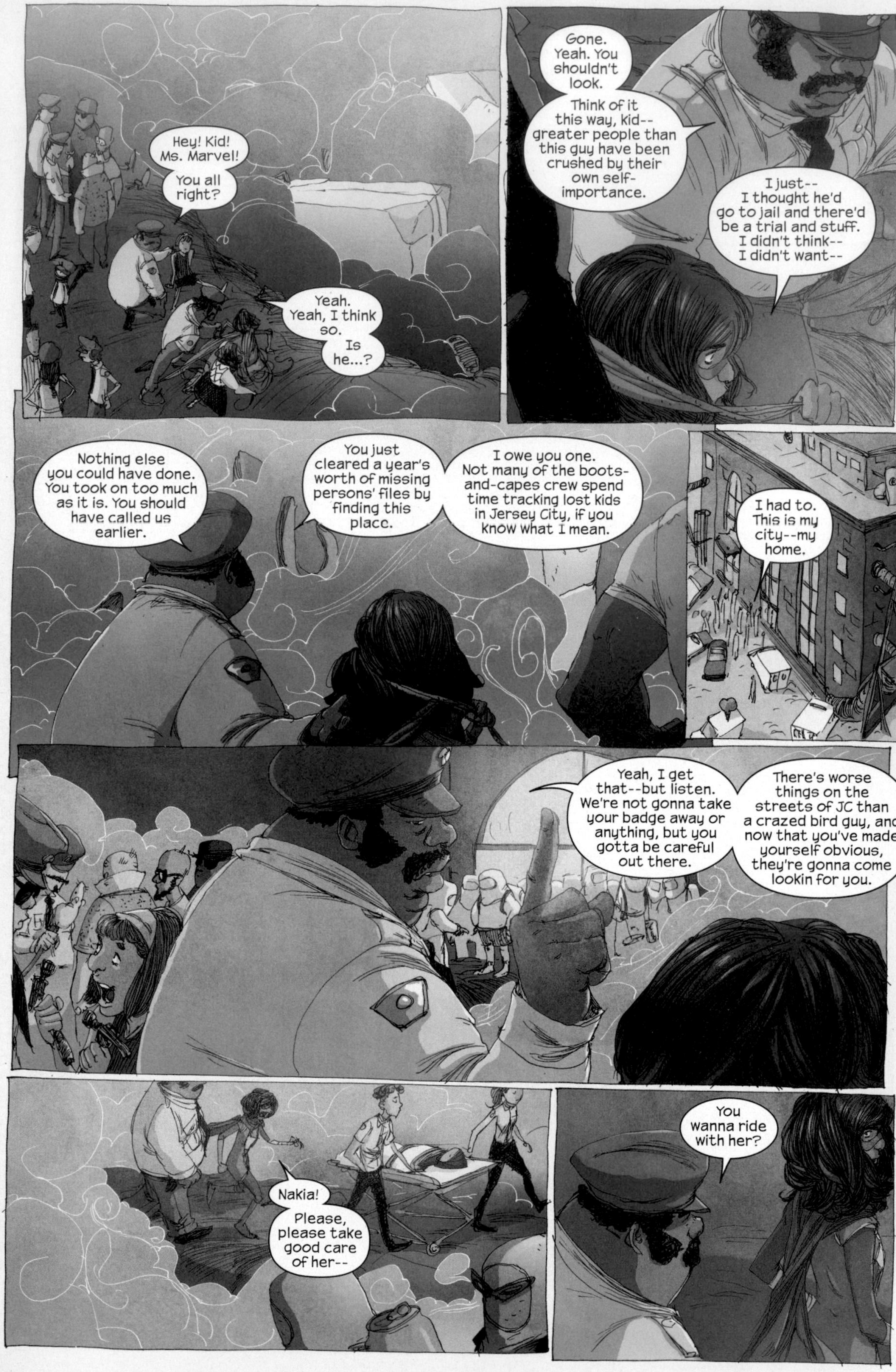
Hey! Kid! Ms. Marvel!
You all right?
Yeah. Yeah, I think so.
Is he...?
Gone. Yeah. You shouldn't look.
Think of it this way, kid-- greater people than this guy have been crushed by their own self-importance.
I just-- I thought he'd go to jail and there'd be a trial and stuff. I didn't think-- I didn't want--
Nothing else you could have done. You took on too much as it is. You should have called us earlier.
You just cleared a year's worth of missing persons' files by finding this place.
I owe you one. Not many of the boots-and-capes crew spend time tracking lost kids in Jersey City, if you know what I mean.
I had to. This is my city--my home.
Yeah, I get that--but listen. We're not gonna take your badge away or anything, but you gotta be careful out there.
There's worse things on the streets of JC than a crazed bird guy, and now that you've made yourself obvious, they're gonna come lookin for you.
Nakia!
Please, please take good care of her--
You wanna ride with her?

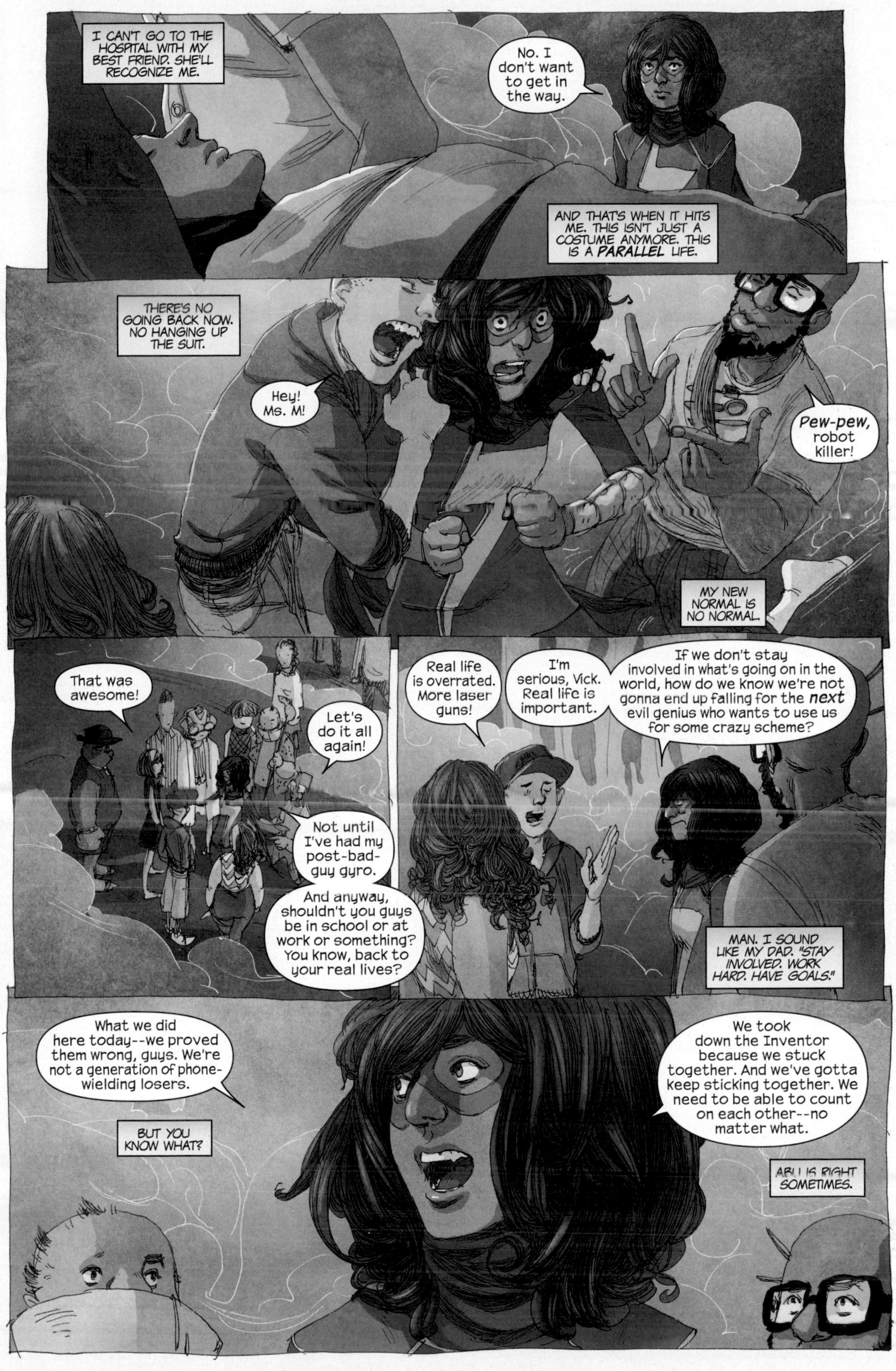
I CAN'T GO TO THE HOSPITAL WITH MY BEST FRIEND. SHE'LL RECOGNIZE ME.
No. I don't want to get in the way.
AND THAT'S WHEN IT HITS ME. THIS ISN'T JUST A COSTUME ANYMORE. THIS IS A PARALLEL LIFE.
THERE'S NO GOING BACK NOW. NO HANGING UP THE SUIT.
Hey! Ms. M!
Pew-pew, robot killer!
MY NEW NORMAL IS NO NORMAL.
That was awesome!
Let's do it all again!
Not until I've had my post-bad-guy gyro.
And anyway, shouldn't you guys be in school or at work or something? You know, back to your real lives?
Real life is overrated. More laser guns!
I'm serious, Vick. Real life is important.
If we don't stay involved in what's going on in the world, how do we know we're not gonna end up falling for the next evil genius who wants to use us for some crazy scheme?
MAN. I SOUND LIKE MY DAD. "STAY INVOLVED. WORK HARD. HAVE GOALS."
What we did here today--we proved them wrong, guys. We're not a generation of phone-wielding losers.
BUT YOU KNOW WHAT?
We took down the Inventor because we stuck together. And we've gotta keep sticking together. We need to be able to count on each other--no matter what.
ABU IS RIGHT SOMETIMES.

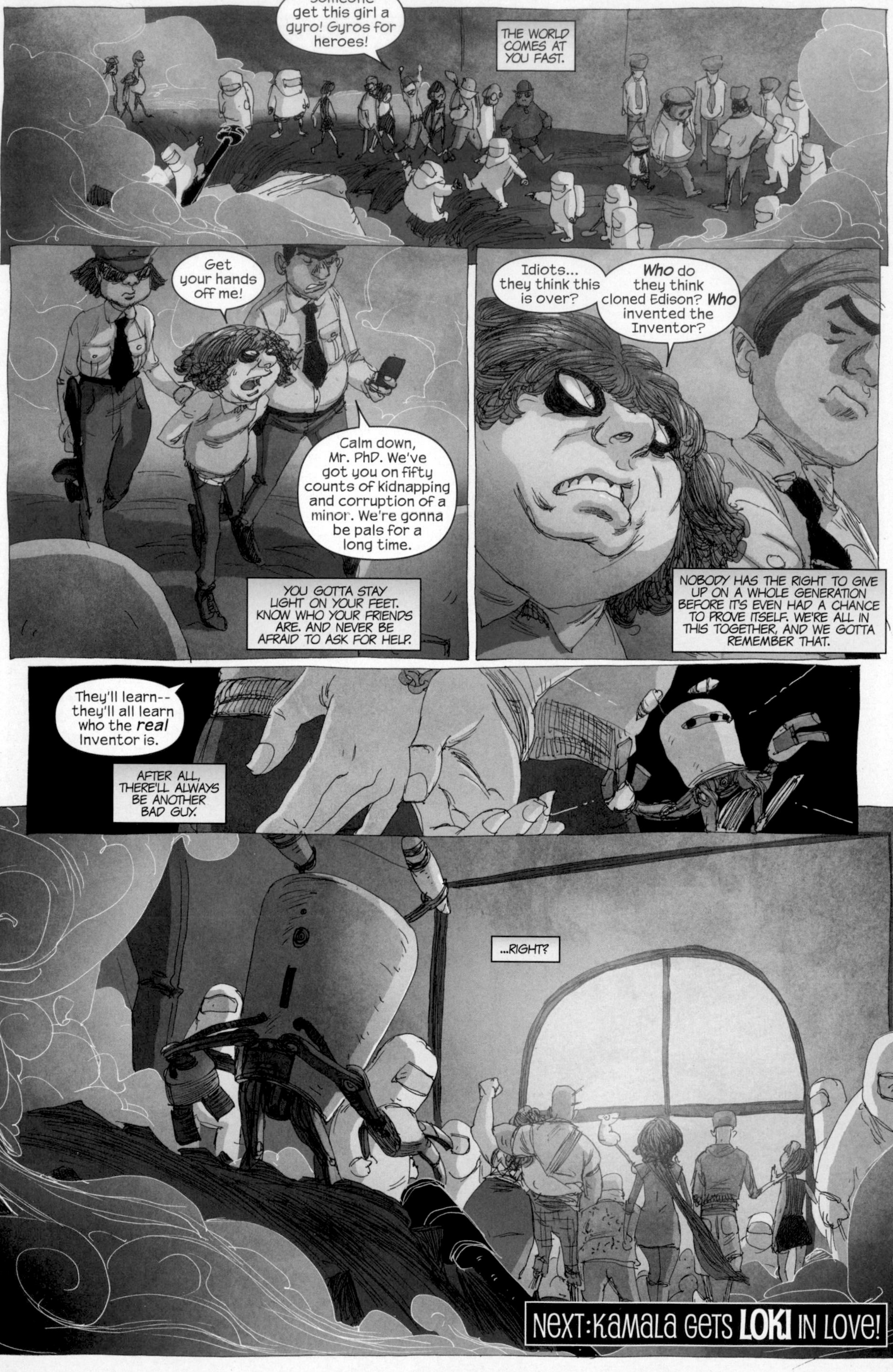
Someone get this girl a gyro! Gyros for heroes!
THE WORLD COMES AT YOU FAST.
Get your hands off me!
Calm down, Mr. PhD. We've got you on fifty counts of kidnapping and corruption of a minor. We're gonna be pals for a long time.
YOU GOTTA STAY LIGHT ON YOUR FEET. KNOW WHO YOUR FRIENDS ARE. AND NEVER BE AFRAID TO ASK FOR HELP.
Idiots... they think this is over?
Who do they think cloned Edison? Who invented the Inventor?
NOBODY HAS THE RIGHT TO GIVE UP ON A WHOLE GENERATION BEFORE IT'S EVEN HAD A CHANCE TO PROVE ITSELF. WE'RE ALL IN THIS TOGETHER, AND WE GOTTA REMEMBER THAT.
They'll learn--they'll all learn who the real Inventor is.
AFTER ALL, THERE'LL ALWAYS BE ANOTHER BAD GUY.
...RIGHT?
NEXT: KAMALA GETS LOKI IN LOVE!

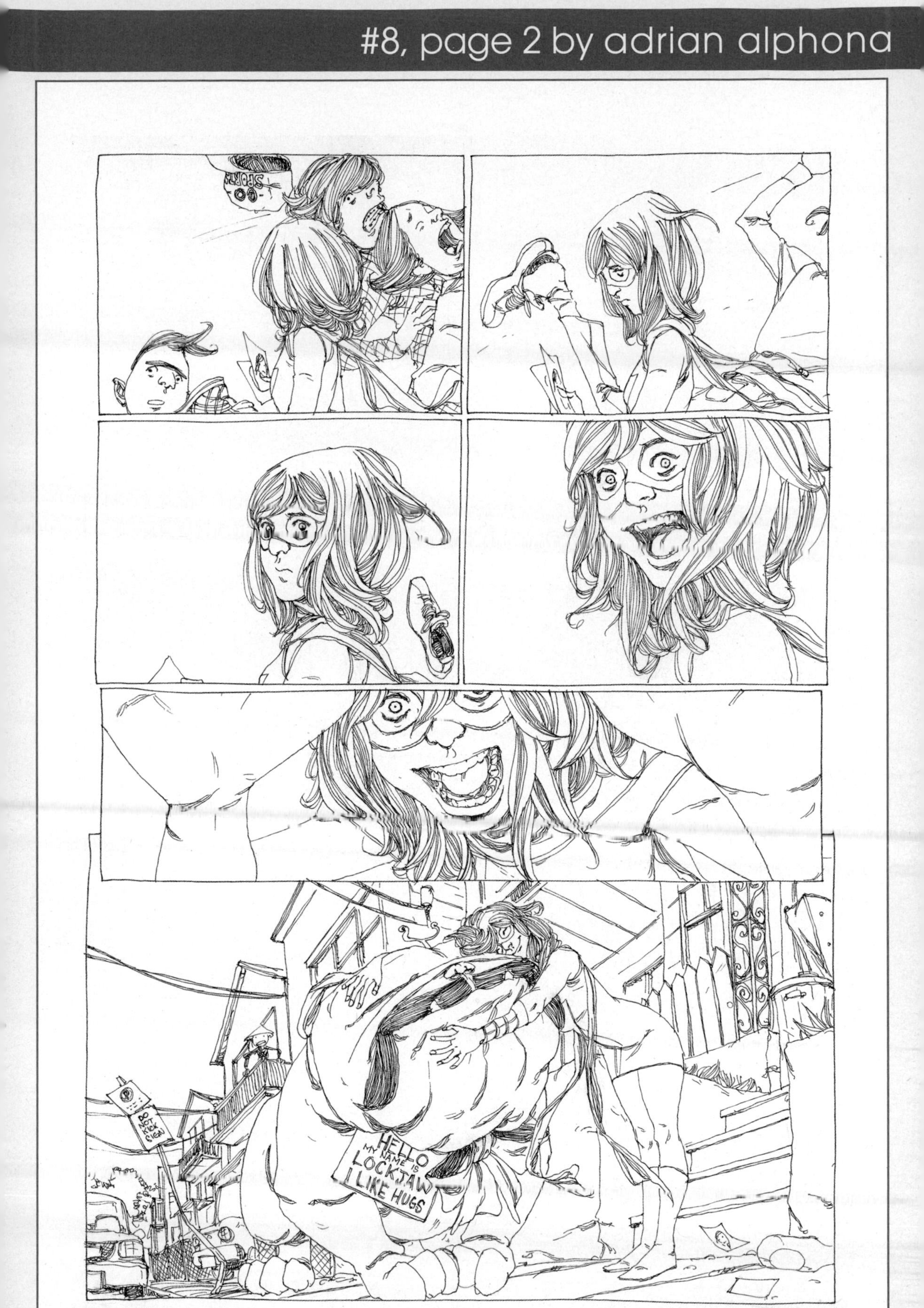
DO NOT KICK SIGN
HELLO MY NAME IS LOCKJAW I LIKE HUGS

#8, page 15 by adrian alphona

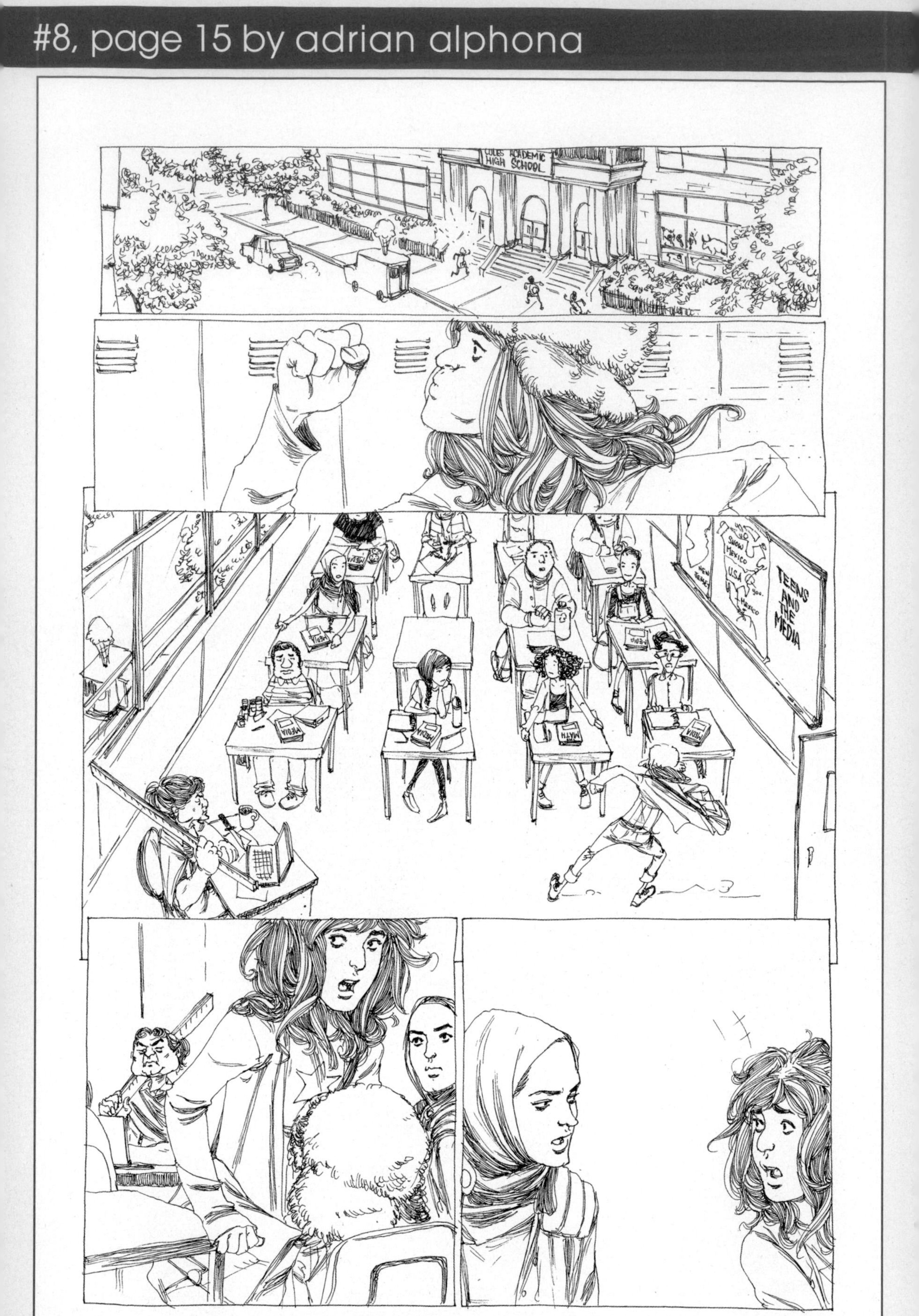
COLES ACADEMIC HIGH SCHOOL
TEENS AND THE MEDIA
USA
MEDIA
MATH

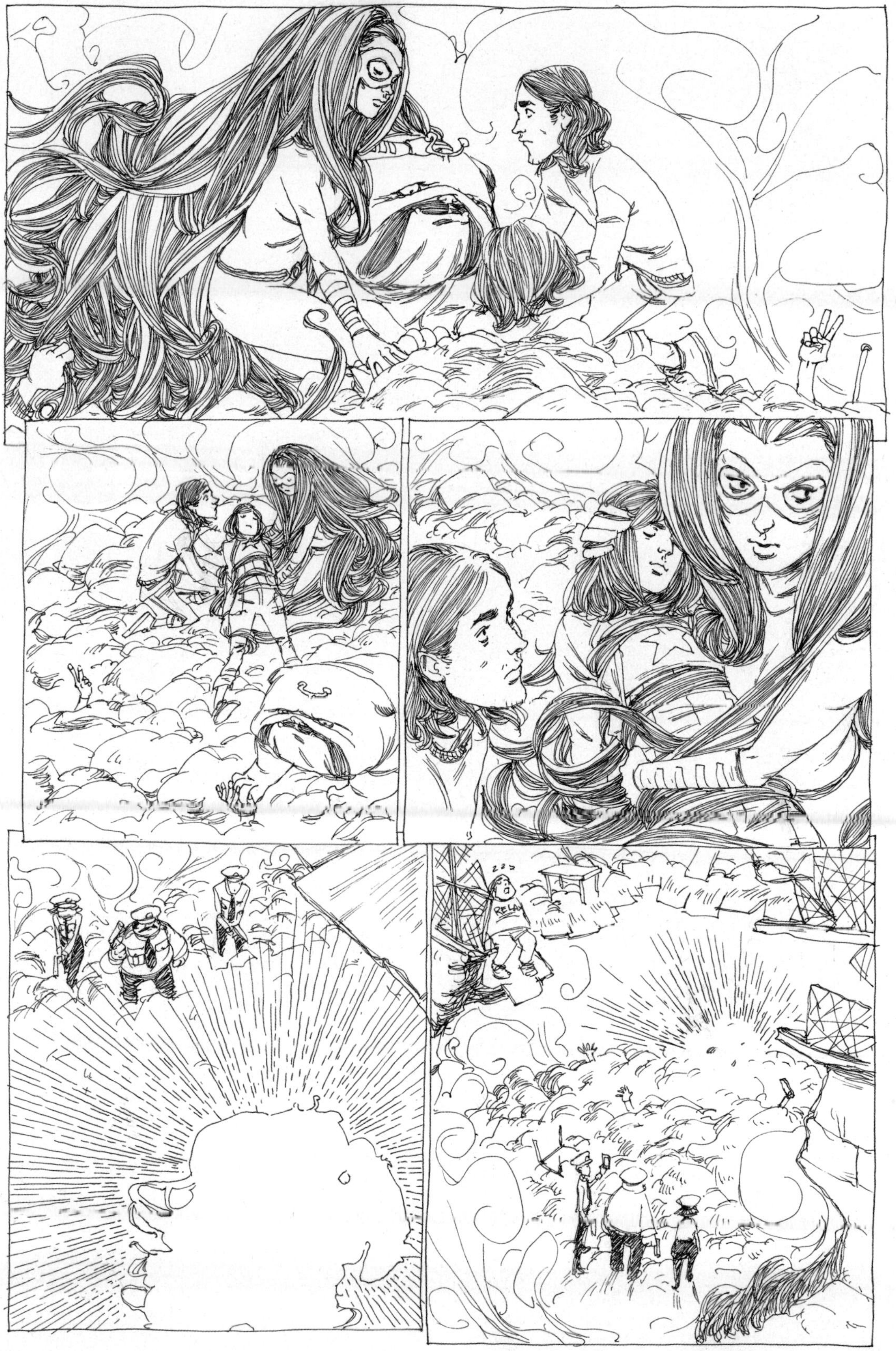
RELAX

#10, page 3 by adrian alphona

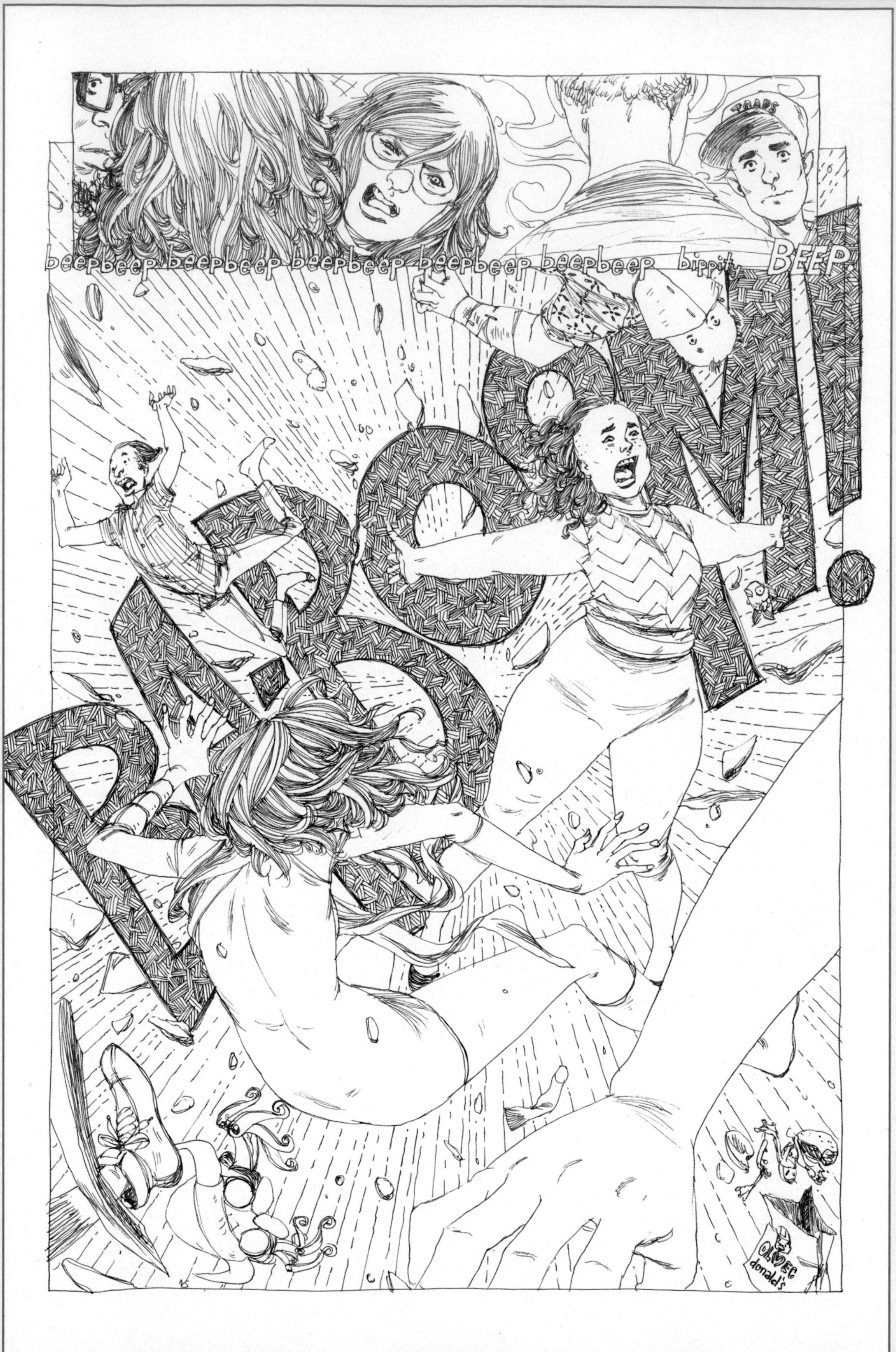
beepbeep beepbeep beepbeep beepbeep beepbeep bippity BEEP!
donald's

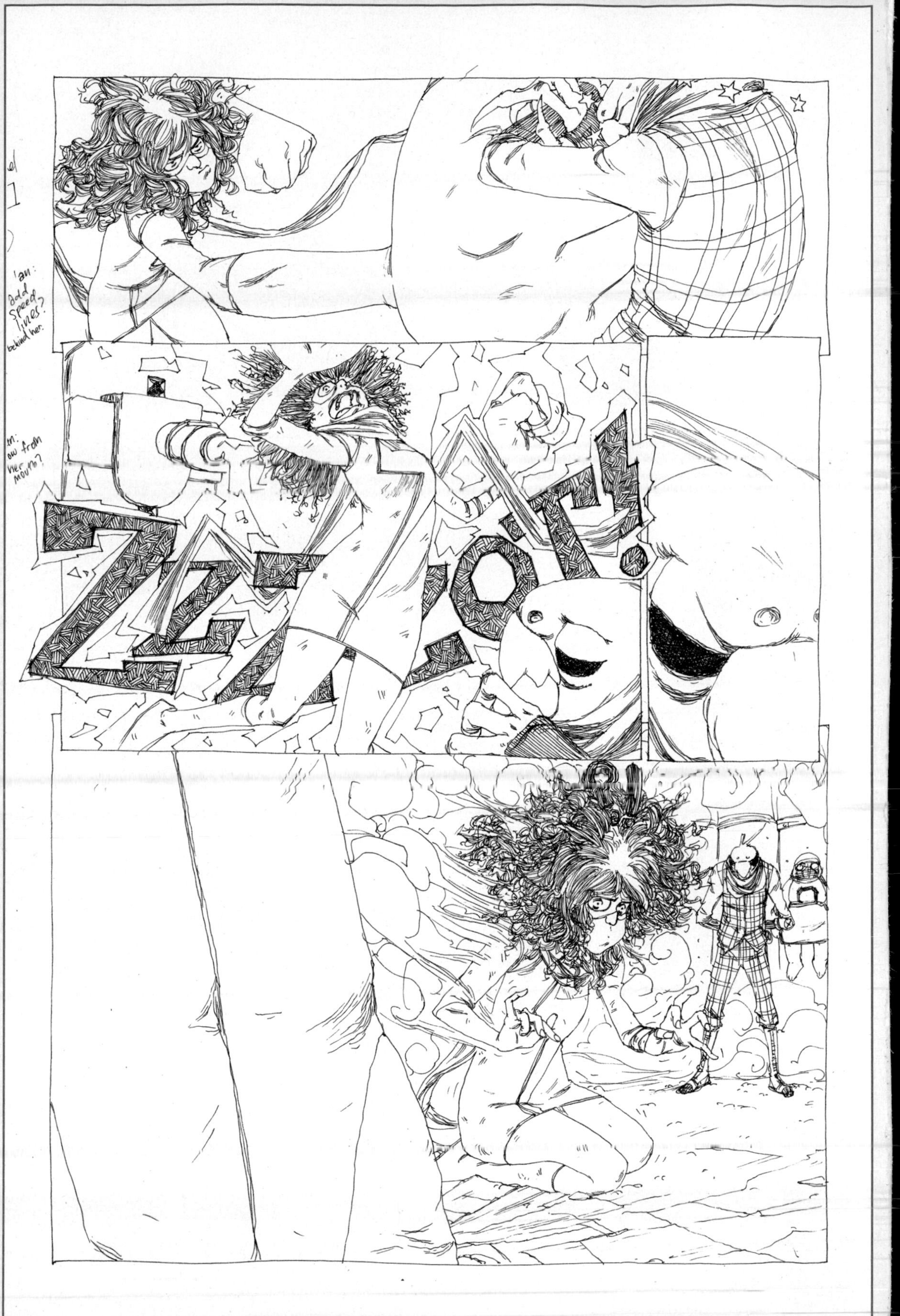
'an: add speed lines? behind her.
n: ow from her mouth?

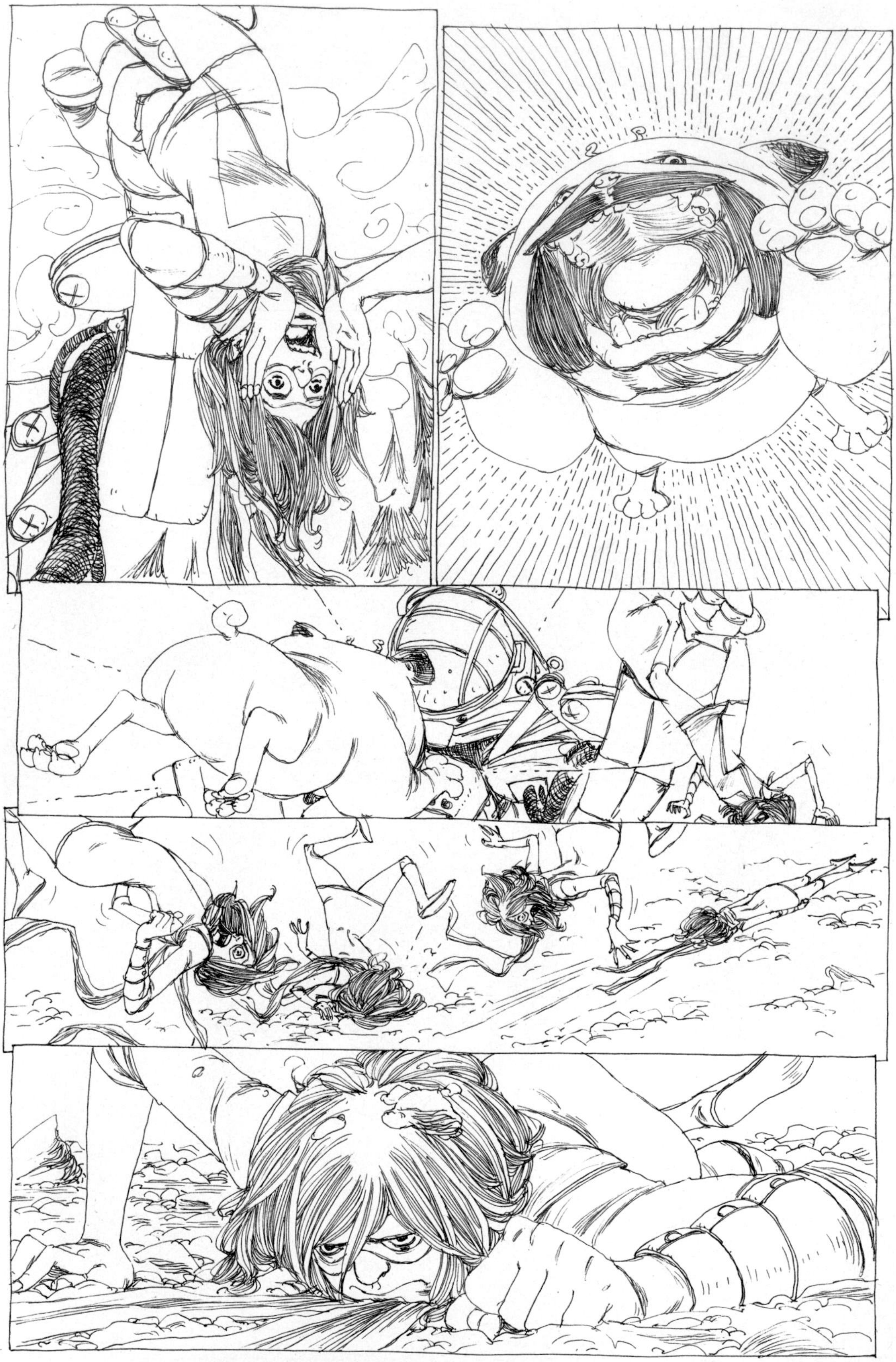

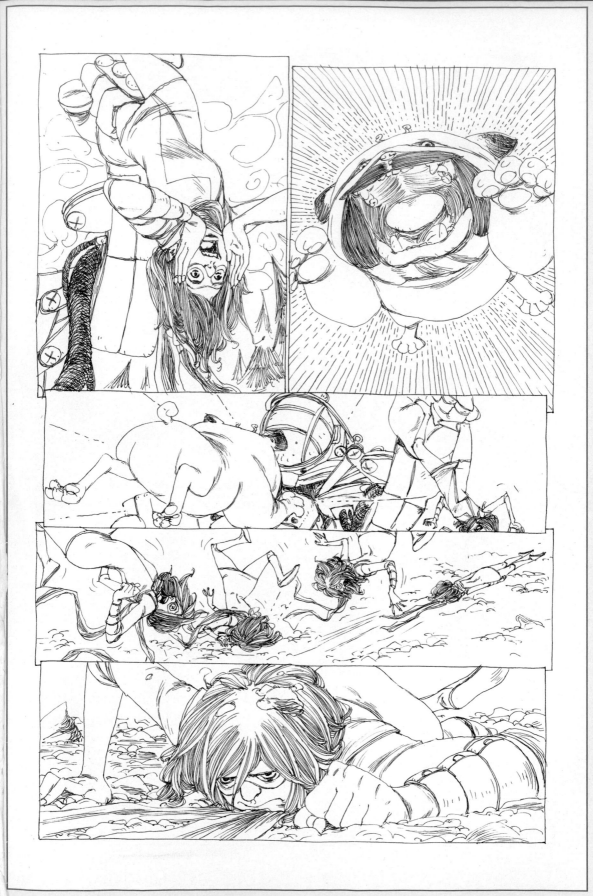